John T. McNeill

A noted church historian, Dr. McNeill is Professor Emeritus in Church History at Union Theological Seminary, New York. Formerly he taught Church History at Toronto, Canada, and was professor of History of European Christianity at the University of Chicago.

Since retirement, Dr. McNeill has been continually active both as a writer and as a teacher, and he is currently visiting professor in the Divinity School of the University of Chicago.

One of the editors of the Library of Christian Classics, Dr. McNeill has written many other books, including: *Christian Hope for World Society*, *A History of the Cure of Souls*, and *The History and Character of Calvinism*.

JOHN KNOX PRESS
Richmond, Virginia

UNITIVE PROTESTANTISM

The Ecumenical Spirit
and Its Persistent Expression

JOHN T. McNEILL

JOHN KNOX PRESS
RICHMOND, VIRGINIA

TO THE MEMORY OF

EMILY L. McNEILL

FIRST AND BEST OF MY TEACHERS

IN FILIAL DEVOTION

Library of Congress Catalog Card Number: 64-10527

©M. E. Bratcher 1964

Printed in the United States of America

CONTENTS

PART I

THE UNITIVE PRINCIPLE IN THE REFORMATION MOVEMENT

PART II

EARLY PROTESTANT EFFORTS TOWARD CHRISTIAN REUNION

CONTENTS

PART III

THE SURVIVAL AND REVIVAL OF THE UNITIVE PRINCIPLE

PREFACE

THE first formulation of materials from which this book has developed was a course of lectures on "Movements Toward Christian Reunion," given in the Divinity School of the University of Chicago in the summer of 1926. This course was revised and condensed for the Summer School in Theology of Knox and Victoria Colleges, Toronto, and was subsequently given to a group of students in these co-operating institutions (now united as Emmanuel College). In November, 1927, and March, 1928, papers on aspects of the subject were read before the Church History Teachers' Club of Chicago and the Western Branch of the American Society of Church History. In 1928 articles were published in the *Journal of Religion* on "Calvin's Efforts toward the Consolidation of Protestantism" (July) and "Cranmer's Project for a Reformed Consensus" (October). The former article has been considerably revised and extended to form Chapter V of this volume; the latter, with slight alterations, constitutes Chapter VI. In the *Canadian Journal of Religious Thought* were published "Catholic Protestantism" (November-December, 1928), and "Luther and the Constitutional Principle of Protestantism" (May-June, 1929). Most of the paragraphs of these articles are embodied, with other matter, in Chapters II and III of the book, respectively; but the first article has also contributed to the *Introduction* and a section of the second has been incorporated in Chapter I. My cordial thanks are extended to

5

PREFACE

Professor Shirley Jackson Case, editor of the *Journal of Religion,* and to Professor George Brockwell King, managing editor, and the Editorial Board of the *Canadian Journal of Religious Thought,* for permission to republish these materials. I gladly acknowledge also a deep debt of gratitude to former colleagues and associates in Toronto and to present colleagues in Chicago for suggestions received, and to many of my students in both centers for their stimulating interest in the historical aspects of the problem of Christian unity.

JOHN T. McNEILL.

PREFACE TO THE REVISED EDITION

THIS is a book about Protestantism, calling attention to an element in it by which it is now emerging into another existence. The divisions and rivalries of Protestant sects were from my first awareness of them distasteful and depressing to me. An exploration of some Reformation and seventeenth-century sources taught me to reject the stereotype in which Protestantism appeared as the cause or natural concomitant of an assertive individualism and doomed by its very nature to progressive fissiparation. Certain experiences and studies in connection with the formation of the United Church of Canada stimulated my interest in searching out what appeared to be an unfortunately neglected aspect of modern church history. The 1930 preface indicates briefly how parts of the book began to appear in print. Further attention to aspects of the Reformation and to the background history of the ecumenical movement has only deepened my assurance of the validity of the main contentions. Through the years I have had to reply negatively to a good many inquiries about the possibility of a new edition. When I received from the John Knox Press the proposal that, "for the benefit of current discussion on the ecumenical movement," the book be reissued with an added chapter, I very gladly complied. In chapters I to VIII a number of textual corrections have been made. The conclusion of chapter VIII has been shortened and the former General Conclusion omitted as no longer useful. I wish to thank my friend, Dr. Samuel Mc-

PREFACE TO THE REVISED EDITION

Crea Cavert, for expert comments on a draft of chapter IX. I am grateful also to Dr. Tadashi Akaishi of the John Knox Press for painstaking correspondence over details of the revision.

John T. McNeill

Elmsdale, East Middlebury,
Vermont
June 28, 1963

INTRODUCTION

WE have all been nurtured in the platitudes by which Protestantism has been traditionally described. According to a common opinion, the Protestant spirit is essentially one of atomic individualism. The Protestant, it is supposed, is one who pushes on from nationalism in religion to sectarianism, and from sectarianism to a religious solitude of pure private judgment freed from authority and association. His formal recognition of the authority of the Bible provides no effective check on individual opinion, since every one is free to interpret the Bible. His experience of justification by faith is assumed to be quite unshared and unsocial. And whereas, in fact, Luther taught the priesthood of every Christian as a function to be exercised on behalf, not of himself, but of every other Christian—an intensely social conception—it is constantly asserted that his doctrine of priesthood merely means "Every man his own priest." Many of Protestant heritage, finding a certain satisfaction in the sanction of their own individualistic inclinations, and thoughtlessly confusing individualism and liberty, habitually repeat these unsupported generalizations. Those emotionally unfriendly to Protestantism press a little further the same interpretation. They habitually represent it as anti-social in its inner character and a disastrously disintegrating agency in its outward influence upon society.[1]

[1] For some authors illustrating the above statements see G. B. Smith and Others, *Religious Thought in the Last Quarter-Century* (1927), chapter on "The Interpretation of Protestantism" (pp. 70ff.), by the present writer. Reprinted from *The Journal of Religion*, VI, 504ff. (July, 1926).

INTRODUCTION

A color of truth is lent to such assertions by extreme utterances in some Protestant quarters, and by tendencies exhibited in certain chapters of Protestant history. The very name which has attached itself to the movement has served to enforce this view. Because on one occasion the political champions of Luther's teaching lodged a protest against the annulment, by their opponents, of a previous mutual agreement, the designation of "Protestant" was applied to all of like persuasion. It has been gravely perpetuated, and although never officially adopted by the greater communions to which it was applied, has, no doubt, by its negative suggestion, helped to create a psychological predisposition to the belief that Protestantism bears in its heart a principle of destructive protest, and that its history is to be summed up as a series of assaults upon ecclesiastical and social order. To those within and without the Protestant ranks who accept this interpretation, the rising tide of unionism to-day must present an arresting question.

Contemporary Protestantism is stirred by a fresh impulse which in wide areas has become a vigorous movement. Its severed communions are seized by a common desire to seek their own liberation into a wider fellowship by means of union. Most Protestants appear to be convinced that a progressive unification of similar groups is both desirable and possible. They may divide on questions of the order in which the groups should coalesce, or on the details of any specific union project, and they may differ widely in the degree of haste with which they are willing to move, but in regard to the principle of union few and

10

faint are now the voices raised in opposition. Denominational rivalries are vanishing, and denominational assertiveness is old-fashioned. Within the greater Protestant groups the principles now in the ascendant are those of integration, comprehension, and catholicity.

The changed outlook may owe something to the business man's commendable demand for economy in administration. In an age of economic interpretations it is in this direction that we naturally look first for an explanation. But we have in recent years been forcibly reminded that nobody has surpassed the Puritans in business economy;[2] yet in violation of the principle of economy they parted from the Established Church and from each other, both in sorrow and in anger, to form detached sects. Religious people have generally shown a willingness to suffer some economic inconveniences for the sake of their religious ideals. Whatever the business spirit may have contributed to this newly emerged tendency in Protestantism, it can hardly be deemed the source and energizing power of it all.

Observation of the character of the movement suggests, indeed, a very different interpretation. Fundamental to it is the craving, not to reduce the cost but to enrich the content of religion. The Protestant communions have, in fact, for a generation or more ardently coveted one another's spiritual goods. They have already taken large booty from each other, and they have deeply realized that there is no legal propriety in things spiritual. They have peacefully penetrated one another, each sharing with the rest what

[2] See, for instance, R. H. Tawney, *Religion and the Rise of Capitalism.*

11

was once its own peculiarity. This process has gone so far as greatly to reduce the psychological uniqueness of every group.

The mutual craving knows scarce any limitation. Not only are the various groups ambitious to possess themselves of the heroes and martyrs, the prayers and hymns, the theological insights and social ideals of the others; each veritably craves identification with all. Paul rebuked the incipient denominationalism of the Corinthians by reminding them of the wider heritage from which, by such a policy, they were excluding themselves. To-day the Protestant churches are deliberately overleaping the fences of their narrow patrimonies as separate bodies and are seeking the freedom and the riches of the whole living residue of the Christian tradition. The final hindrance to the complete appropriation of what they hold to be their rightful spiritual heritage lies in their separate organization; hence they are facing the problem of removing that hindrance. Because of the wider range of unhindered fraternity which unionism offers, it bears the aspects of a movement both of liberation and of cultural increment. It presents to the individual an increased volume of interests, contacts, obligations; a fuller functioning of life in services, larger opportunity and influence, and a consequent enrichment of thought and emotion. It thus promises fundamental satisfactions, the desire for which, once thoroughly awakened, will hardly be denied.

The process of interpenetration and mutual appropriation was formerly largely unconscious. It has now become conscious and purposeful, with the objective of corporate union. The air is full of expectation.

Students in preparation for the ministry exhibit a fresh interest when the subject comes under review in the classroom. Church gatherings attend upon the words of any one who can offer guidance or interpretation. Among laymen who observe the divisive influence of sectarian organization in community life, as well as among ministers who are aware of the history of the denominations and their common origin, one frequently hears eagerly expressed the hope of a general consolidation of Protestantism. Many think of this as a stage in the complete unification of Christianity. Ecclesiastical recognition of the new spirit is seen in the large amount of committee work now being expended on union proposals in many countries. Certain impressive achievements in the working out of the union principle are already recorded—achievements which none but a bold prophet would have ventured to forecast a generation ago. Such results are now widely regarded as but first-fruits of a universal harvest. The movement is confidently expected to sweep over the churches and remake the church. This is the religious enthusiasm of the hour. Should it prove to be that of the century, it will have done its work.

Why should Protestantism, after four hundred years of history, enter upon this new phase? Have we here simply a response to the demand of the present age with its after-war craving for reintegration? It is to be remembered that union sentiment and action in Protestantism had gained much momentum before the Great War, and it is quite possible that the movement has been as much retarded as accelerated by it. Is it, then, a simple reaction of human nature,

13

a shrinking back from the results of long-exerted divisive tendencies to which Protestantism is necessarily prone? It would seem probable that if Protestantism is essentially divisive, any unitive movement that might arise would be detached from and unfavorable to it, and would be feared and shunned by it in turn. Many anticipated this direction of things some years ago, but to-day it is apparent that the reverse tendency is becoming dominant. May it not be, then, that the phenomenon of unionism is primarily to be explained as the outcropping of an element original to Protestantism, though hitherto largely frustrated?

The distinction pressed by Troeltsch between early and modern Protestantism is not here a subject of inquiry; but it may be noted for the purpose of comparison. Assuredly, in respect to questions of authority, of the supernatural, and of toleration, a wide difference is to be recognized between the Protestantism of the sixteenth and that of the twentieth century. It has, however, been reasonably contended against some observations of Troeltsch, that the roots of the New Protestantism lie mainly in the Old rather than in elements extraneous to it.[3] Just as Protestantism itself sprang, under the stimuli of a changing world-order and new educational resources, out of elements long obscured but still preserved in medievalism, so the new Protestantism has gradually rather than abruptly succeeded the old as factors obscured within the old emerged and became dominant. According to this view, the part played in the making of *Neu-*

---

[3] Hoffmann, H., *Der neuere Protestantismus und die Reformation*, pp. 25ff., p. 46,

protestantismus by the sects which the early Protestantism unchurched and by the Enlightenment which it resisted, was stimulative but not necessarily constitutive; and, for that matter, both the sects and the Enlightenment owed much to the Reformation. The present-day temper and outlook of Protestantism must be accounted for mainly by the emergence, under the stimuli of these factors, of certain minor and long apparently latent characteristics of the original movement. It is easily possible to indicate, for example, in the thought of the Reformers, suggestions of an historic and humanistic view of Scripture, of a widening of the limits of toleration, and of a rationalism that discounts the miraculous.

It is not important to our thesis to urge any particular interpretation of *Neuprotestantismus*, but the one suggested above bears some parallel to the argument of this book. Indeed, our claim is somewhat more positive. It is here contended that the ideal of Christian unity was a pronounced original characteristic of Protestantism, that it was by no means entirely inactive at any period, and that in the contemporary movement it has resumed vitality and, favored by a social environment that intensely craves integration, now promises to become dominant.

The emergence of Protestant unionism constitutes a challenge to the student of Reformation history. It is surprising to observe how little light is shed upon it by historians. So massive is the body of facts with which the investigator of sixteenth century movements has to wrestle, that in most instances he exhausts his energy in arranging mere events and results. The motives, ideals, and objectives which give real character to a movement are in this case often obscured. Because schism and disruption followed in the wake of the Reformation, it is often assumed that they were its conscious objectives. It is high time that investigators devoted some attention to the problem of ascertaining in what degree the Reformation cherished the principle of unity and sought its realization.

Indeed, merely in the interests of truth and proportion, and quite apart from the present reunion tendency, a fresh survey of the Reformation from this point of view would be fully justified. No history of the Reformation as a whole has given more than incidental and cursory attention to the subject of union advocacy and effort within the movement. The drive toward separatism has been taken as the main theme. Variations of opinion, party alignments, and group conflicts have been handled with keen analysis and refined elaboration. Cohesive and catholic elements have been passed over lightly, as the untimely and ineffectual efforts of impractical dreamers. The student has been led to think of the few irenical spirits of the period who have been called to his attention as puny and insignificant figures making pleading gestures on a stage filled with contending giants. He has hardly been permitted to entertain the surmise, much less to realize the fact, that all the greater Reformers, with the exception of Luther in certain moods and special crises, were consistent advocates either of a Protestant or of a wider Christian union.

The following chapters are offered as a contribution to a new interpretation of Protestantism. The familiar older interpretation, both by its adherents and by its opponents, has emphasized in it the thought of salvation as an individual matter, and minimized or neglected the elements of communion and organic solidarity. These elements have indeed begun to receive recognition on the part of a few, chiefly German, investigators, but no general study of the subject has been made, and no work has appeared in which they are made a substantive part of the movement as a whole. The tendency of the social historians has been to regard Protestantism as a concomitant of the nationalism and individualism which marked the social life of the age, and as wholly sympathetic with these movements. In the present study both these viewpoints are challenged as inadequate, and the view is advanced that Protestantism, while not unaffected by the nationalistic and individualistic movements that preceded and accompanied it, possessed an inward unitive principle by virtue of which it resisted, with a measure of success, the forces of disintegration. The assertion of this principle by the Reformers is indicated with reference to their teaching on the communion of believers, their claim of catholicity against the sectarianism of Rome, and their conciliar ideal of church government. The practical efforts which they made toward the realization of the unitive principle in the formation of wider communions are treated as serious and important factors in Reformation history. Finally, the line of connection is traced between the expressions of this principle in the sixteenth century and the modern and contemporary unity movement in Protestantism.

The facts employed do not, of course, constitute a

history of the Reformation or of its consequences. That they do, however, considerably supplement the materials contained in existing works on the subject and bring to light some of the little-prized resources of Protestantism, is a permissible claim. The writer does not anticipate the immediate and undisputed acceptance of his thesis by all readers, much less of every detailed contention in support of it. His purpose will be attained if the book is instrumental in revealing to impartial students some important considerations the neglect of which has, he believes, hitherto prevented an integral conception of the character of original and later Protestantism. Many facts and viewpoints excluded from treatment here have been carefully borne in mind while the book was in preparation; but it seemed best to work within the limits that have been adopted. Experience in the teaching of Reformation history and exchange of opinion with other teachers, and with graduate students, on many of the points discussed, have strengthened the conviction gained in research that the interpretation here put forth is simply demanded by the facts, and that, however inadequately it may now be presented, it is destined ultimately to receive acceptance. Of the validity or error of this conviction the reader is now the judge.

PART I

THE UNITIVE PRINCIPLE IN THE REFORMATION MOVEMENT

CHAPTER I

PROTESTANT COMMUNION: THE RELIGIOUS BASIS

WHEN Luther wrote: "The holy Christian Church is the principal work of God, for the sake of which all things were made,"[1] and when Calvin avowed: "I take God and his angels to witness that never since I became a teacher of the church have I had any other purpose than the church's advancement,"[2] they were but voicing the common devotion of the sixteenth-century Reformers. Such words would ring with the same sincerity if uttered by Melanchthon or Bucer, by Zwingli or Bullinger, by Cranmer or Knox. The zeal that consumed them was a zeal to be of service to the Christian Church. In their acceptance of the Apostles' Creed they affirmed their faith in "the Holy catholic Church" and in "the Communion of Saints"; and they regarded the latter of these expressions as simply an explanation of the former. The Reformation conception of the church began with the idea of the *Communio Sanctorum*. What was the content of this idea? We shall call Luther and Calvin to answer; but before they appear it will be necessary to realize something of the earlier connotation of the phrase.

[1] "Die heilige Christliche Kirche ist das fürnehmste Werk Gottes, um welches willen alles geschaffen ist." *Sämtliche Schriften*, IX, 1386.

[2] "Ipsum et angelos testes habeam nihil ex quo officium doctoris in ecclesia suscepi, mihi fuisse propositum quam ecclesiae prodesse." "Johannes Calvinus Lectori," (preface to the final edition of the *Institutes*). *Corpus Reformatorum*, XXX, 2.

1. The Conception of Communion Before the Reformation

The Christian Church took its rise in the *koinōnia*, or fellowship, of those who shared a profound and transforming experience which centered in Jesus Christ. Its chief functions were to interpret that experience in terms of social living, to extend the number of those who shared it, and to perpetuate it to after generations. From the beginning of Jesus' ministry his followers had mingled personal discipleship with group loyalty, and the latter developed with great intensity when the physical presence of the Master had been withdrawn. The Eucharist took a central place in the Christian's experience, since it served both as a means of making Christ's presence a continuous reality and as a visible pledge of the inviolable fellowship of the group. A hostile environment promoted group solidarity by tending to confine the Christian's social relations within the circle of the fellowship. There alone he was likely to be understood, respected, and befriended, and there he came to fullest and freest self-realization in the exchange of mutual service. He profited by this corporate solidarity in concrete satisfactions. He felt a spiritual enrichment in the stimulus of an intensely religious fraternalism within the Christian community, in which faith, hope and love and the other virtues and graces of the Christian life were purposefully cultivated. Further, under the sanction of charity conceived as religious duty and privilege, the group offered economic relief and security to the individual, and the individual sacrificed private gains to maintain the group life. Christians were expected to bear one another's bur-

22

dens and to share one another's benefits. These
relationships extended beyond the local society. The
local church realized itself as the manifestation of a
wider organism of which Christ was the Head, and
which early in the second century began to be referred
to as the Catholic Church.

This conception tended to expand, in response to
experience, in two directions. Intense belief in im-
mortality, and those spontaneous and religiously cultivated attachments which death could not destroy in
the survivor, made very thin the veil between this life
and the after-life. Hence the Christian's communion
was thought of as not confined to his earth-dwelling
associates in the visible church, but as extending to
those who had passed the gates of death and joined
the glorious ranks of the church triumphant. But
again, the Christian looked upon the world-society as
the church's mission field, out of which were to be
won new recruits into the army of the redeemed.
The thought could not be dismissed that those yet
to be Christians, even if they were not yet born,
already in the mind of God belonged to the sacred
fellowship. In these two ways the conception of communion was extended to limits that became imper-
ceptible. At the same time, in one sense, it underwent
a process of restriction. Observation made it all too
apparent that the external church of the baptized
contained some members who could not be thought
of as candidates for heaven and therefore did not
truly belong to the communion of saints. As Augustine was fond of saying, there were tares mingled
with the wheat. It was humanly impossible to distinguish with certainty between the wheat and the

tares; adjudication of the point was to be left to the omniscience of God.

Thus the notion of the *communio sanctorum*, which came to be asserted as a substantive part of Christian doctrine in course of the development of the Apostles' Creed, involved elements which made it impossible to identify it with the visible church. It meant a real but invisible communion, whose membership, past, present, and future, was known only to God. Augustine's *City of God* affords, amid much peripheral and extraneous matter, the most impressive literary statement of this phase of Christian experience and thought. Bryce eloquently wrote of this influential treatise: "The greatest mind of his generation consoled the faithful for the fall of their earthly city, Rome, by describing to them its successor and representative, the City which hath foundations whose builder and maker is God."[3] But Augustine not only consoled; he also challenged and encouraged. His heavenly city, the home of God's elect, was the social embodiment of perfect love, justice, and peace, and served as a model and pattern of perfection for the Christian society on earth. He closely related without identifying the *ecclesia externa* with the *civitas Dei*, that he might bring aid to the catholic visible church to which he was passionately devoted. In his intention, even more than in the application of his ideas in the Middle Ages, the picture of the celestial society was employed as the objective toward which the struggling and defective earthly society was to strive.

In the Middle Ages the idea of an other-world com-

[3] *The Holy Roman Empire* (New York, 1917), p. 94.

munion shared by the living lost nothing of its vivid-
ness. Each celebration of the Eucharist tended to
revive it in pious minds. It did, however, lose something of its grandeur. With the growth of the notion
of vicarious merit distributed quantitatively on codi-
fied terms under papal administration, the democratic mutuality of the early conception largely passed
away, and the desire was created merely to share
parasitically in the supererogatory works of the saints
which swelled the "Treasury of Merit." It was the
radical thinkers rather than the official champions of
the medieval church who recaptured the earlier idea
of communion which Augustine had clothed in Platonic
idealism. In the fourteenth century, to meet the
needs of an age of decline, Wyclif, a pronounced
Augustinian, set it forth again with scholastic elaboration. For him the true church is the expression of
God's eternal will, timeless and invisible, consisting
of all the predestinate—*universitas fidelium predestinatorum.* It bears an indeterminate relation to the
apparent (*pretensa*) or visible church, but we cannot
know how far the former interpenetrates the latter.
The predestinate form a unified body in the bonds of
charity. This intangible, invisible, and timeless church
is a real entity, having a corporate unity in Christ its
Head, and is rightly called "holy mother church."
No one is a member of holy mother church who is
not predestinate, and everyone who is predestinate,
regardless of his present status, is a member of holy
mother church.[4] In such teaching Wyclif is invok-

[4] Wyclif, *De Ecclesia,* ed. J. Loserth (Wyclif Society), pp. 7, 19, 28f.,
37, 107. Cf. Workman, H. B., *John Wyclif, a Study of the English
Medieval Church,* II, 6-20, and McNeill, J. T., "Some Emphases in
Wyclif's Teaching," *Journal of Religion,* VII, 1927, 447ff.

ing the heavenly ideal to shame the earthly reality, and the result is to leave the church visible seriously discredited. This does not mean that Wyclif repudiated the notion of a church visible, or even dissociated himself from the historic church. But to his eyes the latter appeared in so corrupt a state that his drastic reform proposals seemed, and still seem, such as would have largely destroyed the existing order before replacing it.

These opinions were essentially repeated by Hus, whose *De Ecclesia* is largely dependent on Wyclif's treatise of the same title. The catholic church, he taught, consists of the whole body of the predestinate, the living, the dead, and those yet to be born.[5] This is the holy catholic church which Christians profess in the creed. He distinguishes between "catholic" and "Roman," and denies that Peter was ever the head of the holy catholic church. The utmost he will grant to Rome is that "a holy Pope in conjunction with holy cardinals are a holy church which is a part of the holy catholic and apostolic church."[6] One of the charges on which Hus was burned was that of having called Wyclif "a catholic man and an evangelical doctor." But while he quoted and praised Wyclif he cited the authority of Augustine, and his doctrine of communion is consciously based on Augustine's. In his attitude to the existing institution he is considerably less radical than his English master.

---

[5] "Ecclesia est omnium predestinatorum universitas, quae est omnes predestinati, praesentes, praeteriti, et futuri."

[6] *Works*, Nürnberg ed., I, 244ff.; Schaff, D. S., *The Church by John Hus*, pp. 3, 5, 66.

2. ETHICAL-SOCIAL CONCEPTION OF COMMUNION IN LUTHER AND CALVIN

Luther first looked into the *De Ecclesia* of Hus late in 1519;[7] and early in 1520 he wrote to Spalatin that he and Staupitz were Hussites without knowing it, as were also, for that matter, Paul and Augustine.[8] In his studies on the Psalms and on Romans his ecclesiology had already taken on its outlines, and the main elements of Hus's doctrine were comprised within it. Like Wyclif and Hus, he had felt strongly the influence of Augustine. He conceives of the true church as "a spiritual and eternal city of God" (*eyn geystlich ewige Gottis Stadt*), in which all the saints (that is, the faithful) are members.[9] He does not, however, dwell on the speculative suggestions of this phraseology, but emphasizes the social and ethical aspects of Christian communion. On the whole he is distinctly less metaphysical and more ethical than his Augustinian predecessors.[10] His high predestinarianism, exhibited in an extreme form in his treatise on the *Unfree Will* (1525),[11] is kept in the background of his interpretation of communion. For him, as for Wyclif and Hus, the true church is the mystical body of Christ, not the visible organization of the baptized or the clergy who rule them. Its membership, however, is thought of as delimited by the operation of

[7] Letter to Staupitz, October 3, 1519; De Wette, W. M. L., *Dr. Martin Luthers Briefe, Sendschrieben und Bedenken*, I, 341.

[8] "Ego imprudens hucusque omnia Johannis Huss et docui et tenui: docuit eadem imprudentia et Johannes Staupitz: breviter sumus omnes Hussitae ignorantes: denique Paulus et Augustinus ad verbum sunt Hussitae." *Ibid.*, p. 425.

[9] *Werke* (Weimar ed.), II, 743.

[10] Cf. Holl, K., *Gesammelte Aufsätze*, I, *Luther*, pp. 78f.

[11] "De Servo Arbitrio.," *Werke*, XVIII, 600-787.

saving grace and the consequent active faith, rather than by divine predestination to that salvation. Accordingly, the church consists of true believers who have laid hold on salvation by the faith which has been implanted in them by the agency of the Word.[12] Shortly after reading Hus's tract, and while in expectation of Rome's act of excommunication, he published his "Sermon on the Sacrament and the Brotherhoods,"[13] and his "Sermon on Excommunication."[14] In the former of these works he links communion with the Eucharist. The meaning or function of this sacrament is the communion of all the saints; hence it has come to be called *communio*, and *communicare* is used in the sense of "to go to the sacrament." This is because Christ and all the saints form a spiritual body, like a city state in which the citizens are all members one of another and of the whole city.[15]

By "communion" Luther means to suggest no merely inward experience, but a vividly realized and dutifully cultivated fellowship with Christ and all the faithful. On the one hand the members jointly share

---

[12] Cf. *Werke*, IV, 400. In this he may have served himself heir, as H. Strohl suggests, to the Franciscan tradition which emphasized the preached Word as over against the miraculous action of the sacraments. *L'Épanouissement de la pensée de Luther*, p. 290.

[13] "Von dem hochwürdigen sacrament des heiligen wahren leichnams Christi und von den Brüderschaften." *Werke*, II, 738ff.

[14] "Ein Sermon von dem Bann." *Werke*, VI, 63ff.

[15] "Die bedeutung oder das werck disses sacraments ist gemeynschafft aller heyligen: drumb nennet man es auch mit seynen teglichen namen Synaxis oder Communio, das ist gemeynschafft, und Communicare auf latein heyst diss gemeinschafft empfahen, wilchs wir auff deutsch sagen zum sacrament gehen, und kumpt daher, das Christus mit allen heyligen ist eyn geystlicher corper, gleych wie einer stat volck, eyn gemeyn und corper ist, eyn yglicher burgher des andern glydmas und der ganzen statt." *Werke*, II, 743. Cf. J. Köstlin's analysis in his *Theology of Luther*, Engl. ed., I, 334-44.

in a spiritual reciprocity with Christ.[16] "Christ, with all saints, takes on our estate (*gestalt*), strives with us against sin, death, and evil, wherefore we take on his estate, and clothe ourselves in his righteousness, life, and holiness."[17] It is clear, says Luther, that this sacrament is "nothing else than a divine sign in which Christ and all the saints with all their works, sufferings, services, graces, possessions, are pledged, given, and appropriated for the consolation of all who are in distress and affliction."[18] On the other hand, emphasis is laid on the reciprocal and mutual relation between believers. In the sacrament "we make our own the infirmities of all other Christians, take on us their estate, and make theirs all the good in our power." Indeed, "we are changed into one another."[19] To the "brotherhoods," or special organizations for sacramental fellowship, he would oppose the general communion of saints, the universal Christian brotherhood in which, without special vows and restrictions, the Christian is free to serve the whole community of Christendom.[20] From this wider fellowship, he argues in the "Sermon on the Ban," formal acts of excommunication cannot exclude the true Christian. The Christian who has faith, though excommunicate, has still the fundamental qualification for membership in the communion of saints: not that he should despise the sacrament;

[16] The sacramental elements themselves suggest to Luther two phases of this participation. The bread represents Christ's life and good works, the wine his sufferings and death, in both of which the worshiper participates. *Werke*, II, 749.

[17] *Ibid.*, p. 748.

[18] *Ibid.*, p. 749.

[19] *Ibid.*, p. 749.

[20] *Ibid.*, p. 756.

instead he should long for it and spiritually participate in it. Faith is that which for Luther gives the
sacrament its efficacy; and he makes finally essential
only the inward attitude and not the outward act.[21]
The sacrament takes a position important but sec-
ondary as instrumental to faith and communion.

Nowhere, then, is communion conceived of with
more of vital activity than by Luther.[22] It is a relationship in which living Christians share in an intense experience, with the most important results.
This thought is set forth even more explicitly in the
"Tessaradecas consolatoria" of February, 1520. Communion is here interpreted as "a communicating of
spiritual goods or blessings—faith, hope and charity,
and the other graces and gifts—which all become
communia through charity." "This," says Luther,
"is the communion of saints in which we glory."[23]
But the expression also means a sharing of burdens
and penalties. There is no isolation in these experiences. "If I suffer, I do not suffer alone: Christ and
all Christians suffer with me, according as he saith,
he that toucheth you toucheth the apple of mine eye."
It is indeed this active communion that constitutes the
church; and "communion of saints" means the same
thing as "holy catholic church," in which good and
ill are mutually shared and all things belong to all,
as is suggested in the Eucharist."[24] Such is the com-

[21] *Werke*, II, pp. 749f.

[22] See also pp. 33ff., below.

[23] *Werke*, VI, 131.

[24] "Hoc est quod dicimus: 'Credo in spiritum sanctum, sanctam
Ecclesiam catholicam.' Quid est credere Ecclesiam sanctam quam
sanctorum communionem? Quo communicant autem sancti? Nempe
bonis et malis: omnia sunt omnium, sicut figurat sacramentum altaris
in pane et vino, ubi unum corpus, unus panis, unus potus ab Apostolo
dicimur." *Ibid.*, p. 131-32.

munion of saints and the Church of Christ: whoever denies this is an unbeliever. Even in death we are not alone, but comforted by the companionship of the whole church.[25]

Thus in Christian communion the individual is completely rescued from his solitariness in life, death, and the hereafter. The church consists essentially in the personal interrelations of its members, among whom there is a community in the possession of religious goods.[26] Membership in it becomes an intimate association of personalities, obligated by solemn pledges to mutual charity and reciprocal service, and functioning harmoniously together as parts of a living organism.

This view of the Christian communion is substantially shared by all the Reformers; but further illustration must be confined to Calvin. The essentials of Luther's thought reappear in that of Calvin, but with more of the Augustinian emphasis on predestination as the constitutive principle of communion.[27] In the manner of Wyclif and Hus, Calvin makes frequent quotation of Augustine, but he combines Augustinian and Lutheran conceptions. "To God alone," he says, "must be left a knowledge of his church, of which

---

[25] "Adeo scilicet nobis Christus noluit mortis viam esse solitariam, quam omnis homo horret, sed comite tota ecclesia viam passionis et mortis ingredimur." *Ibid.*, p. 132.

[26] Cf. Kattenbusch, F., *Die Doppelschichtigkeit in Luthers Kirchenbegriff*, p. 31.

[27] Th. Werdermann, "Calvins Lehre von der Kirche in ihrer geschichtlichen Entwicklung," in *Calvinstudien, Festschrift zum 400 Geburtstage Calvins*, ed. J. Bohatec, p. 261, quotes with approval the words of Max Scheibe in his *Calvins Predestinationslehre*: "Die Erwählungsidee ist konstituerend für den Kirchenbegriff. Der Wert des Glaubens an die Kirche wird durch sie festgestellt, indem sich als inhalt dieses Glaubens die Überzeugung des Heils nie verlustig zu gehen, ergibt." Cf. *Ibid.*, pp. 279-80.

his secret election forms the foundation."[28]   The
Lutheran emphasis on the Word is also present, and
such expressions as "God inspires us with faith, but it
is by the instrument of his gospel,"[29] accord with
Luther's view; but in general this element is, logically
at least, subordinated. The difference from Luther has
to do only with the origin, not with the content of the
communion. All the elect are knit together, as the
different members of a body of which Christ is the
sole Head, and are "called not only to the same in-
heritance of eternal life, but to a participation of one
God and church."[30]   Christians must accordingly conduct themselves as sheep of one flock. "And hence
the additional expression (in the creed) 'communion of
saints,' "[31] an important clause, since "it admirably expresses the quality of the church, as if it were said that
the saints are united in the fellowship (*societatem*) of
Christ by the law that they mutually communicate to
each other all the blessings which God bestows on
them." The Scriptures (Acts 4. 32; Eph. 4. 4) distinctly
teach a real community (*communitas*), though this does
not exclude diversity of gifts or private property.
There is the greatest comfort (*consolatio*) in the word

---

[28] "Cujus fundamentum est arcana illius electio," *Inst.*, IV, i, 2; *C. R.*,
XXX, 747. (In the following citations of Calvin's works I have frequently profited by Beveridge's translations, but have in all cases
used the *Corpus Reformatorum* edition. In translations given I have
usually found it desirable to alter Beveridge's language for the sake of
accuracy, often I fear at the expense of elegance.)

[29] *Inst.*, IV, i, 5; *C. R.*, XXX, 749.

[30] *Inst.*, IV, i, 2; *C. R.*, XXX, 747.

[31] Calvin uses the expression "sanctorum communicatio," as if he
wished to give point to his idea of participation. *Inst.*, IV, i, 3, *Ibid.*
Compare his Genevan Catechism (1545), which defines the church as
"corpus et societas fidelium, quos Deus ad vitam eternam praedestina-
vit." *C. R.*, XXX, 747; Müller, E. F. K., *Die Bekenntnisschriften der
reformierten Kirche*, p. 125.

"communion," since it creates the assurance that all things conferred by God upon his members are ours.[32]

The emphasis on the individual's obligation to the corporate body may receive one further illustration from Calvin. On Eph. 4. 16 he says, "The edifying of itself in love" means that "no increase is advantageous unless it answers the needs of the whole body. He errs who seeks to grow by himself. . . . If we wish to be considered members of Christ, let no man be anything for himself, but let us all be whatever we are for each other.[33] This is accomplished by love; and where love does not reign there is no edification but a mere scattering of the church."[34]

Both Luther and Calvin, then, made the idea of communion applicable to the social contacts of Christians. Originating in a divine act, it was to be socially realized on a human plane. Both described the church in terms of the communion of its members, and thought of communion as active social intercommunication and reciprocal service. Whether the Christian society was delimited by reference to predestination or to active belief,[35] they agreed in stressing its corporate character.

3. Communion and the Priesthood of the People

Nothing in the teachings of the Reformers, and especially of Luther, is more characteristic than the

---

[32] *Inst.*, IV, i, 3. *C. R.*, XXX, 747-48.

[33] "nemo sibi aliquid sit sed alii aliis simus quicquid sumus."

[34] *C. R.*, LXXIX, 203.

[35] Werdermann regards even Calvin's idea of the "company of the predestinate" as not alien (*nicht fremd*) to Luther's thought. *Op. cit.*, p. 279.

emphasis upon the priesthood which is exercised by believers. Yet no other Reformation principle has been so widely misunderstood and so frequently misrepresented. Luther's teaching on this for him highly important point is in fullest accord with the conception of communion which has received attention in the foregoing paragraphs. But by an unwarranted detachment of the passages on priesthood from those on communion, and through the neglect of any close inspection of the actual statements of Luther on priesthood, an extraordinary misconception of his view has long prevailed. Not to cite extreme examples of this widespread misrepresentation, let us observe how the matter is stated in one moderate and, in general, scholarly work. In the Introduction to Dr. R. H. Murray's *Political Consequences of the Reformation* (1926), we read (p. xxi) that although "the appeal of the Bible was the soul of the Reformation," nevertheless:

The reformer asserted the priesthood of the believer and this assertion carried with it the right to examine for oneself regardless of any *Ita scriptum est*. Thus was provoked the habit of inquiry that lies at the very base of individualism. The interpretation of the Bible was left to the ever-varying necessities of the individual. Men were convinced that the salvation of each soul was dear in the sight of God, and they were convinced that nothing and no one must stand between the soul and its Creator. As the national state emerges, so does the individual, with all the advantages as well as the drawbacks of his newly found liberty.[36]

---

[36] Reprinted by permission of Little, Brown & Company, publishers, Boston, Massachusetts.

A. M. Hunter, in *The Teaching of Calvin*, has fallen into the same common error (an error from which much that he shows familiarity with in this book might have saved him), when he says (p. 13), "The Reformation declared every man to be a priest toward God, independent of the help of other mortals in securing the blessings of the Christian salvation."

This paragraph is typical of the trite platitudes that pass for historical exposition, in which, in one form of language or another, modern individualism is, without citation of text, represented as deriving from Luther's doctrine of priesthood. But the platitude is false.

A few German scholars (with whom is to be associated the French Luther authority, H. Strohl) have, indeed, pointed out the injustice of the whole conception of Luther as an individualist. K. Holl was among the most pronounced in his emphasis upon the corporate aspect of Luther's religion.[37] F. Kattenbusch, in a recently published careful review of the sources and literature of Luther's doctrine of the church,[38] has established the point more firmly. For him Luther is no individualist: he "does not know that he ever stood in danger of becoming" one. His experience itself was not isolated, and he was always concerned for the church.[39] In a living, personal way he perceives the church as *communio sanctorum*, "and this communion is marked by the interchange of commonly possessed religious goods."[40]

But Kattenbusch has not concerned himself to indicate the relation of this high doctrine of vital communion to that of the priesthood of believers, with which, in fact, it is closely interwoven in Luther's thought. An examination of the principal passages

[37] *Gesammelte Aufsätze*, I. See also Holl's posthumous article, "Martin Luther, à propos de l'étude de M. Jacques Maritain," in *Revue de théologie et de philosophie*, Août-Décembre, 1927, pp. 260ff.

[38] *Die Doppelschichtigkeit in Luther's Kirchenbegriff* (1928).

[39] *Op. cit.*, pp. 4f., "Das augustinische 'Gott und die Seele! Weiter nichts? Weiter nichts!' hat ihn nie innerlich regiert." His piety is personal, even subjective, but never "privatisch." *Op. cit.*, p. 4, and footnote 1.

[40] *Ibid.*, pp. 21f., p. 31.

in which Luther states this doctrine will furnish the best illustration of the point, and will show how very far the reformer was from teaching individualism in connection with it.

Far from destroying the idea of priesthood, Luther is giving to it an expanded content. Over against the Romanist conception of the exclusive priesthood of the few, he affirms the priesthood of the whole body, in which, indeed, the priesthood of the few continues, but in a functional and representative form. The official priesthood is now a ministry, and a summation and representation of the priesthood of all, which is bestowed by Christ. The lay priesthood is exercised socially and mutually, never atomically. "Every man his own priest" is not for a moment the thought of Luther; on the contrary, it is every man his neighbor's priest. Instead of saying that "No one must stand between the soul and God," Luther is saying and reiterating that it is the function of every Christian to lead souls to God.

Luther is by no means the originator of this doctrine,[41] but he and the other Reformers made it so central and gave it such profound religious content that rather than "the appeal to the Bible," it may be rightly called "the soul of the Reformation." So far as his expression of it is concerned, it first appears clearly in a letter of December 18, 1519.[42] It was developed in his *Sermon on the Mass*, 1520, and in his

[41] It rested, of course, upon the New Testament. Emerton finds it anticipated in Marsilius of Padua's statement that "all believing Christians may be called *viri ecclesiastici*" (*Beginnings of Modern Europe*, p. 169). It is really implied in the position of the whole Conciliar party. But Luther gave it fresh emphasis and clarity.

[42] Enders, *Briefwechsel*, II, 279, and editor's note, p. 280. K. Holl, *op. cit.*, I, 273.

great treatises of that year. In the *Address to the Nobility* we are told that the bishop's consecration "is just as if in the name of the whole congregation he took one person out of the community, who all possess equal power, and commanded him to exercise his power for the rest."[43] Priests differ only in function from the people. "A cobbler, a smith, a peasant, every man, has the office and function of his calling, and yet all alike are consecrated priests and bishops and every man in his office may be useful and beneficial to the rest, that so many kinds of work may be united in one community, just as the members of a body all serve one another."

When in the treatise, *On Christian Liberty*, he contrasts "kingship" with "priesthood," he indicates that it is by virtue of the former that the Christian is "the most free lord of all": by virtue of the latter he is "the most dutiful servant of all." The universal

---

[43] *Werke*, VI, 407. The harmonization of the people's priesthood with that of an ordained ministry offers no problem to Luther's thought. The latter is for him a natural specialization of the former; the minister's function is representative of the general priesthood from which it springs. "Our priest or bishop," he wrote in 1533, "stands before the altar, having been duly and publicly called, and formerly in baptism consecrated, anointed, and made a priest of Christ." When he distributes the bread and wine "We all kneel down behind and about him, man and woman, young and old, master and servant, mistress and maid, the aged and the children, as God brings us together, all true and holy priests together, sanctified by the blood of Christ, anointed and consecrated in baptism.... We do not let our pastor utter the ordinance of Christ for himself; but he is the mouth by which we all say it together with him from our hearts (*er ist unser aller mund und wir alle sprechen sie mit im von hertzen*). . . . This is our mass, and the true mass . . . " (*Von der Winkelmesse und Pfaffenweihe*, 1533. *Werke*, XXXVIII, 247). This idea is common in his earlier works. For characteristic expressions of it in writings of 1523, see below, pp. 121ff. For Luther the evangelical ministry is a representative priesthood exercised *vice et nomine omnium*, and undertaken only *consensu universitatis seu ecclesiae*. The emphasis of Luther on the representative principle in the conception of the ministry was carried over into Calvinism, where the idea found logical expression in a representative polity.

priesthood, while it projects from itself a specialized ministry, rests upon the priesthood of Christ. It is a dignity far higher than kingship, because "by that priesthood we are able to appear before God, to pray for others, and to teach one another mutually the things that are of God."[44] By it believers are "reciprocally and mutually one the Christ of the other, doing to our neighbor as Christ does to us."[45] "The good things we have from God ought to flow from one to the other and be common to all." "A Christian man does not live in himself, but in Christ and his neighbor: in Christ by faith, in his neighbor through charity."[46] Luther even goes so far as to say, "My faith and righteousness ought to be laid down before God as a covering and intercession for the sins of my neighbor, which I take upon myself."[47]

That any reader should find in these entirely typical passages the foundation of an assertive individualism, is difficult to understand. In point of fact, they teach nothing of the kind, but emphasize mutual obligation, each for all and all for each. Individualism yields completely to conceptions highly social and communion-forming. The priesthood of believers is not for Luther the believer's privilege to live his life in jealous isolation and independence. Its reference is not to individual privilege, but to social duty and social experience. It is not self-regarding, but other-regarding. It binds the individual to the group under inviolable obligations of love and service. It is a doc-

[44] *Werke*, VII, 57.
[45] "Invicem mutuoque sumus alter alterius Christus facientes proximiis sicut Christus nobis facit." *Ibid.*, p. 66.
[46] *Ibid.*, p. 69.
[47] *Ibid.*

38

trine fundamentally unitive and in no sense divisive. It is a phase of communion, and the way of realizing it, while it is also a religious and ethical interpretation of everyday life and conduct.[48]

4. THE INVISIBLE CHURCH AS THE PATTERN OF THE VISIBLE

Such an ethical-social conception of communion could only be realized by means of some form of visible organization. This naturally leads us to ask what was the relation between the invisible and the visible church in Reformation thought. Recent special studies have made it clear, nor, indeed, was there ever good reason to doubt, that the Reformers had no thought of repudiating the principle of a visible church. Luther is further from such a position than Wyclif, and almost, if not quite, as far from it as Calvin. He aimed at extensive reforms, but thought of these not as destructive of the church, but as needed restorative agencies. They were needed because the visible body had, in his view, to a great degree lost relationship with the invisible Ideal. The idea of invisibility was again, even more purposefully than in Augustine and Wyclif, invoked not merely to explain

---

[48] Since these paragraphs were written the notable study of Luther's ecclesiology by Professor Paul Althaus, *Communio Sanctorum: die Gemeinde im lutherischen Kirchengedanken*, I. *Luther*, has appeared. Althaus follows out with industrious research the suggestions of Holl, and exhibits with ample citations the Reformer's conception of communion. His study dwarfs the present incidental treatment of that subject, but at the same time tends wholly to corroborate the viewpoints here expressed. On Luther's idea of the priesthood of believers he remarks: "Das Priesterthum ist geradezu das Gemeinde bildende Prinzip, die Wirklichkeit der *communio sanctorum*" (p. 69). In an appendix he combats the recently expressed view of E. Kohlmeyer, "Die Bedeuting der Kirche für Luther" (*Zeitschr. f. Kirchengesch.* XLVII, 466ff.) that Luther ceased to stress this conception after 1519.

a traditional belief in terms valid for the new age, but to awaken a desire and arouse a demand for the realization of ideal conditions of communion in the visible body. The idea functioned in the cause of practical church reform. The spiritual qualities, which in the contemporary state of decline had seemingly passed out of the external and could be posited only of the unseen church, were to be given visibility again as the renovated visible society took on the character of the invisible model. This fact is implied in Luther's whole position. The exaltation of the invisible *communio sanctorum* as the model of social communion, the downright condemnation of the defects of the existing papal church, and the detailed statement of projects of reform are intimately related elements in Luther's teaching. He was not primarily concerned with speculation about the invisible church; rather he was its representative and advocate in his work as a reformer of the visible.

This is a legitimate deduction from a general view of his reforming activities; and it finds support in his writings. As early as 1518 Luther argued that the *communio* is twofold: inner and spiritual and outward and physical.[49] The spiritual consists of the one faith, hope, and love; and the outward is a participation in the sacraments of these, the signs, that is, of faith, hope and love, and extends to "the communion of things, custom, conversation, habitation" and other contacts pertaining to the bodily life.

---

[49] "Est autem fidelium communio duplex: una interna et spiritualis, alia externa et corporalis. Spiritalis est una fides, spes, charitas in deum. Corporalis est participatio earundem sacramentorum, id est signorum fidei, spei, charitatis, quae tamen extenditur usque ad communionem rerum, usus, colloquii, habitationis." *Werke*, I, 639.

His spirited reply to Alveld[50] offers corroboration of this view. Here Luther's interest is to confute the doctrine that the Roman is the true church, and he is led far in his assertion of invisibility and the headship of Christ. Yet he recognizes an intimate relation between the visible and the invisible in which, as the body is a representation of the soul, so is the bodily community a representation of the spiritual community.[51] He is led to set down a clear distinction between a "spiritual inner" and a "bodily external" *Christenheit*, not that he would "divide them from each other"; but "just as when I speak of one man and in respect to his soul call him a spiritual man, in respect to his body, a physical man."[52] Thus even in the height of his claim against Rome, he links closely the visible with the invisible church. Clearly then, this external or corporal communion is the bearer into routine social living of the values of the *communio sanctorum*.

On the basis of these and similar utterances, W. Köhler has argued for a progressive "materializing" of Luther's idea of the church.[53] Kattenbusch, in his

---

[50] "Von dem Papstthum zu Rom wider den hochberühmsten Romanisten zu Leipzig," 1520. *Werke*, VI, 285ff.

[51] "Das ist wol war, das gleichwie der leyp ist ein figur odder bild der seelen, alzo ist auch die leyplich gemeyn ein furbild diszer christenlichen geystlichenn gemeyne." Luther is arguing that "even on earth" the church has no head but Christ. The bodily community must have a bodily head, as the "spiritual" has a spiritual head: but the spiritual cannot have a bodily head. *Ibid.*, p. 295.

[52] *Ibid.*, p. 297.

[53] "Die Entstehung der Reformatio ecclesiarum Hessiae, 1526, A. D." *Deutsche Zeitschr. f. Kirchenrecht*, 3 Folge, XVI (1906), 199ff., esp. pp. 212f.; *Christliche Welt*, 1907, pp. 371ff. Köhler contends against Riecker's view that "Protestantism is not church-forming"—a view developed in defense of the state control of religion. For Böhmer's judgment of this matter, see below, p. 121. K. Holl charges Köhler

valuable study cited above,[54] commends Köhler's statement of Luther's fond wish to see the church made visible.[55] According to Kattenbusch there were for Luther not two churches, visible and invisible, but these two were aspects of one concrete reality.[56] Quoting Schelling's remark that spirit is the invisible of nature and nature the visible of spirit, he holds that the community of faith was for Luther the invisible of the community of love (the visible church) and *vice versa*.[57] The *communio sanctorum* manifests itself in organized cult-congregations and craves such manifestation. Invisible and visible are related as "Spirit" and "Word." In the *Kultgemeinde* in which the Word is preached the *communio sanctorum* is recognized and its existence assured.[58] Köhler's remark on the *Sermo de virtute excommunicationis*, that "the church moves out of the sphere of faith and incorporates itself in a visible community,"[59] seems a just description of the tendency of the Reformer's thought at all periods rather than of any extended process in his thinking. Through Word and sacraments and Christian social living in an organized group, the invisible was to be rendered visible.

with error, and inconsistency in his statement of the evolution of Luther's thought, and particularly his use of the term "Materialisierung," but he quotes Köhler's statement in 1916 that Luther never was a "spiritualist" but retained a connection between the community of believers and the concrete, organized church. *Gesammelte Aufsätze* I, 260, 261, footnote 3. Köhler's view that Protestantism was church-forming from the beginning is in accord with Holl's treatment: *op. cit.*, I, 273f., 288f.

[54] *Die Doppelschichtigkeit in Luthers Kirchenbegriff.*

[55] *Op. cit.*, p. 16.

[56] *Ibid.*, pp. 46f.

[57] *Ibid.*, p. 70.

[58] *Ibid.*, pp. 71, 90, 107. Cf. Holl, *op. cit.*, I, 292f.

[59] *Christliche Welt*, 1907, p. 375.

In Calvin's thought the relation of the invisible and the visible is rather more explicitly stated. He repeatedly appeals to belief in the invisible as a means of encouragement in the distresses of the age. The invisibility of the church, never quite complete,[60] is the church's misfortune and humiliation, and is considered as an act of God's judgment for disobedience. In the "Address to the King of France" with which Calvin prefaced the *Institutes*, he notes the frequent virtual disappearance of the church among the Jews, and cites (as frequently) Elijah's mistake, 1 Kings 19. 11. "How long after the coming of Christ did it remain without form? and how often thereafter, through wars, seditions, heresies was it so oppressed that no part of it flourished?" God, who knows his own, may sometimes withdraw from human view the external evidence of the church. This, he confesses, is a terrible punishment of God upon the world; but we should not resist. In past ages God has suffered the disobedient to be so plunged in thick darkness that no face of a true church appeared.[61]

In lamenting the disorder of the church visible he elsewhere remarks: "For although the sad devastation which everywhere meets our view may cry out that no church remains, let us know that the death of Christ is fruitful, and that God marvelously preserves his church, while placing it, as it were, in concealment (*in latebris*). Thus it was said to Elijah,

---

[60] Werdermann justly remarks: "According to Calvin there is not a church which is entirely invisible: at most there is one that is not completely visible." *Op. cit.*, p. 312. This judgment is fully borne out by reference to Calvin's commentaries. See his comments on Isa. 52. 13, *C. R.*, LXV, 251; Isa. 60. 4, *C. R.*, LXV, 357; Isa. 64. 10, *C. R.*, LXV, 414; Zech. 11. 17, *C. R.*, LXXII, 319; Dan. 12. 1, *C. R.*, XL, 288ff.

[61] *C. R.*, XXX, 23f.

'Yet have I left me seven thousand,'" etc.[62] Thus for him the true church is invisible in the sense of being driven to invisibility by human sin, or, in punishment of the latter, withdrawn by God from men's sight. This idea is frequently met with in Calvin and in Calvinism; it owed something to Augustine.[63] Mere invisibility is the abnormality and deformity of what should be the visible counterpart of the perfect pattern. The task of a reformer, then, was that of bringing the invisible to visibility again. Luther saw the reviving church as Israel leaving Babylon. In 1522 he lamented that though Babylon had been left behind, little progress had yet been made toward Jerusalem.[64] Calvin regarded the later triumphant chapters of Isaiah on the return from Babylon as in process of fulfillment in the Reformation. "These things were fulfilled in some measure when the people returned from Babylon; but a far brighter witness was given in the gospel. . . . Have we not indeed in our

---

[62] *Inst.*, IV, i, 2. *C. R.*, XXX, 747.

[63] Cf. *Inst.*, IV, ii, 3. *C. R.*, XXX, 770, where Calvin quotes Augustine *ad Vincentium*, Ep. 48.: The church "is sometimes obscured, and as it were beclouded (*obscuratur et tanquam obnubilitatur*) by a multitude of scandals; sometimes in time of tranquillity she appears quiet and free; sometimes she is covered and tossed by billows of tribulation and trial." In the *Second Helvetic Confession*, 1562, this idea is expressed in similar language: God in his just judgment sometimes permits the truth and the catholic faith to seem to be almost extinguished, no church longer surviving, as happened to Elijah and at other times. However, God has still many true worshipers amid the darkness. "Hence the church may be called invisible, in the sense, not that its people are invisible, but that it is withdrawn from our sight and known only to God." Müller, *op. cit.*, p. 199. Cf. the Hungarian Confession of 1562, Ch. V, 7.-9. in Müller, pp. 428ff. It is in this sense that the Westminster Confession states: "Unto this Catholick visible Church Christ hath given his ministry, oracles, and ordinances of God. . . This Catholick church hath been sometimes more, sometimes less visible." Chap. XXV, 3, 4; Müller, *op. cit.*, p. 598; Schaff, *op. cit.*, III, 658.

[64] *Werke*, X (2), 39. Cf. p. 25.

44

own time seen the fulfillment of this prophecy? How
many children has the church brought forth these
thirty years in which the gospel has been preached?"
The church is "the principal theater of God's glory,"
and God exhorts and incites to joy despairing believers
who are "moved by a singular affection" and "prompt-
ed by a pious love" of the church, and are zealous
for her deliverance.[65] He acclaims Luther as the appointed leader of the revival by which the obscured
church is coming to manifest life. "At the time when
divine truth lay buried under this vast and dense
cloud of darkness, . . . then Luther arose, and after
him others, who with united efforts sought out plans
and methods by which . . . the church might be
restored from this calamitous state to a somewhat
tolerable one. We are still, at the present day, going
forward in the same course."[66] Calvin believed that
notwithstanding calamities, he was living "in the
springtime of the reviving church,"[67] and that he was
an agent of God's purposes by which it was to be
revived.

5. The "Marks" of a True Church

The line at which the invisible church becomes
manifest is for all the Reformers alike, in the true
preaching (and hearing) of the Word and the right
administration of the sacraments (that is, their administration according to the Word). Luther laid
down these marks of recognition of the true church
in his answer to Ambrosius Catharinus in 1521. The

---

[65] *Comm. on Isa.* 66. 8-10. *C. R.,* LXV, 444f. Cf. *ibid.,* 61. 9.
C. R., LXV, 379.

[66] *De necessitate reformandae ecclesiae. C. R.,* XXIV, 472-73.

[67] Letter to Melanchthon, 28 June, 1545. *C. R.,* XXXX, 98.

church must have signs by which its members may recognize it and assemble with it. These signs are found primarily in the preaching of the gospel, and secondarily in the right administration of the two sacraments. [68] This is a constant factor in the teaching of Luther and Melanchthon, and is briefly stated in the *Augsburg Confession*, Art. VII, which says: "The church is the congregation of saints [German ed.: "of all believers"] in which the gospel is truly preached and the sacraments rightly administered [Germ.: "according to the gospel"]."[69]

In Calvin's treatment this conception is stressed, and utilized to establish authority in the visible church. The true church, the object of creedal belief, "is manifest to the eye of God only," but we are enjoined to give attention also to the church which is "so-called with reference to man," and to "cultivate (*observare*) its communion." This makes it of first importance that we should recognize it; and we are enabled to do this by certain marks or symbols which God has authorized, "foreseeing that it was in some degree expedient for us to know who are to be regarded by us as his sons." By the presence of these marks "the form of the church arises and stands forth manifest to our eyes. Wherever we see the Word of God sincerely preached and heard, wherever we see the sacraments administered according to the institution of Christ, there we cannot have any doubt that the

[68] "Quo ergo signo agnoscam Ecclesiam? oportet enim aliquod visibile signum dari, quo congregemur in unum ad audiendum verbum dei. Respondeo: Signum necessarium est, quod et habemus, Baptisma scilicet, panem et omnium potissimum Evangelium: tria haec sunt Christianorum symbola, tesserae et caracteres." *Werke*, VII, 720.

[69] Schaff, P., *Creeds of Christendom*, III, 11-12.

Church of God has some existence."[70] Where the preaching of the gospel is reverently heard and the sacraments are not neglected, there for the time the face of the church appears (*ecclesiae apparet facies*) without deception or ambiguity, and she must be recognized, adhered to, and obeyed.[71]

Thus Calvin, characteristically referring all benefits to God, would tell us that God, by Word and sacraments, graciously renders visible and recognizable the true church which is the communion of saints. While the church invisible is and remains the true church, she is never purely invisible, though, in dark times, very nearly so. A reformation or revival of the church, then, means the glorious increase of her visibility, the prosperity of the earthly counterpart of the heavenly model.

In later Protestantism the principle of "the Word" had its doctrinal and its educational aspects. It required attention to preaching and teaching, and led to thought and research. Attempts to force it into purely dogmatic channels broke down again and again. An educational momentum was gained which naturally broke bounds and entered into scientific and critical activity, with important results in the modern world. Similarly, as we have already seen, the sacramental practice had great social importance. Particularly in Lutheranism it furnished, in addition to the ethical impulses noted above, an emotional center for the higher life which carried over into

---

[70] Hinc nascitur nobis et emergit conspicua oculis nostris ecclesiae facies. Ubi enim cunque Dei verbum sincere praedicari atque audiri, ubi sacramenta ex Christi instituto administrari vidamus, illic aliquam esse Dei ecclesiam nullo modo ambigendum est. *Inst.*, IV, i, 8, 9. *C. R.*, XXX, 753-54.

[71] *Inst.*, IV, i, 10. *C. R.*, XXX, 754.

mysticism and poetry. In Calvinism there sprang from it a highly important social praxis which must now receive attention.

Calvin adds as a third factor, logically subordinate, though practically essential, the mark of discipline. Discipline is employed primarily to hedge the sacrament from profanation and avoid scandal, secondarily to establish social righteousness. "The object in view is to prevent the occurrence of scandals, and when they arise to remove them. . . . Now, this cannot be done without connecting with the office of the ministry a right of summoning those who are to be privately admonished or sharply rebuked, a right, moreover, of keeping back from the communion of the Lord's Supper those who cannot be admitted without profaning the high mystery." From this discipline no believer, however highly placed in political society, is exempt.[72] As the saving doctrine of Christ is the life of the church, discipline is its sinews (*pro nervis est*); "for to it it is due that the members of the body . . . adhere together."[73] The body of Christ cannot be defiled by putrid members without dishonor to the Head. . . . Regard must be had to the Lord's Supper, which might be profaned by a promiscuous admission.[74] For their own good, too, offenders must be faithfully rebuked and, if needful, denied communion till they come to repentance.[75] In the administration of the discipline, meekness, clemency, and humanity are to be constantly exercised.[76]

[72] *Inst.*, IV, i, 5. *C. R.*, XXX, 896.
[73] *Inst.*, IV, xii, 1. *C. R.*, XXX, 905.
[74] *Inst.*, IV, xii, 5. *C. R.*, XXX, 907.
[75] *Inst.*, IV, xii, 6. *C. R.*, XXX, 909.
[76] *Inst.*, IV, xii, 8-11. *C. R.*, XXX, 910-12.

The right which Calvin asserted to summon to discipline and enforce appearance before the ecclesiastical courts involves the exercise by the church of privileges which modern churches do not exercise or claim. In practice it meant the co-operation of the police with the ministers in the attempt to bring to visibility the kingdom of God in the whole society. The *Ordonnances Ecclésiastiques* of 1541[77] set up the mechanism of this alliance of church and city, and the records of the council show the system in operation.[78] Calvin believed that "as the magistrate ought to purge the church of offenses by corporal punishment and coercion, so the minister ought, in his turn, to assist the magistrate, that there be not many who transgress. Thus they ought to combine their efforts, so that one becomes a help to the other, not a hindrance."[79] Persistent church offenders thus become civil offenders, and unrepented sins become public crimes.

6. CALVIN'S VOCATIONAL IDEALISM AND THE DISCIPLINED COMMUNITY

Into this system of discipline was woven Calvin's vocational idealism.[80] Recognition as a Christian depended, *inter alia*, upon a man's behavior in his calling. Prodigals and spendthrifts were excluded from communion. The church had no place for the idler, the waster, or the economic parasite, whether rich or poor. Calvin takes literally 2 Thess. 3. 10, "He

---

[77] *C. R.*, XLIX, 283–87.

[78] Reyburn, H. Y., *John Calvin, His Life, Letters, and Work*, pp. 339, 341; Foster, H. D., "Calvin's Program for a Puritan State in Geneva," *Harvard Theological Review*, I (1908), pp. 391-434.

[79] *Inst.*, IV, xi, 3. *C. R.*, XXX, 895.

[80] *C. R.*, L, 72; 93.

that worketh not shall not eat," and describes with scorn a class of indolent persons who get their living by going from house to house. "He that lives to himself so as to be unprofitable to the human race deserves to be called ἄτακτος [disorderly] and to be put away from the society of believers." Christians are to shun such drones, who have no honest way of livelihood.[81] On the other hand, industrious application to one's calling was encouraged, and business was set free from all except moral restrictions.

The religious interpretation of the common man's occupation as "vocation" or "calling" was not achieved in the Middle Ages. There are hints of it in Tauler[82] and in *Piers Plowman*, but it was Luther who first vigorously proclaimed it.[83] Luther gave a high religious significance to the occupation as "Beruf," or calling; but he interprets it mainly in terms of passive resignation to the will of God. Calvin would have the Christian in his calling in active association with God's will. A man's vocation, said he, is "the chief part of the human life, and that which is of most importance before God."[84] If Luther gave a highly important religious character to ordinary work, Calvin introduced a vocational activism under religious sanc-

---

[81] "Cum ejusmodi fucis qui nullum habent honestum vitae genus in quo se exercent." They are pests and blots on religion and their indolence and inertia are accursed of God. *C. R.*, LXXIX, 211-13.

[82] Winkworth, S., *History and Life of John Tauler* (New York, 1858), pp. 127, 263.

[83] Weber, M., "Die Protestantische Ethik und der 'Geist' des Kapitalismus," *Archiv für Sozialwissenschaft und Sozialpolitik*, XX (1904), p. 36, note 1; p. 37, note 2, finds no word corresponding to Luther's "Beruf" among the Latin peoples. Weber's able essay occupies Vol. XX, pp. 1-54, and Vol. XXI (1905), pp. 1-110, of this periodical.

[84] *Brieve instruction contre les Anabaptistes, C. R.*, XXXV, 81.

tion which has had revolutionary results in modern economic and social history.[85]

Unlike Luther, Calvin admits that a change of vocation is without blame if it serves the glory of God.[86] He likewise sets open to the Christian, though under the restrictions proper to the religious communion, the vocation of mercantile business, and allows a reasonable interest on money.[87] When in this way business became, like other occupations, for the Calvinist a means of honoring God, it escaped its medieval disrepute, and under a cautious religious sanction entered upon the triumphant course of its modern progress. Calvinist frugality and hatred of waste, coupled with the energy and productivity of consecrated endowments, tended to the accumulation of wealth. For this reason Calvin has come to be re-

---

[85] Cf. Weber, *op. cit.;* Troeltsch, E., *Die Soziallehren der Christlichen Kirchen und Gruppen*, pp. 653ff.; *Protestantism and Progress*, pp. 83ff.; Tawney, R. H., *Religion and the Rise of Capitalism*, pp. 79ff.; Doumergue, E., *Jean Calvin, les hommes et les choses de son temps*, V, 624ff.; O'Brien, G. A. T., *An Essay on the Economic Effects of the Reformation.*

[86] Weber, *op. cit.*, XX, 41ff.; Doumergue, *op. cit.*, V, 644.

[87] Letter to a friend, *de usuris*, C. R., XXXVIII, 245ff. Calvin argues that interest is condemned in Scripture only where it is accompanied by cruelty and fraud, and defends the merchant's gains on the ground of his "industry" in his calling. He is careful to lay down a series of restrictions in the interests of private justice and the public welfare. Cf. Tawney, *op. cit.*, pp. 104ff.; Troeltsch, *Soziallehren*, pp. 707ff. Both Troeltsch and Tawney regard the mercantile environment of Calvin in Geneva as suggesting his liberalizing business ethics. Says Tawney, p. 105: "Since it is the environment of the industrial and commercial classes which is foremost in the thoughts of Calvin and his followers, they have to make terms with its practical necessities. It is not that they abandon the claim of religion to moralize economic life, but that the life which they are concerned to moralize is one in which the main features of a commercial civilization are taken for granted." (From *Religion and the Rise of Capitalism.* Reprinted by permission of Harcourt, Brace and Company, Ltd., publishers, New York.) In other words, Calvin did not deliberately lead Christians to become business men, but tried to make of business men such Christians as he could. Business had to be sanctioned in order that it might be subjected to religious discipline.

garded as the chief prophet of modern capitalism and industrialism.

Whether, with Weber, we regard Calvin's teaching on vocation as "intramundane asceticism"[88] or, with Th. Ziegler, as "mundane Christianity,"[89] we must recognize in it the primacy of religion. It would be wholly erroneous to identify with Calvinism the secular and anti-social activities of the mere money-getter.[90] The latter flourishes in what has historically been a Calvinistic environment only in the degree in which Weber's generalization is true that "the religious root of modern economic humanity is dead; to-day the concept of a calling is a *caput mortuum* in the world."[91] For Calvin the common task offers a divine opportunity and constitutes an ever-pressing summons to arduous social service. It is never to be dissociated from the social obligations of Christian communion. A man's powers and wealth are held in stewardship for social uses. Quoting 1 Cor. 13, Calvin argues that "all the gifts which we possess are deposits of God intrusted to us for the purpose of being distributed for the good of our neighbor." We are members of a body in which "no member has its

[88] "Innerweltliche Askese," Weber, *op. cit.*, XXI, 1ff. Doumergue objects to this expression, as, with its medieval suggestions, misleading. See especially his spirited article: "Calvin, Epigone or Creator," in *Calvin and the Reformation, Four Studies*, published by the Princeton Theological Review Association, 1909.

[89] "Weltliches Christentum"; quoted by Doumergue, *Jean Calvin* V, 641.

[90] O'Brien completely misconceives Calvinism when he says that capitalistic individualism "is strictly analogous to the insistence of the Protestant on the removal of all restraints by the church. It is private judgment translated into the realm of industry," *op. cit.*, p. 91. The idea of "all restraints by the church" being removed by Calvinism is amusing. O'Brien betrays no direct knowledge of the works either of Luther or of Calvin.

[91] *General Economic History*, Engl. ed., New York, 1927, p. 368.

function for itself, or applies it for its own private use, but transfers it to its fellow members (*ad socia membra transfundit*)." The benefits are mutual, but we should "chiefly study our neighbor's advantage" and make our own subordinate to his.[92] Charity goes beyond the church: it is to be exercised toward the unworthy because of the image of God in them.[93] "Everyone should consider that he owes himself to his neighbors and that the only limit of his beneficence is the failure of his means."[94] Service to one's neighbor is primarily a means of giving glory to God. "The Christian should be so trained and disposed as to consider that during his whole life he has to do with God (*ut sibi in tota vita negotium cum Deo esse reputet*)." With this high conception he will give over vain thoughts, pride, and ostentation, avarice, lust and luxury, and fulfill Christ's demand for self-denial (Matt. 16. 21).[95] We are to concentrate upon our own calling, as a means of glorifying God. If a man deserts it for incidental activities, he displeases God, "and besides there will be no harmony between the different parts of his life." This conception of occupation as a God-pleasing service to society will alleviate life's burdens. "In all our cares, toils, annoyances, and other burdens it will be no small alleviation to know that all these are under the control of God." Everybody will bear his burden without repining, consoled by the thought that within his proper calling "no work will be so sordid and vile

---

[92] *Inst.*, III, vii, 5.   C. R. XXX, 509-10.
[93] *Inst.*, III, vii, 6.   C. R., XXX, 511.
[94] *Inst.*, III, vii, 7.   C. R., XXX, 512.
[95] *Inst.*, III, vii, 2.   C. R., XXX, 506.

that it will not be resplendent and very precious in the sight of God."[96]

The Calvinist régime in Geneva gave the model for an important type of modern social organization which, in a severe temper, combines theocracy and democracy. The type is to be recognized to-day not only in such antiquated survivals as the blasphemy laws sometimes invoked to suppress propaganda, but also in measures vigorously embraced by up-to-date people: such as the prohibition of the liquor traffic in America and its restriction in other lands. The Disciplined Community of Geneva has reappeared, with modifications imposed by environment, in Presbyterian Scotland, Puritan England and Puritan New England; and in many minds it still remains a potent social ideal. Something of the tradition lives to-day in America, as André Siegfried has recently intimated, amid much loose generalization, in a popular interpretation of American life. He refers to "the Calvinist point of view that the group, and not the individual, is the social unit and the foundation of the religious structure," a point of view which he says is incomprehensible to the Latin mind.[97] The influence of Calvinism in America can be overstated; but the strength of group-consciousness in Calvinism is not likely to be.

Judged by some of its manifestations, the Calvinist Disciplined Community appears in history as disappointingly legalistic and repressive. The work

[96] *Inst.*, III, x, 6. *C. R.*, XXX, 532. Calvin urges faithfulness and continuity, but holds that a change of vocation is not forbidden if it is made with good reason and not merely from discontent. *Comm. on* 1 Cor. 7, 20. *C. R.*, LXXVII, 415. This was novel and important advice.

[97] *America Comes of Age*, p. 34.

of Calvin himself is marked by these qualities, and
the list of trivial and major tyrannies exercised under
the laws of Geneva has been made familiar to countless readers. Discerning minds have always recognized
in Puritan theocracies not only the unpleasant trivialities of the legislation, but also the rich and positive
conceptions which repression was mistakenly employed to serve. Too frequently, however, in Calvin's
case the explanation has been given in purely theological terms. It has not been observed that his predestinarianism was really modified by a profound
social sense. The communion of saints could not
flourish in a society of unrestrained sinners. No
moralist or psychologist could be more aware of the
importance of environment as determining moral
habits and social behavior. From an environment
resigned to depravity what good men, such as he could
conscientiously admit to communion, would be likely
to arise? The total environment must be made conducive to the Christian virtues, must at once reflect
and help to sustain the character of the Christian
communion itself. The church was to be made "not
simply an institution for the worship of God, but an
agency for making men fit to worship him."[98] The
vigor of the system was due to the deep religious conviction, the devotion to the will of God, that accompanied it. There is doubtless a tendency to copy
the externals of Calvin's Disciplined Community with
out reference to its religious dynamic; and Calvinist
discipline has sometimes declined into mere legalism.
In such experiments we see only the soulless corpse
of Calvinism. Unless men view the laws that restrict

---

[98] Fairbairn, A. M., in *Cambridge Modern History*, II, 364.

their conduct as instrumental to some grand life-purpose, or as the condition of some prized social bond, they will tend to regard such laws as tyrannical and intolerable. Calvin ultimately won Geneva, by means not always praiseworthy, it is true, to the sincere acceptance of his social ideal.

His model of the Disciplined Community has the profoundest lessons for the modern sociologist. It was essentially the product of the thought of Calvin —under the stimulus in some degree of Bucer, his elder Strassburg associate—on the means of maintaining the purity of the fellowship whose sign and bond was the sacrament of the Eucharist, the seal of Christian communion. The defensive discipline of the church became the enforced standard of the civil society. The Protestant emphasis on communion thus gave rise to a social tradition of the very first importance in modern history.

7. CONCLUSION

In the church concept of the Reformers and their adherents the element of communion is paramount. They interpreted the creedal tenet of "the Holy Catholic Church" in terms of the *communio sanctorum*, and identified the latter both with the invisible communion of the saved and with the true visible church in the world which they felt themselves called to restore. Communion was for them fraught with ethical content. It involved in a high degree a corporate consciousness, a group solidarity, and the recognition of an obligation mutually to bestow religious benefits and render social services. The sanctity and centrality of communion were strongly felt and asserted in Lutheranism. It was associated with the mystery of the Eucharist, and its values were impressed under the idea of the priesthood of every Christian, an office conceived of not in an individualistic but in a social sense as obligation to aid his fellow Christian and "be a Christ" to him. In Calvinism the sanctity of the sacrament of communion was further guaranteed by exacting tests of behavior. The standards of behavior were such as were adapted to the promotion of communion and its social product—the welfare not primarily of the individual, but of the group of communicants and of the entire community. This communion-guarding discipline was extended to become the ethical standard of the whole community, and with its concern for vocational activity as God-honoring service to the community, instituted a distinctive and historically important type of social organization. The Disciplined Community shaped by Calvin as a consequence of his emphasis upon the sanctity of communion has profoundly affected modern religious, social and economic life.

The movement of modern thought has rendered antiquated many of the doctrinal presuppositions which attended the formulation of the principle of communion by the Reformers; and the principle itself has rarely, if ever, since received the attention which they claimed for it. Theology has been concerned largely with these presuppositions rather than with the communion concept; Protestant ethics have been denatured by dissociation from communion; and the trivialities and inhumanities of Calvin's discipline have called forth the adverse judgments of historians who reached no realization of the inner character of the society.

Yet the instinctive communion interest has remained in Protestantism, as it must, of course, remain while Protestantism bears any relation to historic Christianity. Nor does it seem improbable that it will be maintained and revived in conjunction with the modernism and humanism with which Protestantism is more and more pervaded. Indeed, it is among the more progressive Protestant groups that the values of communion are most prized, or at least most craved. Hence their manifest interest in its enrichment and widening by means of organic union. The sense of communion to-day seems to be rising to the foreground of the Protestant consciousness. It deserves from thinking minds an attention which it has not received. For it is scarcely an exaggeration to say that the principle of communion lies at the basis of religion itself. Certainly, no religion that does not stress it will meet the needs of modern society with its keenness of social intelligence and lack of social consecration.

Should this emphasis be renewed in contemporary Protestantism, similarly important social results would assuredly follow. It is not to be supposed, of course, that a revived sense of the values of the Christian fellowship would to-day express itself in legal and coercive measures. Yet it would certainly result in a quickening of social-mindedness that would once more take the whole community as its field of operation. Christianity would again endeavor, in ways more suitable to the spirit of our time and more in accord with its own original character, to impart to the whole body politic the social values realized and cultivated within the pledged fellowship itself. The harmonious interchange of esteem, confidence, love, and practical service, the mutually advantageous relation of the individual and the group, the exhilaration of the common pursuit of great ends, are still, however abuses or cynicism may obscure the fact, normal to the experience of a Christian Church, as of old to the associated followers of Jesus. By laying stress on this point Protestantism might not only attain to corporate unity, but become, more than it has been in the past, an integrating social force. An enlivened appreciation of its religious resources in the communion of saints would inevitably exert a profound influence on the whole community of humanity, where it would tend to transform the economic nexus into a communion of workers, and the state into a communion of citizens, and to revitalize the entire social order.

CHAPTER II

PROTESTANT CATHOLICITY: THE ECUMENICAL OUTLOOK

1. The Unattained Ideal of Catholicity in Christianity

None of the founders of Protestantism boggled at the creedal phrase, "Holy Catholic Church." As holy and catholic, however, the church was for them only imperfectly visible. It was the object of faith and effort only in a restricted sense of actual observation and experience. The association, in other quarters, of the church with subjection to papal government, they indignantly rejected. Their indignation is historically comprehensible, even if it often ran to unjustifiable extremes. The moral deterioration of the Roman Church rendered the description "holy" very inapplicable to it. The facts that go to illustrate this statement have long been well known, and have no place in the present study. Happily, the historical student of to-day is in a position to view these facts with less passion and more justice than was possible to zealots for righteousness of the time, whose very senses were smitten by the offensiveness of conditions in the papal church. He can at least appreciate the fact that the causes of decay lay only to a slight degree in the designs of wicked men, and that it was possible for men of worth to support the old church order in the hope of helping in its transformation. He can see too that holiness in the church has always been an ideal far from general attainment, and that the Reformation attempt to attain it was almost as far from succeeding as that of the Middle Ages, although in both Romanism and Protestantism the value and potency of the ideal have been incalculable.

In respect to catholicity the case is similar. Since catholicity first came to be a conscious note in Christian thought—and for this we should probably go back from Ignatius to Paul—it has been an unattained but potent principle. The term is, of course, an elastic one that does not yield readily to historical definition. Some appreciation of the idea may be gained, however, by recalling that it has always suggested both inclusiveness and selection. Catholicity thus involves ecumenicity, or the co-ordination of all the parts of the church far-flung throughout the world, "wherever the glory of Christ has been shed abroad."[1] It presupposes also some standard by which elements regarded as unchristian are to be excluded. It has reference to a body of Christians of unlimited extent in the earth, but always to an integrated body of recognizable character. It rejects all that remains unintegrated while including all that is capable of integration in the experience, belief, cult, purposes, and psychological disposition of the whole living organism. The Ecumenical period, through all its confusions, exhibits an insatiable craving to realize catholicity as a fact in church life, and to formulate the terms by which it might be clearly discerned. But catholicity was more and more thought of in terms

[1] "Nos Catholici in omni terra sumus, quia omni terrae communicamus, quocunque gloria Christi diffusa est." Augustine, *Ennarationes in Psalmos*, lvi, in Migne, *Patrol. Lat.*, XXXVI, 669.

not of what it embraced, but of what it repelled. A rigid principle of uniformity triumphed, and much that might have proved of value was left unintegrated either because it was merely local or because it was held to be alien in nature to the experience of the corpus.

The Eastern mind, with its speculative habits, proved more concerned for accuracy in the definition of the terms of belief; the Western, with its governmental interests, for the solidification and regimentation of the universal organization. The difference was early perceptible and proved more pronounced as the Eastern and Western churches grew apart. In the East orthodoxy has always been the church's chief care as well as her chief boast. The church, in fact, became a series of organically largely independent churches, bound together by adherence to orthodox formulæ. Creedal orthodoxy became the norm of catholicity, and the living voice was silenced by the authority of the dead letter. In the West orthodoxy was more fluid, and, in the process of centralization under Rome, the standards of the Ecumenical period were freely interpreted or added to by fresh decisions for which Rome took responsibility. In respect to movement and adaptation to a changing environment, the advantage of the West over the static, literal East was immeasurable. But the advantage was offset by the nullification of the idea of ecumenicity itself. The Councils of the fourth and fifth centuries had spoken in the name of the whole extended body animated by the Holy Spirit. Rome spoke in the name of Peter, the apostle on whom all authority in the church had been conferred by Christ.

Orthodoxy was the voice of the Pope, the vicar of Christ and head of the church militant. The idea of catholicity lost the early sense of universality, and was constantly associated instead with the oracles of Rome. Rome's rising demands for obedience permanently alienated the Easterns, while Eastern immobility was wholly unattractive to the Western mind. The strenuous efforts of the late Middle Ages to restore the unity that had been formally disrupted in the eleventh century were in the nature of things foredoomed to failure.

In both Eastern orthodoxy and the medieval papacy, then, catholicity had received only partial expression. Indeed, within both, and between the two, insuperable barriers had been raised against its complete expression. How, then, did Protestantism, in its inception, relate itself to the principle of catholicity to which, by acceptance of the traditional creed, it professed to adhere?

2. THE CLAIM OF CATHOLICITY IN LUTHER

When we begin to examine the evidence that bears on this inquiry, one of the first facts to come to notice is the insistence with which the claim of catholicity was made by the leaders of the Reformation. They were far from regarding themselves as heretics, schismatics, or sectaries. Among their deepest convictions was the assurance that they were the perpetuators of the catholic church of which Rome had become the betrayer.

The excommunication of Luther by the Church of Rome was threatened, but not effected, by the bull *Exsurge Domine* of 1520. On receiving it Luther took the initiative, and by solemnly burning it may be said to have excommunicated the Pope. In repudiating Rome Luther meant to indicate not his own, but Rome's exclusion from the catholic church. Both before and after this event he constantly represented his own teachings as catholic, and those of his opponents as hostile to catholic doctrine. In 1520 he more than once complained that the Romanists were virtually demanding an alteration of the Creed to make it read: "I believe in the church of Rome."[2] In his reply to the bull he marvels that the papists condemn what is not false, heretical, or scandalous, but true, catholic, and edifying.[3] Koestlin notes that he continued to speak of his own statements as catholic doctrine (*pro Catholicis dogmatibus*), and that he defended his *Operaciones in Psalmos* of 1519–1521 as doing no violence to the pure catholic faith.[4] He was well aware that his conception of catholicity was at variance with that inculcated by Rome. He was none the less assured that it was not a novel or revolutionary conception, but one deeply rooted in the past and answering to the experience of the church. He thought his views traditional, and honestly defended them on that ground. In controversy with the Zwinglians he used the argument that it is a dangerous

[2] "Von dem Papstthum zu Rom wider den hochberümten Romanisten zu Leipzig." *Werke*, VI, 300. "An den christlichen Adel deutscher Nation." *Ibid.*, p. 412.

[3] "Quis ergo non miretur tanta ingenia Papistarum, qui invenire potuerunt offensivum esse in Ecclesia, quod tamen nec falsum nec haereticum nec scandalosvum, sed verum, Catholicum, edificatorium sit, et tamen hoc ipsum damnant?" "Adversus execrabilem Antichristi bullam." *Ibid.*, 602.

[4] Koestlin, quite inadequately, I believe, explains Luther's catholicity in terms of the invisible church. *The Theology of Luther*, tr. Hay, 1897, I, 421f.

thing to diverge from the faith of "the entire, holy, Christian church maintained harmoniously from the beginning, that is, for more than fifteen hundred years, throughout the whole world."[5]

The respective views held by Luther and the Romanists about 1520 on the subject of catholicity may be best understood by reference to antecedent discussions. The Roman principle had been concisely formulated in the *Dictatus Papae*, four centuries before Luther was born, in the words: "No one can be regarded as a catholic who does not agree with the Roman Church."[6] This definition accords with the presupposition of Luther's papal opponents. To Luther, as he looked upon the history of Christianity, it seemed a manifest departure from the fundamental idea of catholicity, which is universality; and he regarded it as a late corruption introduced by antichrist.

Most authors at this point enlarge upon Luther's conception of the invisibility of the true church. This doctrine has, as we have seen, its own place in Luther's thought and should not be minimized. The invisible church functioned in the teaching of the Reformers as a pattern of perfection to which it was hoped the visible church would approximate. But Luther never was so obsessed by the idea of the invisible church as to become oblivious of the church which is both visible and catholic. Purely in its visible aspect the catholic church of Luther was not that of Leo X. His conception of the visible catholic church was in part, as was the idea of invisibility, derived from a soter-

[5] De Wette, *Briefe*, IV, 348.
[6] "Quod catholicus non habeatur qui non concordat Romanae ecclesiae." Mirbt, *Quellen zur Geschichte des Papsttums*, 4 Aufl., p. 146.

iology of predestination; it was also in part the product of his survey of church history, and had been vividly and permanently impressed on his mind in the Leipzig Disputation (1519).

In preparation for this debate Luther had made a careful scrutiny of the ancient fathers and councils. This led him to a confident rejection of the divine right monarchical principle of church power.[7] It forced upon his mind the fact that Christianity was vastly wider than Romanism. Against Eck he cited the Greek Church as proof that the "rock" passage in Matthew is not applicable to the Pope, whose connection with "My Church" is with a section of it only. This argument Eck tried to dismiss with contempt: the Greeks, in separating from Rome, he said, became exiles from the faith of Christ.[8] Luther insistently returned to the point, expressing the hope that Eck, "with Eccian modesty," will spare so many thousands of saints, since the Greek Church, though separated from Rome, has endured and will endure. Eck in turn, while he avoids condemning the Greek fathers, has little hope for the salvation of any in the modern East except a few who hold the Roman obedience (*qui Romanam obedientiam tenent*).[9] Here was Romanism in its baldest form; and Eck's expressions were calculated to confirm the differentiation that had arisen in Luther's mind between "catholic church" and "Roman obedience."[10]

---

[7] "Potestatem monarchicam jure divino a Christo institutam." *Werke*, II, 258.

[8] "Taceat, ergo, queso, Reverendus pater, et nobis non insultet cum Grecis et orientalibus, qui, a Romana deficientes ecclesia a fide quoque Christiana facti sunt exules." *Werke*, II, 262.

[9] *Ibid.*, pp. 266, 269.

[10] Of Eck's argument on the damnation of the Easterns Luther remarked: "qua blasphemia nihil potest detestabilius dici." *Ibid.*, p. 276.

In the town of Leipzig, with its hatred of the Bohemians, Eck was happy to enlarge also upon the infallibility of the Council of Constance in its dealings with Hus, whose views, he pointed out, were shared by Luther. Luther thought the Hussites had been uncharitably treated; and Eck succeeded in giving the impression of the identification of the Lutheran and the Hussite movements.[11] Luther thus found himself championing groups upon which the Romanist hurled the epithets "schismatic" and "heretic." He had no doubt that his own position was the more ecumenical and catholic. If he frequently uses the word "Christian" in preference to "catholic," he uses it consciously in an ecumenical sense, in opposition to the sectionalism of Rome. In Eck's vocabulary the word "catholic" is simply replaced by *"Romana obedientia."* Henceforth for Luther the catholic or universal Christian Church was to be distinguished with perfect clarity from the Roman obedience.

But Luther was, in 1519, still within the Roman obedience, and in it there was still, he supposed, one rôle that he might play. Probably here again Eck helped him to see his way. In the Disputation Eck urged him to give more attention to Saint Bernard's *De Consideratione.* Luther learned from Bernard another lesson than that which Eck intended. While Bernard placed the Pope above the patriarchs, he still more obviously constituted himself the censor of the Pope. It is not surprising that Luther's letter to Leo X of the following year should have two references to this work of Bernard, in one of which he says, "I

[11] *Ibid.*, p. 272.

imitate Saint Bernard in his book *De Consideratione* addressed to Eugenius, a book which ought to be known by heart by every pontiff." Probably by this date, however, Luther had little expectation that his advice would be considered at Rome. All that followed only served to make it plainer to him that no opinions which did not tend to confirm the papal "obedience" would be held by the Romanists to be catholic.

It was, then, the narrowness of Rome's alleged catholicity that antagonized Luther. It was to be confined to the Roman obedience, and even to those within that dominion who silently acquiesced in conditions and proffered no advice. Could that be catholic which was so far from comprehending the entirety of living Christianity? The answer was clear. Because his church was ampler than the Roman, he viewed with composure the launching of the bulls against him; and he burned *Exsurge Domine* with a lighter heart because it was Eck's own handiwork and "condemned what was catholic," as its author had done at Leipzig.

3. The Claim of Catholicity in Calvin

An adequate examination of Calvin's teaching regarding the catholic church would require more space than is here available.[12] The evidence that he pos-

---

[12] E. Doumergue has given an extended treatment of Calvin's ecclesiastical ideas in Vol. V of his *Jean Calvin*. A. M. Hunter, *The Teaching of Calvin*, Chaps. VIII–X, gives valuable illustrations. An arresting discussion is that by P. Wernle, *Der evangelische Glaube*, III, *Calvin*, pp. 49ff.; 355ff. Wernle traces the progressive enrichment of Calvin's church concept through the editions of the *Institutes*. In the present study the final edition is almost exclusively utilized, as representing Calvin's completed thought.

sessed the catholic idea and ideal of the visible church is overwhelming and generally recognized.[13]

Calvin refers the article in the Creed on the "holy Catholic Church," to the church which is invisible, but also to that which is visible.[14] He finds two uses in Scripture of the word "church" in its general sense. It means, first, the invisible church, including the church triumphant; and, secondly, "the whole multitude of mankind scattered throughout the world who profess to worship one God and Christ, who by baptism are initiated into the faith; by partaking of the Lord's Supper profess unity in true doctrine and charity, agree in holding the word of the Lord, and observe the ministry which Christ has appointed for the preaching of it." We are, he adds, under obligation "to cultivate the communion" of this universal visible church.[15]

In the Geneva Catechism the following is the explanation of the word "catholic" in the Creed: "This word means that as there is but one Head of the faithful so they ought all to be united in one body. Thus there are not several churches, but only one, which is extended throughout all the world."[16]

Calvin's ever-recurring phrase "the church of God,"

[13] It is emphasized, for example, by F. Heiler, who has no sympathy with the puritan temper of Calvinism, but who recognizes catholicity, not only in its polity but in its worship. Heiler commends the Roman Catholic Imbart de la Tour's article, "Pourquoi Luther n'a-t-il créé qu'un christianisme allemand?" in *Rev. de metamphysique et de morale,* 1918, for its emphasis on Calvin's "impressive catholicity." *The Spirit of Worship,* pp. 97, 182. *Evangelische Katholizität,* p. 143.

[14] "This article of the creed relates in some sense (aliquatenus) to the external church." *Inst.,* IV, i, 3.

[15] *Inst.,* IV, i, 7. *C. R.,* XXX, 752-53.

[16] "Omnes in unum corpus coalescere oportere, ut una sit ecclesia per totum orbem diffusa, non plures" (pas plusieurs Eglises, mais une seule, laquelle est espandue par tout le monde)." *C. R.,* XXXIV, 39.

often simply shortened to "the church," is intended to convey the notion both of invisible and of visible catholicity. The constant trend of his argument is that the Romanists abuse the word "church" in applying it, or at least in applying it exclusively, to themselves. They "use the name of 'church' to oppress the church."[17] "There is no reason why the papists should affright us when with blown cheeks they thunder the name of the church."[18] He scathingly rejects their claim to be called the catholic church.[19] He cannot accord to them the name "church" without reservation, but, applying the tests of word and sacraments to some special groups among them, he states: "Although we are unable to concede *simpliciter* the name of 'church' to the papists, we do not deny that there are churches among them."[20]

He repeatedly refers to the church as the mother of the faithful. In treating of the visible church he says, in accord with traditional doctrine: "What God has thus joined, let not man put asunder. To those to whom he is a father, the church must also be a mother (*ut quibis ipse est pater, ecclesia etiam mater sit*)."[21] The church is to be called "a queen, and the mother of all pious souls."[22] We are to rejoice in her prosperity and be grieved by her adversity.[23] "The symmetry of the church consists of a multiplex unity . . . as in a symphony there are variant sounds, but

[17] *C. R.*, XXXV, 611.
[18] "quum plenis buciis detonant nomen ecclesiae." *Comm. on Ezek.* 2. 6. *C. R.*, LXVIII, 70.
[19] *Ibid.*, 2. 8. *C. R.*, LXVIII, 73.
[20] *Inst.*, IV, ii, 12. *C. R.*, XXX, 776.
[21] *Inst.*, IV, i, 1. *C. R.*, XXX, 746.
[22] *Comm. on Psa.* 47. 4. *C. R.*, LIX, 468.
[23] *Comm. on Isa.* 52. 1. *C. R.*, LXV, 243.

suited to each other with such fitness as to produce one concord."[24] The universal unity of the church is thought of primarily in relation to the sole headship of Christ whose body and whose completion (*complementum*) it is.[25] Baptism connects us with the church; it is a link which binds the members so that they live one life.[26] To maintain communion in the Church of God is a solemn obligation. We must be one body if we would be kept together with him as the Head; but if we break up into different bodies, we depart from him also.[27] "It is a wicked and sacrilegious divorce to sunder those who agree in the unity of Christ."[28] Calvin's devotion to "the church," which is reiterated with the greatest frequency, is always a devotion to "the catholic church" or the church of God in all her parts. Unified in the headship of Christ, she is to be extended into and beneficially operative in the whole world. "The restoration of the church may be regarded as the restoration of the whole world."[29] He exults over the sons and daughters to be born to the church in every corner of the world.[30] "The true stability of the church, the restoration of the world, consists in this, that the elect be gathered into the unity of the faith, so that

[24] "Symmetria ecclesiae multiplici (ut ita loquar) unitate constat . . . sicut in symphonia varii sunt cantus, sed tal proportione inter se temperati, ut unum efficiant concentum." *Comm. on 1 Cor.*, 12. 4. *C. R.*, LXXVII, 497.

[25] *Comm. on 1 Cor.* 12. 12; *Eph.* 1. 23. *C. R.*, LXXVII, 501; LXXIX, 159.

[26] *Ibid.*

[27] *Comm. on 1 Cor.* 1. 13. *C. R.*, LXXVII, 316.

[28] *Comm. on Rom.* 16. 17. *C. R.*, LXXVII, 288.

[29] "Restitutio ecclesiae . . . renovatio totius orbis." *Comm. on Isa.* 55. 12. *C. R.*, LXV, 292.

[30] *Isa.* 55. 5. *C. R.*, LXV, 286. Cf. 60. 4. *Ibid.*, 357.

with one consent all may lift their hearts to God."
The stability of the world depends on the welfare of
the church.[31] The divisions of the church, the "fright-
ful mutilation of Christ's body," caused Calvin profound pain.[32] He wished "to maintain the church universal in its unity, which malignant minds have always
been eager to dissever."[33] Having quoted the *Interim*
on the marks of the true church, he comments, "The
marks which they set down for discerning the church,
viz., pure doctrine, the right use of the sacraments,
and the holy unity thereon depending, I willingly
receive." It is noteworthy that he here records
no objection to the strong claims of corporate unity
set forth in the *Interim*, but merely proceeds to
attack the episcopal-succession doctrine of continuity.[34]

Nothing in Calvin's teaching is expressed with
more emphasis than his horror of schism. "Such is
the value which the Lord sets upon the communion
of his church that all who contumaciously alienate
themselves from any Christian society in which the
true ministry of the word and sacraments is maintained, he regards as deserters of religion. . . . Revolt
from the church is denial of God himself." To break
communion is wicked (*scelerato*) dissent; there is no
more atrocious crime. So long as the true word and
sacraments are maintained, we are bound to maintain

---

[31] *Isa.* 51. 16. *C. R.*, LXV, 237.

[32] "Nemo enim est, vel modico duntaxat pietatis sensu praeditus,
quem non excruciet ac moerore conficiat foeda haec, horrendaque
corporis Christi laceratio." *Vera Christianae pacificationis et Ecclesiae
reformandae ratio. C. R.*, XXXV, 591.

[33] *Inst.*, IV, i, 9. *C. R.*, XXX, 754.

[34] *C. R.*, XXXV, 610.

communion, even though the church "swarm with many faults."[35]

Against the Roman charge of schism Calvin replies with heated indignation. He quotes Cyprian, whom he praises for his emphasis on the headship of Christ. The reformed are, he claims, sufficiently absolved from the charge unless the apostles, "with whom we have a common cause," are to be called schismatics too.[36] Indignantly and repeatedly he retorts upon Rome the charge of schism. "With what fairness," he asks, "is the blame for the present commotions imputed to us, when they have not been in the least degree incited by us? Nay, with what face do those charge us with the crime of disturbing the church who themselves are marked out as the authors of all these disturbances? Verily the wolves complain against the lambs."[37] The claim of Rome to be called the mother of all the churches is denied on the ground that Rome has lost all trace of the true church and "severed all the nerves of that holy communion which ought to exist among the faithful."[38] In the fresh activities of Rome he saw only new occasions of the sectarian discord which he deplored. He closes his critique of the Acts of the Council of Trent with the exhortation which characteristically mingles zeal for reforming action with reliance upon God: "Therefore since the churches are scattered . . . as to what concerns the universal body of the church, we commend it to the Lord's care. Let us not meanwhile

---

[35] *Inst.*, IV, i, 10, 12. *C. R.*, XXX, 754-55.

[36] *Inst.*, IV, ii, 6. *C. R.*, XXX, 772.

[37] *De necessitate reformandae ecclesiae.* *C. R.*, XXXIV, 499.

[38] "Ut nervos omnes sanctae, quae inter fideles esse debet, communionis absciderit," *op. cit.* *C. R.*, XXXIV, 524.

be indolent or careless; let each do his utmost; let us all contribute whatever we possess of counsel, of zeal, of talent to build up the ruins of the church (*ad instaurendas ecclesiae ruinas*)."[39]

4. The Claim of Catholicity in the Other Reformers

This matter might profitably be pursued further as it affects Luther and Calvin, but some consideration must now be given to the attitudes of other Reformers. Melanchthon fully shared Luther's view, and coupled with it a more intense desire for the realization of the corporate unity of the catholic church. The Jesuit Grisar, in the chapter of his work on Luther which he devotes to Melanchthon, adversely remarks on this in the following terms: "The wrong idea which he came more and more to cherish amounted to this: The true doctrine of the catholic church of Christ, as against the Roman Catholic Church of the day, is to be found in 'the Epistles of the apostles and in the recognized ecclesiastical writers.' Without succeeding in finding any position of real safety, he insists on the necessity of sharing the 'consensus of the catholic church of Christ,' and of belonging to the true, ancient and sublime 'coetus ecclesiae' over which rules the Son of God."[40]

In the address to Henry VIII with which the 1535 edition of the *Loci Communes* opens, Melanchthon refers to his work as an attempt to assemble the "catholic doctrine of the church of Christ," praises

---

[39] *Acta synodi Tridentinae cum antidoto.* C. R., XXXIV, 506.

[40] *Luther, Engl. ed.*, III, 368. It is to be inferred that for the Jesuit writer the "position of real safety" is not "the consensus of the catholic church of Christ," but obedience to the chair of Peter.

the king's (presumed) interest in composing the
differences in the church, and asserts his own devotion to that cause, and his sincere veneration for "the
catholic church of Christ" and desire to be found
in agreement with her good men and doctors.[41] In a
further address "to pious students of divinity" which
then follows, he again professes his agreement with,
and intention to uphold against all fanatical opinion,
the "consensus of the catholic church of Christ."[42]
Which, it may be asked, should be regarded as the
more "catholic," these sentiments of Melanchthon or
Rome's flat demand of subjection to the papal monarchy? Melanchthon's writings are replete with similar statements. Catholicity is a major emphasis in his
teaching, and is set by him in contrast to the par-
ticularism of Rome.

Zwingli's idea of the church is primarily that of the
whole body of the believers of which Christ is the
Head and ruler.[43] This body of the faithful is "the
church or communion of saints, the spouse of Christ,
the church catholic."[44] It is usual to say that catholicity is here swallowed up by invisibility. Staehelin
remarks that for Zwingli the church exists empirically
only in the individual congregation.[45] This interpretation is substantially that adopted by Jackson.[46]
It is, I am convinced, based upon an incomplete ex-

---

[41] "Ego ex animo veneror Ecclesiam Christi Catholicam, ejusque
sententiam omni studio amplector. Nec velim unquam a judiciis
bonorum et doctorum in Ecclesia dissentire." *C. R.*, XXI, 333, 340.

[42] *Ibid.*, 342.

[43] "Caput omnium credentium qui corpus ejus sunt." *Conclusiones*,
vii. Schaff, P., *Creeds of Christendom*, III, 198.

[44] "Haec est ecclesia seu communio sanctorum, sponsa Christi, ecclesia catholica." *Ibid.* (sec. viii).

[45] Staehelin, R., *Huldreich Zwingli, sein Leben und Wirken*, II, 207f.

[46] Jackson, S. M., *Huldreich Zwingli*, p. 387.

amination of Zwingli's statements. In his *True and False Religion* Zwingli describes the church as the assembly, not of the clergy, but of the whole people.[47] In order to guard against the identification of clergy and church he points out the original sense of the word *ecclesia*, and makes the Latin equivalent, *concio*—"a public gathering." It is primarily its popular, not its local character, on which the emphasis is laid. Two pages are then devoted to the application of the word *ecclesia* both in the Old and in the New Testament, to include all outwardly attached to religion. With this conception is contrasted "another kind of church," alluded to in Eph. 5. 25-27, the church which Christ loved, the stainless spouse of Christ. This is the church which does not err, since it is firmly fixed upon the Word of God. Though diffused throughout the world, it is unknown to men, and will never assemble till the last day. Finally he discusses particular or local churches. It is important to note here Zwingli's explicit statement that these local churches together constitute the "one church, the spouse of Christ, which the Greeks call 'catholic' and we call 'universal.'"[48] This, he adds, in emphasis upon his starting point, is not a collection of the bishops but of the saints, a communion of all the faithful, and this was meant by the fathers in the Creed.[49]

This, to say the least, indicates a connection between the local churches and the catholic church, which

---

[47] "Ecclesia enim coetus est, concio, populus universus, collecta simul universa multitudo." *C. R.*, XC, 741.

[48] "Sed omnes istae ecclesiae una ecclesia, Christi sponsa sunt, quam Graeci 'Catholicam,' nos 'universalem' adpellamus.'" *Ibid.*, 751.

[49] *Ibid.*

imports into the latter the idea of visibility.[50] The
Fidei Ratio presented by Zwingli to Charles V in 1530
is more decisive. Here he distinguishes three variant
uses of the word "church" in the New Testament.
The first is its application to those who, having been
predestinated, believe; this church is known to God
alone. Secondly, "The church is understood in a
universal sense of those who are reckoned by Christ's
name, that is, who have enlisted under Christ."
This church, while universal, is visible, and defective.
Thirdly, there is "the particular congregation of this
universal and perceptible (*sensibilem*) church. . . .
I believe," he adds, "that there is one universal perceptible church, while it maintains the true confession of which we have already spoken."[51]

Bucer's thought of the church, both in its invisible
and in its visible aspect, is stated essentially in catholic
terms. Here is his definition: "The church is the
congregation and society of those who are thus in our
Lord Jesus Christ gathered out of the world and
associated together, that they may be one body and
members one of another; each one of whom has an
office and work for the common edification of the
whole body and of all the members."[52] Bucer's pre-

---

[50] P. Wernle argues, from various writings of Zwingli, that he was
no mere spiritualist believing in an invisible church. "Das ist nicht der
ganze Zwingli." Instead his emphasis lay in the church as part, in
close association with the state, of the theocratic society. *Der evangelische Glaube*, II, *Zwingli*, 193-201.

[51] Müller, E. F. K., *Die Bekenntnisschiften der Reformierten Kirche*,
pp. 84ff. *Fidei Ratio*, 6, in Jackson, *op. cit.*, Appendix, pp. 465f., quoting Jacobs' translation.

[52] "Ecclesia est congregatio et societas eorum qui in Christo Domino
nostro, ita e mundo congregati et consociati sunt, ut sint unum corpus,
et singuli aliorum membra; quorum unumquemque habet officium et
opus ad aedificationem communem totius corporis, omniumque mem-
brorum." Quoted by W. Pauck, *Das Reich Gottes auf Erden*,

destination does not make less keen his conception of the visibility in organization of the universal corpus Christi. For him, as Pauck observes, "the church, which at first seems to be the invisible community of the elect, is nevertheless an organization of institutional character."[53] Like Calvin, he finds his catholicity authorized in the Old Testament. By an exposition of Isa. 2. 2f. he teaches that all peoples and kingdoms ought to come under the sway of the Church of Christ,[54] that is, "within the communion of the true church."[55]

In Scotland, Knox, without presenting any extended exposition of the character of the church, exhibits the same presuppositions as Calvin and Bucer. Thus he resents and refutes the charge of Tyrie that the Reformed Church of Scotland was "without the societie of the Catholic Kirk." He insists that the church of the Creed is not only catholic but also holy. The Pope is the man of sin, and Tyrie is of his "sect," while the church of Scotland is "visible and beautiful in all her proper ornaments."[56]

In no quarter was the claim of catholicity more vigorously put forward than in the English Reformation Church. By the Tudor theologians, from Cranmer to Hooker, this note is struck and constantly reiterated. The claim was emphatically made by

p. 18. Taking this definition in its context, Professor Pauck remarks: "Besser kann der Charakter der Kirche, die in ihrem wahren Wesen mit dem Reich Gottes identisch ist, als einer organischen Gemeinschaft höchster sittlicher Art kaum ausgedrückt werden." *Ibid.*

[53] *Op. cit.*, p. 14.

[54] "Eo docemur Ecclesiae Christi tandem subiici oportere omnes gentes et regna quae quidem propitium Deum sempiternae salutis esse participes voluissent." *De Regno Christi* (Basel 1557), p. 16.

[55] *Ibid.*, p. 37.

[56] *Works*, ed. Laing, VI, 488f.

Robert Horne, later Bishop of Winchester, and other Elizabethan clergy, in a debate with the Marian clergy at Westminster, March 31, 1559.[57] The works of John Jewel, Bishop of Salisbury, the first distinguished apologist of the Elizabethan Church, abound with evidence which might here be adduced. He repudiates the Roman charge of schism, and spiritedly defends the catholicity of the *Ecclesia Anglicana*.[58]

The evidence, then, for the fact that the Reformers, with no less emphasis than their opponents, asserted the catholicity of the visible church is substantial and impressive. It fully justifies the vigorous, though too casual, observation of Lindsay: "They did not for a moment suppose that in sharing in this movement they were separating themselves from the catholic church of Christ in its visible sense. . . . Neither Luther nor any of the Reformers thought that they were founding a new church and going forth from the visible catholic church of Christ. They refused to concede the name of catholic to their opponents."[59]

5. CATHOLICITY IN THE PROTESTANT CONFESSIONS AND IN PROTESTANT WORSHIP

The claim of catholicity in early Protestantism can be illustrated, not only from the treatises of the leaders, but also from the doctrinal standards adopted by the different groups. The *Augsburg Confession* (1530), the mother of all Protestant confessions, contains, in

[57] Strype, *Annals of the Reformation*, II, Part I, 465f.

[58] "Apologia Ecclesiae Anglicanae," and "Defense of the Apology of the Church of England," Parker Society, *Works of John Jewel*, III.

[59] *Luther and the Reformation* (1900), p. 222. Cf. Ritschl, O., *Dogmengeschichte des Protestantismus*, IV, 257: "Erst Nikolas Hunnius begann damit die 'Papisten' wie sie sonst meistens genannt wurden, unbefangen auch als 'Katholisch' zu bezeichnen." (Hunnius lived 1585–1643.)

preface and conclusion, emphatic protestations of catholicity. The evidence of these passages may be slightly impaired by the fact that they came apparently from the hand of the Saxon Chancellor, Bruck, rather than from the theologians. But they are fully supported by Article XXII of the document itself, which claims that in the Lutheran doctrine there is nothing which is "discrepant with the Scriptures, or with the church catholic, or even with the Church of Rome so far as that church is known from the writers" (German Ed.: "the Fathers").[60]

The *French Confession* (1559) clearly implies the same viewpoint. It requires that believers "guard and maintain the union of the church," and declares that those who commune with Rome "cut themselves off from the body of Christ."[61] The *Belgic Confession* (1561) treats of "the Catholic Christian Church." This is defined as "one catholic or universal church, which is a holy congregation or assembly of believing Christians . . . dispersed over the whole world." Since out of this church there is no salvation, everyone ought to join himself to it, maintaining the unity of the church, submitting to its doctrine and discipline, and separating from those who do not belong to it. These clauses indicate that the visible communion is thought of as catholic. "The body and communion of the true church" is distinguished from "all other sects (*toutes autres sectes*) who call themselves the church." From what follows it is perfectly clear that it is the Roman "sect" that is chiefly in mind.[62]

[60] Schaff, *Creeds of Christendom*, III, 27.
[61] Sections XVI, XVIII, Schaff, *op. cit.*, III, 374, 376.
[62] Articles XXVII-XXIX, Schaff, *op. cit.*, III, 416-421.

The *Second Helvetic Confession* was mainly the work of Bullinger, Zwingli's loyal successor. Written in 1562, it was adopted and published in 1566. The preface is addressed "to all the faithful in Christ in Germany and the nations beyond." This Confession holds a place of great authority among the Reformed. It was subscribed in Scotland, Hungary, Poland, and France, and was favorably received in Holland and England. It quotes at the outset the imperial edict by which the Symbol of Damasus was made the test of the application of "the name of Catholic Christians" and adds: "Since we are all of this faith and religion we hope to be regarded by all not as heretics but as catholics and Christians."[63] It contains a chapter (XVII) on "the catholic and holy church of God." The phrases used are substantially those already quoted from Zwingli. But there is added insistence on the universality and unity of the church catholic. The Donatists, who would confine the church to Africa, and the Romanists, who represent the Roman Church alone as catholic, are, with sly humor, placed side by side for condemnation. The church militant has always had various particular churches which, however, are all to be referred to the unity of the catholic church.[64] It is of no small significance that this representative and most widely accepted document of the Reformed Church not only contains, but strongly emphasizes the claim of catholicity, and repudiates Romanism as sectarian.

The *First Scots Confession* (1560) confines its defini-

---

[63] "Speramus nos ab omnibus habendos non pro haereticis sed pro Catholicis et Christianis." Schaff, *op. cit.*, III, 235-236.

[64] *Ibid.*, pp. 271-273.

tion of the catholic church to the church of the elect which "is invisible, known only to God." The church is, however, locally visible where the Word, sacraments, and discipline are maintained as now in "the Realme of Scotland." The unity of the church is based upon the Word of God, since "the Spirite of God quilk is the spirite of unitie is in nothing contrarious unto himselfe." General councils are contemplated, though with authority limited by Scripture.[65] But the Scottish church at once went further. It approved in 1566, without emendation, the *Second Helvetic Confession*, with its vigorous claim of catholicity, and in its later standards set forth equally unequivocal statements of this doctrine. The *Form of Presbyterial Church-Government*, framed by the Westminster Assembly of Divines and adopted by the Church of Scotland in 1645, affirms: "There is one general church visible held forth in the New Testament. . . . Particular visible churches, members of the general church, are also held forth in the New Testament."[66] The Westminster *Confession of Faith* adopted by the Church of Scotland in 1647, after defining the invisible church, states: "The visible church, which is also catholick or universal under the gospel (not confined to one nation as before under the law), consists of all those, throughout the whole world, that profess the true religion, and of their children; and is the kingdom of the Lord Jesus Christ, the house and family of God, out of which there is no ordinary possibility of salvation."[67]

---

[65] Articles XVI-XX, Schaff, *op. cit.*, III, 458-66.

[66] *Form of Presbyterial Church-Government*, Philadelphia, 1745. Reprinted, New York, 1880, p. 48.

[67] Chapter XXV, Schaff, *op. cit.*, III, 657.

Aside from the rejection of the papal monarchy it was in the matter of worship that Protestantism, and especially the Reformed churches, most radically altered the expression of religion. Prior to the Reformation the Western liturgy had become loaded with excessive detail, and the need for simplification was generally recognized by enlightened minds. But the Roman church shrank from decisive measures. Quignon failed to obtain sanction for his outstanding project of liturgical reform, which Clement VII had commissioned him to draw up, until it was greatly modified. The work of Luther, Melanchthon, and Cranmer carried such efforts a long stage further. The fundamental changes were the elimination of the passages expressive of transubstantiation (which had only been made *de fide* in 1215), and the use of the language of the people. Luther would retain Latin where it was understood, but not where it was an unknown tongue to the worshipers. "I do not wish," he said, "in any wise to permit the Latin tongue to disappear out of divine service;" he would use Greek and Hebrew if they were known. He wished gradually to replace Latin by German hymnody, as in the expression of the fresh experience of the Reformation a body of hymnody should develop.[68] These measures, with his whole conception in the *Formula Missæ* and the *Deutsche Messe*,[69] show a desire to avoid abrupt change, and to continue the essential elements of catholic worship, with the added effectiveness of an understood speech. There was no attempt to make

---

[68] Sehling, E., *Die Evangelische Kirchenordunngen des XVI, Jahrhunderts,* I. 11.

[69] *Ibid.,* pp. 31f.; pp. 10ff.

worship uniform in the Lutheran churches; and answering to the demands of the churches themselves, there grew up a wide diversity of practice. In general, the greater degree of simplification occurred in the churches of south Germany. Adjacent to these were the Reformed churches, in which the simplification went still further.

Calvin and Zwingli excluded from public worship all that was not specifically authorized in the Scriptures. This was a drastic reform. Public worship was for Calvin, as F. Heiler remarks, "a solemn act of homage on the part of the whole congregation." It was a means of realization by the assembled community of the glory of God, in which "the place of meeting becomes a temple where God's glory dwells. . . . The Calvinistic service thus embodies, to a remarkable degree, Old Testament and Catholic cultus ideas."[70] The book of Psalms, with the French translations of Marot and Calvin and the noble tunes of Louis Bourgeois and Claude Goudimel, was well adapted to be the instrument of a worship which was characterized primarily by an awe and wonder-stricken consciousness of the glory of God.[71] In the course of later history the Reformed churches have recovered not a little of what was cast out in the sixteenth century; although in the process of seeking a fuller catholicity of worship they constantly run the risk of mere vulgarity, an element totally absent from the austere Calvinist model.

The Reformation modification of worship was by

---

[70] Heiler, F., *The Spirit of Worship*, pp. 96f.

[71] Doumergue, *op. cit.*, II, 419ff., especially the section "Calvin et le Psautier," pp. 505-24.

no means merely negative. That worship ceased to be the function merely of the specialized priesthood and became a function of the whole body, was surely not an uncatholic reform. Not since primitive Christianity had there been such participation in worship by the lay people. Community religious song, whether Lutheran hymnody or Calvinist psalmody, was an incalculably active factor in building church communion. Catholic worship had fallen into degeneracy. Luther moderately, and Calvin drastically, reformed it. But it may reasonably be argued that in both communions what was gained was more valuable, and not less catholic, than what was rejected.

CONCLUSION

The above citations constitute, it must be recognized, a chain of irrefutable evidence, not only that the leading Reformers asserted the principle of the catholicity and ecumenicity of the visible church, but also that their followers who formed the "particular" churches which they fostered into strength and activity, adhered to the same principle, and believed in their own catholicity to the exclusion of Roman claims. Rome was condemned by them, not merely as corrupt, but also as sectarian. Catholicity has often been obscured in Protestantism, and the terminology in which "catholic" meant "Roman" has been allowed to pass without objection by the successors of those who vigorously protested this confusion in the sixteenth century. It is usually assumed by Romanist writers that Protestantism is by nature uncatholic.[72] But, in fact, the Reformers aimed at a reformed catholicity, a catholicity freed from papal domination and medieval obscurantism. Many who emphasize orthodoxy and continuity, rather than universality, in the concept of catholicity, and can see no catholicity without the characteristic beliefs and practices of the late Middle Ages, will hesitate to recognize the catholicity of the Reformation. Since in their minds it is heretical to reject such elements alien to Protestantism as mariolatry, transubstantiation, and indulgences, those who rejected these cannot be by them regarded as Catholic. It should be remembered, on the other hand, that the Protestants recognized the claims of orthodoxy, and even of continuity, as fully as their opponents. They saw, however, a break in continuity in the history of the Roman Church itself, and differed considerably from the Romanists on the question of what constituted orthodoxy. That obedience to Rome was a matter of faith for the Christian, they, in common with the fathers of the councils of Pisa and Constance, regarded as an heretical position. This was the fundamental difference between the parties; and the difference is irreconcilable.

The Reformation was a revolt, not against the principle of unity and catholicity, but against the privileged and oppressive monarchy of Rome—an uprising not merely of national, but of catholic feeling, against what had become a localized and overcentralized imperialism in Christianity, which made true catholicity impossible. The system had been ren-

---

[72] For example, H. Moreau, article "Catholicité" in Vacant, A., et Mangenot, E., *Dictionnaire de théologie catholique*, II, 2010.

dered antiquated by two hundred years of town democracy, nationalism and new ecclesiastical and political thought. The communion of western Christendom was in a state of growing disintegration. Religion was depressed. The largely secular individualism of the Renaissance, innumerable sectarian discords, and constantly embarrassing national grievances, marked the enfeeblement of the corporate sense. The parish was not a congregation, but an administrative unit. The governmental aspect of unity was not supported by an adequate religious bond. The Roman Church had substituted the idea of "Roman obedience" for the earlier conception of catholicity expressed in a universal free communion. Obedience itself could no longer be exacted. Any hope there was of the rehabilitation of catholicity lay along the rough path of reform. In the Reformation the Christian people were taught to think, to believe, and to sing together, and given a new vision of the high and universal fellowship which is the church catholic. The catholicity at which the Reformers aimed was one of spontaneous, though visible and corporate, fellowship in the obedience of Christ.

With a considerable degree of insight, though not with logical consistency, the early Protestants attempted, in thought and organization, the recovery and promotion of catholicity in Christianity. It was partly through their own faults, partly through the faults of others, and partly through circumstances beyond all human control, that their efforts so largely failed of fulfillment. Powerful interests which the old régime had sought in vain to control were let loose in the sixteenth century to prevent the religious revival from achieving the unitive ends it sought. Will modern Protestantism, with less than its founders exhibited of the letter that killeth, and more of the Spirit that maketh alive, purposefully advance to the long-postponed fulfillment of their dream of catholic unity?

CHAPTER III

PROTESTANT CONCILIARISM: THE CONSTITUTIONAL PRINCIPLE

In the foregoing chapters attention has been called to the fact that Protestantism at the outset was not merely national or sectional, but catholic in spirit and aim. Here it is proposed to indicate the nature of that constitutional principle by which order, liberty, and communion were to be maintained in the Protestant churches. That principle was *conciliarism;* and Protestantism continued the tradition of conciliar, as opposed to monarchical, catholicism.

1. THE CONCILIAR PRINCIPLE IN THE LATE MIDDLE AGES

In the Middle Ages two opposing principles of government were contending within the church. These we may designate as the monarchical and the conciliar principle. In the history of government at large the approximate equivalents are absolutism and constitutionalism. In the former, authority rests with a ruler who is not responsible to the ruled. In the latter, it is the ruled who also rule, though ordinarily through delegated and responsible bodies. These principles have been everywhere in conflict; the history of their conflict comprises a great part of the history of politics.

The conflict does not cease even when cleverly devised phrases seem to offer a theoretic solution. The

Code of Justinian adopts from Ulpian (third century) the famous statement: "The prince's decision has the force of law, since by the royal law passed concerning his authority the people has reposed in him all of its own authority and power."[1] In the practical interpretation of this dictum, the emphasis was sure to be thrown on one or the other end of the balance, that of the derived princely authority, or that of the original popular sovereignty. It is, in fact, the first clause only that has become familiar, for the historic reason that it was the one which became exclusively significant in the operation of Roman government. "In the later Roman Empire popular sovereignty has disappeared; its place has been taken by the imperial will."[2] The same tendency arose early in the development of the French Monarchy, where it reached its culmination in the Bourbon maxim, "*L'état c'est moi.*" The emergence of this absolutism is not difficult to understand. Though it be granted at the outset that the prince exercises authority by delegation from the people, once invested with power, the masterful ruler will assume that the original delegation was irrevocable and unlimited, and will so conduct himself that, through lack of its exercise, popular sovereignty becomes a vanishing memory. The minions of an ambitious lord are wont in such cases to substitute for the notion of popular delegation the claim of divine sanction, thus rendering his sovereignty inviol-

[1] "Ulpianus libro primo institutionum. Quod principi placuit legis habet vigorem; utpote lege regia, quae de imperio ejus lata est, populus ei et in eum omne suum imperium et potestatem conferat." *Digesta*, I, iv, i, ed. Mommsen, p. 7. *Institutes*, I, 2, ed. Krüger, p. 30.

[2] Meynial, Edouard, chapter on "Roman Law" in Crump, G. C., and Jacob, E. F., *The Legacy of the Middle Ages*, p. 385. Cf. Moyle, J. B., *Imperatoris Justiniani Institutio*, p. 45.

able, absolute, and secure—until its abuses and the counter-attacks of the Hotmans and Rousseaus bring on "the Deluge."

In varying degrees this tendency has been exemplified in all monarchies, whether secular or ecclesiastical. The medieval papacy exhibits its rise, development, triumph, and decline. Claiming scriptural and divine institution, and completely repudiating the notion of a derivation of authority from the corpus of which it claimed to be the head, it rose from moral leadership to feudal suzerainty, from suzerainty to absolute sway. The shocks of the Conciliar and the Reformation period have left it in modern times maintaining a pathetic struggle to assert a divine right to rule over an incorrigibly disobedient world.

It is remarkable how closely the history of the late medieval church as an institution parallels that of the Roman Empire a millennium earlier. In both the temporarily successful assertion of the monarchical principle caused reactions destructive of the world unity that had been hopefully attempted. In both the means adopted to secure revenue called forth resentment and so caused a weakening of the structure. As the Germanic kingdoms replaced Roman Government in the West, leaving the East to stagnate under an effete system, so national churches replaced the papal imperium in northern Europe during the sixteenth century, leaving the Latin nations in some degree under Roman obedience. In the case of the empire, however, the causes of decline were in part external, while the disasters to the medieval papacy were due to causes almost purely inherent in the system itself.

Government without representation, in order to maintain itself, must be repressive of the voluntary and spontaneous elements among the governed, whether these are designated as treason and sedition or as heresy and schism. These elements in turn, whatever be our judgment in detail of their wisdom and right, must sooner or later assert themselves, even though they be loudly condemned in the name of heaven. The issue may be one of exploitation of the people for revenue, of taxation without representation and without benefit to the taxpayer; the underlying question is that of effective participation in government by the governed or by groups delegated to represent them.

Medieval writers were, as a rule, insistent in their demands for the recognition of the people's political rights. The great Scholastics have much to say that is now proudly cited by Roman Catholics favorable to political democracy, as anticipating the typical ideas of modern democratic theory.[3] But by the orthodox Scholastics these ideas—the outcome of their efforts to Christianize Aristotle's *Politics*—were applied only to secular states, while in church government the same writers lent royal support to the papal monarchy.

---

[3] Amid the extensive literature on different sides of this subject the reader may profitably consult: Gierke, O., *Political Theories of the Middle Ages*, tr. Maitland; M. de Wulf, *Medieval Philosophy illustrated from the System of Thomas Aquinas*, Chap. XV: Müller, W. "Die Staat in seinen Beziehungen zur sittlichen Ordnung bei Thomas von Aquin," in *Beiträge zur Geschichte der Philosophie des Mittelalters*, Vol. XIX; Ryan, J. A., and Millar, M. F. X., *The State and the Church;* Nations, G. O., *The Canon Law and the Papal Throne;* Murphy, E. J., *St. Thomas' Political Doctrine and Democracy;* Schaff, D. S., "The Bellarmine-Jefferson Legend and the Declaration of Independence," in *Papers of the American Church History Society*, Vol. VIII, pp. 237ff. Murphy has placed in parallel columns certain teachings of Aquinas and paragraphs from the Declaration of Independence. Schaff controverts claims of the dependence of Jefferson on Bellarmine.

Indeed, they so exalted the papacy as to support all its divine-right absolutist pretensions in relation to human society and to encourage their assertion by the Popes themselves. Not long after Aquinas had affirmed "that submission to the Roman pontiff is necessary to salvation," Boniface VIII, in *Unam Sanctam* (1302), made this opinion an authoritative declaration. "We therefore declare, say, determine, and pronounce," says this famous utterance, "that submission on the part of every human creature to the Bishop of Rome is altogether necessary for salvation."[4]

But there were other writers of that age, chiefly of the generation after Boniface, by whom the principles of civil polity were not thus reversed in the ecclesiastical sphere. They saw the ecclesiastical world society subject to the same laws of popular sovereignty as those which the accepted theologians applied in temporal government. This did not necessarily involve a secular, as opposed to a theocratic, conception of society. The theocratic ideal was not, in fact, affected by the democratic view; there was merely a difference in the channel by which divine influence was conceived of as entering human government. While on the one side it was maintained that the mediation of the divine was through the Pope, on the other it was affirmed that authority flowed from the divine Spirit diffused throughout the body of the Christian people, and accordingly that the fundamental organ

---

[4] "Porro subesse Romano pontifici omni humanae creaturae declaramus, dicimus, diffinimus, et pronunciamus omnino esse de necessitate salutis." This is but an emphatic expansion of Aquinas' "quod subesse Romano pontifici sit de necessitate salutis." Mirbt, C., *Quellen zur Geschichte des Papsttums*, 4 Aufl., pp. 200, 211.

of authority was a council of the Christian people or of their delegated representatives.

The assertion of the conciliar principle in the fourteenth century was in part a revival of the spirit and practice of early Christianity and in part an outcome of contemporary conditions. The conciliar reformers appealed to such passages of Scripture as: "Where two or three are gathered together, there am I in the midst of them," and to the example of early church councils. They vigorously asserted the headship of Christ against that of the Pope and the divine right of the group against that of the hierarchy. But they were also deeply affected by the rising force of the many forms of corporate activity that marked the intelligent and progressive society of their time. It was the era of the universities, the guilds, town government and commercial enterprise; of the English Parliament, the Swiss confederacy, the French and Italian communes, the Hansa and Rhine leagues. It was an age till then unparalleled for corporate enterprise and corporate loyalties—an impressive proof of the fact that life is greater than government and creative of it. Even the national monarchies, with all their defects, were calling forth the powerful motive of patriotism; and universal absolutism was doomed.

The papal unity, long gallantly maintained, was broken in the Great Western Schism (1378), and Europe stood in balance between national groups allied behind hostile Popes. The Conciliarists were not, it must be observed, disruptionists, but pacifiers and unionists. Marsilius, their chief inspirer, had written out his ideas under the significant title, *Defensor Pacis* (1324). In this work, long before the Schism, he had charged the Pope with "defacing the beauty of the church, which is her unity." The Conciliarists regarded the papacy itself as, in its absolutist character, an obstacle to unity. They now zealously sought the reunion of the West and the reconstruction of the *Republica Christiana* on a representative basis. They regarded the whole visible church as one body, whose parts were members one of another, and whose Head was a divine and not a human person. They attempted a fundamental constitutional reform, with enough recognition and enough control of nationality and local interests to keep the bond of peace and the solidarity of the catholic communion. The supreme authority was to rest in a general council of delegates from local and national groups.[5]

There were, of course, considerable variations in the plans for this conciliar organization, and the movement suffered from the inexperience of those on whom responsibility rested, in parliamentary government on so vast a scale. It did, however, produce results that were of permanent significance. It achieved one of its objectives—that of reunion. And it made vigorous statements of its governmental principle that were written indelibly upon the mind of Europe. The Council of Constance claimed (1415) to "represent the catholic church militant" and to "hold authority directly from Christ," and asserted its superiority to all, explicitly including the Pope.[6]

[5] Creighton, M., *History of the Papacy from the Great Schism to the Sack of Rome*, Vol. I; Valois, N., *La France et le Grand Schisme d'Occident; La crise religieuse du XVe. siècle; le pape et le concile;* Salembier, L., *Le Grand Schisme d'Occident;* Emerton, E., *The Beginnings of Modern Europe; The Defensor Pacis of Marsiglio of Padua;* Connolly, J., *John Gerson, Reformer and Mystic;* Powers, G. C., *Nationalism and the Council of Constance.*

[6] Mirbt, *op. cit.*, p. 228.

The formal rejection of these statements by the restored papacy, in violation of the pledges of Martin V,[7] did not destroy the vitality of the conciliar idea in reforming minds. Advocates of reform of the generation before Luther, like Gregory of Heimburg and Jacob of Jüterbock, whose work affected the special area in which Luther's activity began, freshly asserted the conciliar principle with zeal and persistence.[8] In the period just prior to the beginning of the Lutheran controversy, the University of Paris, under the influence of such leaders as John Major, the Scottish forerunner of Buchanan and Knox in political thought, repeatedly demanded a council.[9] The principle was repeatedly affirmed and the decree of Constance which embodied it was repeatedly appealed to by the leaders of the Protestant Reformation.

2. LUTHER AS AN EXPONENT OF CONCILIARISM

The fact has often been emphasized that Luther, with special reference to the treatment of Hus at Constance, admitted the fallibility of councils. In this respect, however, he did not differ from many of the medieval exponents of conciliarism. Most of the Conciliarists emphatically asserted the authority of coun-

---

[7] Mirbt, *op. cit.*, pp. 233, 242.

[8] Brockhaus, C., *Gregor von Heimburg, ein Beitrag zur deutschen Geschichte des 15. Jahrhunderts.* Ullmann, C., *Reformers before the Reformation*, Vol. I, pp. 193ff. *Realencyklopädie*, VIII, 556ff. Jüterbock (d. 1465) was a Saxon, and became an Erfurt Professor. He vigorously advocated a general council for reform in an address to the Pope in 1449. Ullmann remarks of Heimburg that he was "fitted above all others to exemplify the thoughts and actions of the German opposition." His chief appeal for a council was made in 1461. He lived chiefly at Nürnberg, and died in Saxony in 1472.

[9] Rénaudet, A., Préréforme et humanisme à Paris, . . . 1494–1517, pp. 333f.

cils while explicitly denying their infallibility. It is
to be noted that Constance itself, in its most height-
ened assertion of authority, did not proclaim itself
infallible. On this point, at any rate, Luther was un-
troubled by that confusion between "authority" and
"infallibility" which has too long afflicted religious
thinking. The attitude taken by Luther may be
illustrated by that of the modern citizen to the national representative assemblies by which he is governed. He is far too sophisticated to suspect them
of infallibility; yet he recognizes their usefulness, and,
while reserving the right of criticism and dissent, in
general willingly submits to their authority. Indeed,
he is their jealous, if discerning, champion. He prizes
them as the necessary safeguard of his liberty against
any possible encroachments of absolutism, and resists
any impairment of their power. Luther and the other
Reformers had not had, in the same degree as the
modern citizen, the opportunity to fix by experience
their loyalties to representative institutions; but they
were essentially on the same ground. They sought in
church polity what he has experienced in state affairs.
They were as far from repudiating conciliarism as
Burke was from abandoning parliamentary government when the Parliament which he addressed on
Conciliation with America took a course in that particular instance which he thought disastrous. Neither
Luther's admission that the council erred nor his assertion of the authority of Scripture constituted a
repudiation of conciliarism. Both these points were
recognized, and the latter was emphasized by the conciliar fathers. The council was necessary, they said,
to bring to recognition the authority of Scripture when

the papacy departed from Scripture. Luther was of precisely the same view. The whole conception of conciliarism tended away from such absolutism as would be involved in any doctrine of the infallibility of any group of men. The espousal of a representative system, even if it be conceived as divinely ordained, does not preclude skepticism of its operations in detail. For Luther the forms of church polity were of human ordering, not of divine appointment. But his preference as between monarchical and conciliar government is strongly and decisively in favor of the latter. His censures on defective expressions of conciliarism must not be confused with any repudiation of the principle.

Gebhardt has indicated how closely Luther paralleled his conciliar predecessors, in the following words: "The proposition that all Christians are of the spiritual order is to be found in John Wessel; the thesis of the right to depose the Pope, in Gerson; the demand that the Pope should be punished when he acts contrary to Scripture, in Dietrich of Niem: all that Luther says on the calling and authority of councils, in Nicholas of Cusa."[10] It may be added that none of the pre-Reformers here mentioned taught that the council is infallible. This statement holds also for Marsilius, Ockham, d'Ailly, and Nicholas of Clamanges. If they held that infallibility resided in the church catholic, they recognized that this was the case only insofar as the church was spiritual—a view which foreshadows the Reformation emphasis on the invisible church. Any given council might not adequately represent

---

[10] Gebhardt, G., *Die Gravamina der deutschen Nation gegen der römischen Hof*, 2 Aufl., pp. 127-28.

the true church. The Scriptures were indeed held by them to be infallible; but the written Word needed a living voice to interpret it, and the church had really no infallible organ of interpretation. All the infallibility that was left to them had passed into the background of the invisible and the intangible. The council was, however, the nearest approximation to an infallible authority. If it blundered, through defective obedience to the Spirit, recourse was to be had to a subsequent council.[11] In accordance with this idea Constance attempted, in the decree *Frequens*, 1417, to provide for a sequence of general councils. Thus the Conciliarists half unconsciously laid down a basis for progressive movement in church order, each succeeding council having the right, in the light of Scripture and the Holy Spirit, to review previous decisions.

But with Luther and his adherents conciliarism was much more than a traditional theory. In crisis after crisis they made vigorous demands and appeals for a free general council. For many years after the controversy began they hopefully looked forward to its settlement by conciliar action.

A few facts must here be reviewed, the significance of which has never been adequately appreciated. On November 28, 1518, Luther, employing almost the

---

[11] For Marsilius see Prévité-Orton, C. W., *The Defensor Pacis of Marsilius of Padua*, pp. 312ff. (*Def. Pac.* Dictio II, Cap. xix, xx.) As in the teaching of the reformers, the authority of the council is subordinate to that of Scripture. On the attitude of Ockham, see Emerton, *Beginnings of Modern Europe*, p. 166. On d'Ailly and Cusanus, see some remarks and references in Kolde., Th., *Luthers Stellung zu Conzil und Kirche bis zum wormser Reichstag. 1521*, pp. 5, 27. Nicholas of Clamanges argues that the Spirit has no control over a carnal and contentious assembly. See Jones, H. W., *The Holy Spirit in the Medieval Church*, p. 199.

very language of the declaration of Constance, and affirming that "a sacred council lawfully assembled in the Holy Spirit, and representing the holy catholic church, is superior to the Pope in matters of faith,"[12] made a solemn appeal to a future free, general council. In the following June-July came the debate of Leipzig, in which Luther was led to declare the Council of Constance in error concerning Hus. Did he thenceforth desist from demanding a council? On the contrary, he continued to advocate it with vigor. Fifteen months later he published his stirring *Address to the German Nobility*. Here he protested against the Pope's claim of the exclusive right to call a council (the "Third Wall") and urged the emperor, princes and nobles of Germany, and whoever could aid in the business, to co-operate in bringing it about: "Whoever can do so, as a faithful member of the whole body, must do what he can to procure a truly free council (*recht frey concilium.*)"[13] The conception of the whole treatise is clearly that the reform is to be carried through by means of a council, or series of councils, free from papal manipulation and control. It is this scheme of reform in which Luther invites his readers' participation. The two sections on specific reforms, in which his whole project is outlined, are entitled: "Of the matters to be considered in the councils," and "What should be done by the temporal authorities or by the General Council."[14] Luther followed the publication of this treatise and anticipated his

---

[12] "Quod sacrosanctum concilium in Spiritu Sancto legitime congregatum, sanctam ecclesiam Catholicam representans, sit in causis fidem concernentibus supra Papam," *Werke*, II, 36f. On some earlier evidences of Luther's conciliarism, see Kolde, *op. cit.*, pp. 11f.

[13] *Werke*, VI, 413.

[14] *Werke*, VI, 415, 427.

reception of the bull *Exsurge Domine*, by repeating, on November 17, 1520, the appeal he had made two years earlier for a free council representative of the whole catholic church.[15]

The holding of a free general council was to prove a matter of insurmountable difficulty, and Luther and his friends appealed for it in vain. If his later demands for a council were not greatly pressed, this was not due to the cooling of his desire for it, but to his growing despair that a "truly free" council could be brought about. There was always the possibility that it would be forestalled by the holding of a carefully planned and guarded papal council, which would combat the very reforms which he was anxious to promote. Luther consistently stressed the difference between a free Christian council and a papal one. The former he thought of as free in the sense of being uncontrolled by the papal monarchy and representative of the community of the Christian people, while he thought of it as Christian in the sense of being in accordance with the Word of God. He came to look habitually upon all the medieval councils as either unfree or unchristian. While he ascribes the beginning of the fall of antichrist to the Council of Constance,[16] he nevertheless condemns it in caustic language for its treatment of the writings of Wyclif and the person of Hus, in which it departed from the truth of Scripture.[17] His *Convocatio concilii liberi*

---

[15] *Werke*, VII, 75f.

[16] *Sämtliche Schriften*, VI, 628f. Cf. XVI, 274f.

[17] "Fateor enim articulum illum Viglephi (omni necessitate fieri) falso damnatum Constantiense conciniabulo seu conjuratione potius et seditione." *Werke*, XVIII, 699. Cf. *Sämtliche Schriften*, XVI, 2272ff., 2749ff., XXVII, 2017.

Christiani, 1534, a bold satire, in the name of the Holy Ghost, on the papal project for a council, is no repudiation of the main principle.[18]

Neither he nor, as we shall see, his supporters grew indifferent to the idea. Their opposition to the council projects of the Popes was due merely to fear that through an unfree and supine council the monarchical principle would achieve a fresh triumph. In 1539 Luther wrote an extended treatise on the subject, called forth by Paul III's preparations for what came to be the Council of Trent.[19] He had now lost hope of any acceptable general council, but still suggested a provincial council for Germany, which the emperor and the princes should call; and he hoped that, should this be done, other lands would follow Germany's example. Luther remained a Conciliarist, though a disillusioned one.[20]

3. THE CONCILIARISM OF LUTHER'S PARTY IN THE IMPERIAL DIETS

Such was Luther's emphasis upon conciliar action for reform that the conciliar idea was deeply impressed upon his followers. No doubt they shared in this a common expectation, but his appeals for a council must have had an influence upon them. It was a

---

[18] *Werke*, XXXVIII, 280ff.

[19] *Von den Konziliis und Kirchen.* *Werke*, L., 509ff.

[20] *Ibid.*, 623. From this and much more evidence, some of which is given below, I cannot agree with Kolde, *op. cit.*, p. 113, who dismisses Luther's conciliarism with the publication of the Edict of Worms, 1521, on the ground that with that crisis began for Luther the period of belief in the invisible church. It is of some interest to find an Anglican writer, somewhat unfavorably disposed to the reformation churches, exculpating Luther from the charge of schism partly on the ground of "his steady appeals through every gradation of ecclesiastical order, to the award of a general council." Manning, H. C., *The Unity of the Church* (1842), p. 328.

Lutheran, Johann von Schwartzenberg, who drew up the report of the Reichsregiment in preparation for the Diet of Nürnberg, 1522–23. This document advised that a council should be convoked at a convenient neutral place, within a year, and that in it there should be lay representation and complete freedom of speech.[21] The diets to 1526 increasingly show agreement with Luther's view. Gebhardt notes Luther's exclusive insistence on the conciliar method of reform, as differing from the attitude taken in the *Gravamina*, or lists of grievances, of the Diets of Worms and Nürnberg (1521–23) in which the method of reform is left open.[22] But by 1526 the "Christian Nobility" who rallied to Luther were intent on the purpose of bringing about a reforming council. It was now the policy of the Lutheran princes to induce the emperor to bring on a council. This the emperor desired, in the hope of Hapsburg advantage; but the Pope's disinclination was an impediment which he had not the courage to cast aside. Whereas Adrian VI had hoped to see a council that would deal with Luther as Constance had done with Hus, Clement VII feared and fought shy of every conciliar project. Charles did not wish to promote a council without his co-operation, fearing a complete triumph of the Lutherans. Even when he was at war with Clement he did not plan permanently to carry on Europe's affairs without the conservative influence of the papacy.

The emperor's *Proposition*, or Speech from the

---

[21] Von Ranke, L., *Deutsche Geschichte im Zeitalter der Reformation*, ed. *Joachimson* (1925–26), II, 42f.

[22] Gebhardt, *op. cit.*, p. 128.

Throne, before the Diet of Speyer, 1526, asked for the execution of the ban against Luther, that "the order of the church in general may be maintained until the meeting of a free council." When, however, Ferdinand, in the emperor's absence, tried to satisfy the princes with a letter from Charles written four months earlier, in which he had promised to arrange with the Pope for the assembling of a council, the imperial free cities jointly pointed out that this plan was now shattered by the opening hostilities between the emperor and the Pope, and that the letter was meaningless.[23] Having discussed the situation, the Diet resolved, "That for establishing religion and maintaining peace and quietness, it was necessary that there should be a lawful general council, or a provincial council for Germany, held within a year." It further resolved to send ambassadors to the emperor's court, urging him to come into Germany and institute a council. After three weeks more of discussion, and without waiting for the return of its ambassadors, the weary Diet made provision for the course to be followed in religion, in the momentous *Recess* of August 27, 1526. It was therein "unanimously agreed and resolved that, while awaiting the sitting of a council or national assembly," each prince should "so carry himself with his subjects in matters of religion as he hopes to answer to God and His Imperial Majesty."[24] Thus was the territorial principle instituted, as an interim measure, pending the conciliar settlement of religion. That it should afterward become permanent cannot have been the expectation or intention of its authors.

[23] Kidd, B. J., *Documents of the Continental Reformation*, p. 184.
[24] Kidd, B. J., *op. cit.*, p. 185.

This result merely followed from the fact that the stipulated action of the emperor was not taken. The Lutherans continued to call for this action, and it is gratuitous to assume that they did not mean what they said.[25]

The demand for a council was reiterated at the Regensburg Diet of 1527, during the papal-imperial war. The defeat of the Pope in this struggle gave Charles an opportunity to press for action in the matter, but Clement succeeded in making peace without consenting to the proposal. Thus, when the Diet met again at Speyer, in 1529, no general or national council had been summoned, and the prospect that one would be held seemed as remote as before. The only factor in the situation that made a council seem desirable to any of the opponents of the Lutheran cause was the operation of the Recess of Speyer, which, by its own terms, would lapse if and when a council should be assembled. But Charles and Clement had now agreed to have "the same friends and the same enemies," and the emperor was determined on stern measures against the Lutherans. Accordingly, he planned to bring about the annulment of the Recess without fulfilling its terms.

A strangely biased and unhistorical construction has habitually been put upon the *Protest* which was framed and signed by the Lutheran party in the Diet of 1529. The evangelical princes found themselves faced by a demand for the unconditional enforcement of the Edict of Worms, which meant the extermination

[25] Grisar offers this judgment in discussing a number of crises in the controversy, but on highly unconvincing evidence. See his *Luther,* Engl. ed., II, 50; III, 430f.; V, 379. H. C. Vedder, *The Reformation in Germany,* p. 352, thinks the "vociferous demands" of the Protestants for a council were insincere.

of Lutheranism. It matters little whether this demand, in its formal statement, issued directly from the emperor himself, or, as has lately been contended, from his brother, Ferdinand, who had his own "East-Hapsburg" ax to grind.[26] The Protest was a response to the imperial *Proposition* as presented to the Diet. This document was so framed as to hold out the promise of a council while removing the only existing guarantee of it. By its terms, and by the *Resolution* of the majority, the Protestants were asked to adopt a policy which would only encourage papal resistance to the conciliar plan of reform, and to admit the abrogation of the unanimous decision of 1526, which, in their view of the matter, was binding until a council should settle the whole issue.

How often have those sentences of the Protest been quoted in which the princes take high ground for private conscience—the least sincere part of their argument, since they made no ado about ruling the consciences of their subjects! In the eagerness to discover at every point Protestant "individualism" and rights of conscience, the real position of the document in the constitutional history of the church has been lost sight of. The Protest of Speyer is primarily the reiteration by the Lutheran princes and cities of the conciliar principle inculcated by Luther himself. It is their protest against the fading of the dream of conciliar pacification and reform which their leader had brightly unfolded to them in his *Christian Nobility* nine years before. "It has always," they say, "been considered in all diets that a suitable means of dealing

---

[26] Johannes Kuhn, "Wer trägt die Verantwortung an der Entstehung des politischen Protestantismus," in *Kultur und Universalgeschichte* (Goetz presentation volume), 1928, p. 215.

with this matter could not be found unless a free general Christian council (*frey gemein christlich Concilium*), or at least a national assembly (*Nationalversammlung*), should be held as early as possible." No other authority is capable of dealing with the business, and they refuse to accept decision in any other court. And because the former Recess of Speyer was of more service to peace and unity than the imperial Proposition, pending a coming council, they are in conscience bound to oppose its annulment.[27]

If Protestantism is to be associated with this Protest, from which its name is derived, the Protest itself should be understood in the light of the long-deferred conciliar proposal with which it was primarily concerned. It was essentially a reassertion of the Lutheran determination to secure peace and reform by means of an unfettered general council. If private judgment is invoked in it, the solution ultimately in view is to be reached by the exercise of corporate judgment in conciliar action.

On October 14, 1529, the princes issued a fresh demand for a "free general Christian council."[28] In the Introduction to the Augsburg Confession in August, 1530, reminding the emperor of his previous promises of 1526 and 1529, they once more called upon him to bring about such a council.[29] Again at the Diet of Regensburg, 1532, the familiar demand was repeated.[30] Why, we may ask, should it be

---

[27] *Sämtliche Schriften*, XVI, 392ff. A free translation of the Protest is given in Vedder, *The Reformation in Germany*, App. VI, pp. 431ff.

[28] *Sämtliche Schriften*, XVI, 592f.

[29] *Ibid.*, 991ff.; *C. R.*, XXVI, 263ff.; Schaff, *Creeds of Christendom*, III, 5f.

[30] *Sämtliche Schriften*, XVI, 2232f.

thought a surprising thing, or an evidence of insincerity in Luther and the princes, that when Vergerio came from Paul III with a scheme for a council to be held at Mantua, only two hundred miles from Rome and far from the German seat of the controversy, Luther told him that Rome's project was a joke[31] and the princes refused to commit themselves to it? On December 21, 1535, the princes indicate a rising despair of the "general, free, Christian council" so long in discussion, but they still stoutly uphold the principle. If such a council, they say, is not to be held, they will at least have testified that they desired it, and that it is legitimate and ordinarily profitable to Christianity[32] and wished for in all lands.

It is true that they had earlier hoped for a council called by the emperor and the Pope, and by implication pledged themselves to co-operate in it. But that was before the notice served on them by Charles V at the close of the Augsburg Diet to return to the papal fold, an action which marked them out as heretics and rebels and led them in self-defense to form the Schmalkald League. Nothing in the preparations for the projected council of Mantua tended to convince them of a willingness to allow the "free general Christian council" which they had always advocated. When on June 4, 1536, Paul III summoned the council, the bull in which it was called unmistakably hinted at the suppression of Protestantism.[33] Luther then drew up the uncompromising *Schmalkald Articles*, in

---

[31] "Es ist nicht euer Ernst . . . es ist nur euer Spott." *Sämtliche Schriften*, XVI, 2294 (November 6, 1535).

[32] "Rechtmässig und insgemein der Christenheit nützlich." *Ibid.*, 2314.

[33] *Magnum Bullarium Romanum*, VI, 224-26.

the preface to which he still expresses his desire for "a true Christian council."[34] Into these articles Melanchthon inserted a conciliatory clause to the effect that "if the Pope would permit the gospel," a *jure humano* episcopacy might be conceded. In an Appendix, which with the Articles was accepted by the Schmalkald Convention (February 15, 1537), Melanchthon included a protest against the papal domination of councils. How, he asks, can the church be purified if the Pope allows nothing to be determined against his will, and concedes to nobody the right to give an opinion except his own members obligated to defend his tyranny? Since the judgments of synods are rightly the judgments of the church, not of the pontiffs, rulers should tame the license of the Pope lest the function of judging and determining from the Word of God be snatched from the church.[35] These sentences are reminiscent of Luther's *Address to the Nobility*, 1520, and can be paralleled by many utterances of the conciliar party some generations earlier. It is of interest too that this passage was long afterward called to remembrance by American Lutherans in support of their synodical polity.[36]

4. THE CONCILIARISM OF CALVIN

Since the polity developed by Calvin and his associates is purely conciliar, it is of some interest to ask

---

[34] *Sämtliche Schriften*, XVI, 2329.

[35] *C. R.*, V, 281 (Latin); *Sämtliche Schriften*, XVI, 2382 (German).

[36] See below, p. 126. Bucer was a signatory of the Schmalkald document just cited, and on other occasions indicated himself a Conciliarist. In 1540 he proposed annual or biennial synods to be called by the Protestant Estates. The conciliar principle was involved in his suggestions of a Protestant conference, for example, in his letter to Bullinger of December 28, 1543, Lenz, M., *Briefwechsel Phillipps von Hessen*, II, 227. Cf. Grisar, *Luther*, v. 176, 7. On the conciliarism of Cranmer, see below, pp. 229ff.

how his ideas of the functions of councils compare with those of the older conciliarism. Calvin explicitly accords authority, not infallibility, to the ancient church councils. Defending the Protestants against the charge of extreme private judgment, he says (1539): "For, although . . . fathers and councils are of authority only in so far as they accord with the rule of the Word, we still give to councils and fathers such honor and rank as it is meet for them to hold, under Christ."[37] Believing that Paul III, having failed to bring about the proposed councils of Mantua and of Verona, was using the promise of a council as a pretext to avoid reform, he urged upon emperor and Diet (1543) the summoning of a provincial council for Germany.[38] Augustine, he says, treated the Donatist heresy in a provincial synod, and the Council of Chalcedon ordered the assembling of provincial synods twice a year.[39]

In this Diet the emperor, without the Pope's consent, promised a council either general or national; and for this he was "paternally" rebuked by the Pope. Calvin published the *Paternal Admonition* with his own comments. By numerous examples he here shows that during the period of the ecumenical councils these assemblies, as well as the provincial councils, were called not by the Popes, but by the emperors.[40] Underrating the constructive phase of Paul III's policy, Calvin believes that the council now called to Trent will never assemble. The projects of Mantua and

---

[37] *Responsio ad Epistolam Sadoleti. C. R.*, XXXIII, 415.

[38] Supplex Exhortatio ad Cæsarem . . . et Principes. . . . *C. R.*, XXXIV, 526, 27.

[39] *Ibid.*, 528.

[40] *C. R.*, XXXV, 261.

Verona have "vanished into a bull." If there should
be any meeting at Trent, the Germans "will hardly
be so silly as to throw themselves into the wolves'
jaws." Caustically he pictures the procedure that
may be expected, since "the cause which is to be
discussed is already condemned."[41] Building on the
emperor's promise he exclaims in closing: "But we
are now in another age. . . . There is an emperor
who will never be induced to bring his faith and
dignity into bondage to Farnese."

Trent, however, did assemble, and in 1547 Calvin
wrote his *Antidote* to the Canons and Decrees of its
First Period. A council has been long "demanded
by the common voice of Christendom." "At no period
was it more necessary to hold a council, if, indeed,
there were any hope that a lawful council could be
obtained." But France has only two "dull and un-
learned" bishops in it. The members are, as was to
be expected, "a hired crew of the Pope's followers,"
as far as possible removed from the character of the
early councils.[42] Calvin proceeds to pour out scorn
upon the whole proceedings.

The general council which Calvin desired "in order
to put an end to the existing divisions in Christianity,"
as with reawakening hope he wrote in December, 1560,
must be "free and universal." He defines its freedom
on three points—of place of meeting, of personnel, and
of procedure. The principle of scriptural authority
is affirmed. While a national council is permissible
to remedy internal conditions, a council calling itself
general must be really representative: a partial though

41 *Ibid.*, 281.
42 *C. R.*, XXXV, 380.

nominally general council will only augment the discord; for universal assent is necessary to the complete unification of Christianity.[43]

Further illustration of Calvin's point of view on councils is hardly necessary to our purpose. For him, as for Luther and Melanchthon, and for the older Conciliarists, the true council of the Christian Church bore no resemblance to a supine assembly of the Pope's partisans. Where hope of a true general council failed he advocated provincial or national synods, to be summoned by the political powers without waiting for papal sanction. In his favorable and unfavorable references to specific councils, and in his generalizations on the subject, Calvin, while constantly denouncing the debasement of the council to the support of the monarchical principle, is an emphatic exponent of the conciliar principle.

5. TYPES OF CONCILIAR POLITY IN PROTESTANTISM

Conciliarism had been repudiated by the Renaissance Popes, but even within the papal church the specter was not laid. The assembling, after many postponements, of the Council of Trent was a recognition, in a degree, of the old principle. The occasion was one of great anxiety to the papal monarchists, fearing as they did a reassertion of the officially rejected propositions of Constance.[44] Papal diplomacy, however, registered a complete triumph at Trent, and the Council became the means of the renewed

---

[43] *C. R.*, XLVI, 285-87.

[44] A useful study of this aspect of the Council of Trent is K. D. Schmidt's "Die Nachwirkungen der spätmittelalterlichen Reformideen während der ersten Periode des Konzils von Trient," in *Studien zur Geschichte des Konzils von Trient*, I.

rejection of conciliarism. Shortly after its conclusion Pius IV, in the bull *Injunctum nobis* containing the "Profession of the Faith of Trent," solemnly obligated the bishops to "true obedience to the Roman pontiff, the successor of the blessed Peter, Prince of Apostles and Vicar of Christ."[45] Since this action there has been no serious prospect of a return to conciliarism in the Roman communion; and the opposing principle of divine right monarchy has been re-enforced by the promulgation of the decree of papal infallibility at the Vatican Council of 1870—a "council" which did little more than register the sovereign will of the Pope.

In the Protestant communions, however, conciliarism has been the normal principle of government. Amid a variety of forms, this is indeed the underlying characteristic of the Protestant church polities. Where the emphasis is laid upon the local application of the principle, we have what is known as the Congregational type of polity. Here the minister and the ruling officers are elected by the body of the congregation, and represent the congregation in ministerial and magisterial authority. This type is, however, almost universally modified by the erection of agencies of control for matters of common concern affecting a group of congregations. In American Congregationalism, these extend to state conferences and a National Council.[46] While there is a jealous care to guard the inherent rights of the congregation, there is also a marked tendency to employ more general elective bodies for work in which the congregations desire to co-operate. These bodies are representa-

[45] Mirbt, *op. cit.*, p. 340.
[46] See the exposition of the subject in Barton, W. E., *The Law of Congregational Usage.*

tive of and responsible, directly or indirectly, to the congregations themselves. In full accord with earlier conciliarism all authority is deputed from the Christian people, whether it is exercised within or beyond the congregation.

The Presbyterial or synodical type is designed to express a high degree of solidarity of the whole communion, together with a distribution of responsibility throughout its congregations and membership. It is parliamentary government in a form rather more complete than is found in secular states. Authority rests ultimately upon the whole Christian people; but the ministers previously set apart to exercise a delegated priesthood take an authoritative place in the setting apart of new ministers. (The same course is followed in practice, though not to the same degree theoretically espoused, in Congregationalism.) Thus in ordination there is a conservative principle, by which the immediate authority of the people (the call of the congregation) is supplemented by the recognition of those previously called to exercise authority. The minister goes to his presbytery (colloquy or classis) only secondarily as a representative of his congregation, primarily as a representative of the whole church, past and present, which has taken action in ordaining him.[47] The congregation has its own lay representative in the presbytery, usually one of those deputed to act as officers in the congregation itself. In this systematic and guarded way, representation, lay and clerical, proceeds from the people to the session, thence to the presbytery, and thence to

---

[47] The doctrine and practice of ordination in Presbyterian, Methodist, and Congregational churches is amply discussed in *A Statement Concerning Ordination*, published by the General Council of the United Church of Canada, 1926.

whatever higher councils the communion may employ. The highest of these bodies is usually national in the extent of its jurisdiction, as in the case of the National Synod of the Reformed Church of France or the General Assembly of the Church of Scotland. Such gatherings as the Synod of Dort (1618–19) and the Westminster Assembly (1643–49) exhibit a temporary application of the conciliar principle on a scale greater than national. Ecumenical councils, constitutionally formed and recurring at stated intervals, have not become operative in Protestantism; though international and world gatherings of an advisory character have become frequent. The expectation on the part of the Westminster Divines of an ecumenical Reformed Church council is enshrined in the *Form of Presbyterial Church-Government,* which states: "Synodical assemblies may lawfully be of several sorts, as provincial, national, and ecumenical." While the hope of the ecumenical completion of the conciliar system, bodying forth the visible catholic church, has remained an unrealized project of Protestantism, the expression of conciliarism in detail has, nevertheless, been more adequate and more successful in the Reformed churches than in medieval Christianity at any period. During the past century and a half there has grown up the extensive and vigorous communion of Methodism, which, although only slightly indebted to Presbyterianism in the origin of its polity, is essentially, even in its "episcopal" sections, organized on the synodical basis.[48]

The late Professor H. D. Foster has indicated the debt of Locke and his followers, including the founders

---

[48] The Parliamentary character of the Methodist Episcopal polity is described by J. M. Buckley, *Constitutional and Parliamentary History of the Methodist Episcopal Church.*

of the United States, to Calvin and the Calvinists.[49]
Undoubtedly, the operation of representative government in the Reformed churches was a potent example
for the political thinkers and organizers. Locke,
Montesquieu, and Rousseau have acknowledged what
in any case would be an obvious indebtedness. But
Calvin and his immediate associates were not the orig-
inators of the system. They added little or nothing
to the old conciliar theory; they merely adjusted its
application to the conditions they had to meet. Foster, indeed, states that Calvin claimed no originality
in his ideas, but he fails to indicate that contemporaries like Buchanan and Hotman had access equally
with Calvin to the older teachings, and were not necessarily dependent on him in the matter. That Buchanan received his chief conceptions through that
sturdy Paris-trained Scottish Nominalist, John Major,
can hardly be doubted.[50] Major had imbibed at Paris
the medieval political and conciliar tradition, and had
confirmed his ideas of popular sovereignty by a study
of the political history of "Greater Britain,"[51] just
as Hotman and Buchanan after him invoked the
history of monarchy in their respective countries
to prove its delegated and responsible character.

Knox may have been indebted to Major, as Buchanan certainly was. But while there was virtually
nothing novel in his "democratic" teachings, his assertion of the "freedom of assemblies" was a forceful de-

---

[49] "International Calvinism through Locke and the Revolution of
1688," *American Historical Review*, XXXII, 475ff. (1927).

[50] See for instance, W. S. McKechnie, chapter on Buchanan's *De jure
regni apud Scottos*, in *George Buchanan: Glasgow Quatercentenary Studies*,
especially pp. 265f.

[51] See his *History of Greater Britain*, English tr. in Scottish Text
Society Publications, ed. by D. A. Patrick.

fense of the corporate freedom of the church, and of her conciliar organs of self-government. The point may be illustrated by some sentences from a famous dialogue between Knox and Lethington in 1561, as recorded in Knox's *History*:

Maitland of Lethington: "The question is whether the Quenc allowis such Convocationis."

Knox: "Yf the libertie of the church should stand upon the Quenis allowance or dysallowance we should be assured not only to lack assemblies, but also to lack the Evangell . . . tack from us the fredome of assemblies and tack from us the Evangell."[52] The warfare of the church of Scotland, from Knox and Melville to Chalmers and Candlish, has been primarily an effort to assert the corporate freedom of its "courts," or councils, against state intervention. Parliament has finally conceded the whole claim, in the Church of Scotland Act of 1921.*

Calvin, indeed, had struggled for the right of self-determination for the church in Geneva, but had permitted a considerable degree of interference by the secular power, for example, in the appointment of ministers. In the Scottish situation he would prob-

---

[52] Knox, *Works*, ed. Laing, II, 296. In striking contrast is Art. XXI of the Anglican *Thirty-Nine Articles*, formerly incorporated in the *Forty-Two Articles* of 1553: "General councils may not be gathered together without the commandment and will of princes." Anglican opinion on this Erastian precept has greatly changed, however. In 1896 E. T. Green in a scholarly study of the *Articles* said: "There can be no doubt that the union between church and state is loosening all over Christendom, and in the event of its being everywhere dissolved the commandment and will of Princes will have no concern for the Councils of the church." *The Thirty-Nine Articles and the Age of the Reformation*, p. 142. The *Westminster Confession*, XXIII, 3, gave the civil magistrate "power to call synods" but this was annulled in the terms in which the Confession was accepted by the church of Scotland. See C. G. McCrie, *The Confessions of the Church of Scotland*, pp. 222f.

*See below, pp. 325f.

ably have been less abrupt than Knox. Knox's clearly phrased assertion of conciliar freedom was historically momentous, particularly in the fact that it was asserted in opposition to the claims of both royal and papal absolutism, whereas earlier Conciliarists had in general sought the aid of princes against the monarchy of the Pope. This was accompanied in Knox by great stress upon the doctrine of Christ's headship. The historical importance of his stand is undeniable, but it can hardly be said to rest so much on the originality of his theory itself as in the boldness of its application.

Indeed, the Protestant exponents of conciliarism in general deserve credit for their application rather than for any origination of the theory. The fundamental ideas at the basis of their bold experimentation in representative church government came to them, consciously or unconsciously, from the conciliar thinkers of the late Middle Ages. But while Conciliarists and Erastians in controversy with the papacy applied the doctrine in such a way as to leave the church at the mercy of the secular power, Knox, Buchanan, and the French Monarchomachi so interpreted it as to guard the autonomy of the church in her own sphere.

6. ANGLICAN AND LUTHERAN MODIFICATIONS OF CONCILIARISM

The statement made above that conciliarism has been the normal principle of Protestantism may be called in question by some critic. How does this apply, it may be asked, to Anglicanism and Lutheranism?

In both these communions the principle has suffered certain modifications. The church has been during long periods in part denatured by the pressure of the state. The Church of England too, divided on the question of its affinity with Protestantism, has shown within itself a recurrence of the medieval conflict between the monarchical and the conciliar ideal. The age of Anglican reform was the age of Tudor absolutism; and in the fight against the Puritan and Presbyterian popular movements the national church tended to revert to a monarchical basis. This was represented by the retention of the episcopate as a self-perpetuating order, exercising, under the claim of a peculiar apostolic character, considerable monarchical power. The eighteenth century witnessed the control of the church by the national government, to such a degree that her own traditional representative institutions were deprived of their functions. Parliament took over most of the functions of the provincial Convocations of Canterbury and York. From 1717 these bodies ceased to govern, and by the early nineteenth century Convocation was known only to "a few antiquarians."[53] The political liberation and the revived church consciousness of the nineteenth century (two movements that within Anglicanism appeared to be mutually hostile) combined to bring about the revival of these provincial councils in 1861. Similar was the history of the diocesan councils; after long disuse they appeared and resumed importance in the nineteenth century. The formation of the National Assembly, authorized by Parliament, in 1919, marks a notable fresh aspect of the Anglican reappropriation of the conciliar principle. The ideal

[53] Makower, F., *Constitutional History of the Church of England*, 1895, p. 371, quoting Warren, *Synodalia*. Lathbury, T., *A History of the Convocation of the Church of England* (1853) is a useful history.

of a "constitutional episcopate," set forth by a committee of the Lambeth Conference in 1920, further indicates the trend of the present age. Recent controversies over Prayer Book revision seem to point to a further assertion of freedom from Parliament.[54] Whether a larger degree of freedom from Erastian interference will be matched by an increasing recognition of conciliarism is not certain, but both tendencies seem to be active at present. In the degree in which the church is Protestant it will be conciliar; but in this connection it is well to recall a remark of the greatest constitutional historian of Anglicanism: "As far as the ecclesiastical law of England is concerned," says Makower, "the designation 'Catholic' forms no antithesis whatever to the designation 'Protestant.' "[55]

Within the Lutheran churches the defective expression of conciliarism seems more exclusively a consequence of state encroachment. The fact that Luther regarded the forms of church government as undefined by scriptural authority, led to considerable variation in Lutheran polity and probably helped to subject the church to the state. Exercise of the conciliar principle may be discerned in the conventions of the Schmalkald League, and in sundry conferences of theologians. In the church order of Pomerania synodical meetings were employed, though virtually without legislative power.[56] But, broadly speaking, the conciliar principle found little expression in Lutheranism, and was never sturdily contended for till much

---

[54] For a review of the discussion see the editorial columns of the *Review of the Churches* VI 141ff. (April. 1929).

[55] *Op. cit.*, p. 178.

[56] Sehling, E., *Die evangelische Kirchenordnungen des XVIten Jahrhunderts*, IV, 392ff.

later times. The churches were governed by consistories appointed by the state, in other words, by the prince. This condition has been due, it is true, in no small degree, to the fact that Luther, in a time of discouragement as regards the people's share in reform, invited the princes to take authoritative action in church affairs. In sanctioning the territorial system with state-appointed consistories, Luther departed from his own ideal, or, rather, postponed any effort to obtain its fulfillment. As Böhmer emphatically says:

Nothing is falser therefore than to represent the so-called territorial system of church government as the form of church polity that most closely corresponds to Luther's ideals. On the contrary, we may assert that the territorial system stands . . . in direct contradiction to Luther's principal conception of religion.[57]

In addition to what has been said above about Luther's advocacy of conciliar reform, it may be useful here briefly to indicate his positive conception of church organization as it developed in the early twenties. At this time there seemed no immediate promise of the free general council to which he had appealed. Accordingly, he proposed the local organization of community churches which in association together would form a widespread church. In May, 1523, he published, in defense of the action of the people of Leisnig in forming a congregation with a carefully planned representative committee of control,[58] a treatise entitled: *That a Christian assembly or congregation has the right to judge all doctrines, to call,*

[57] Böhmer, H., *Luther im Lichte der neueren Forschung;* 3 Aufl. (1913), p. 164.
[58] For the constitution see Sehling, *op., cit.* I, 596ff.

install and dismiss teachers: proof and reason from the Scriptures.[59] This is a vigorous claim, on the basis of the priesthood of believers, of the rights of the Christian community. It is conciliarism in its elemental, congregational form. When he opposes "God's Word" to "bishops and councils," he is obviously referring to the unfree, papal councils.[60] All Christians are called to be priests, but they are to select those who shall exercise the ministry on their behalf.[61] This is Luther's favorite idea of a representative priesthood in the specialized ministry as projected from the priesthood of the whole body.

Another and more extended statement of the same year was his advice to the Estates of Bohemia on instituting ministers.[62] This he took care to issue immediately in German, thus indicating, as Grisar says, that in preparing it, "he was thinking of Germany, and above all of Saxony."[63] Here he reasserts at length the doctrine of the priesthood of the whole Christian people. On the basis of 2 Pet. 2. 9, he contrasts the priesthood that is "spiritual and common" with that which is "special and external." All have the right to preach and administer the sacraments, but for the sake of order and convenience one or more in every community should be "chosen or accepted to exercise this right in the name and for the sake of all who nevertheless have the same right." The right is not to be publicly exercised except by consent of the whole

[59] *Werke.* XI, Cf. K. D. MacMillan, *Protestantism in Germany*, pp. 39f. (MacMillan quotes with approval the above sentences from Böhmer.)
[60] *Werke*, XI, 409.
[61] *Ibid.*, p. 412.
[62] *De instituiendis ministris Ecclesiae* (October, 1523).
[63] *Luther*, Engl. ed., II, 112.

body or church (*nisi consensu universitatis seu ecclesiae*). Those whose hearts God has touched should
accordingly meet as a congregation and choose their
bishop. When a sufficient number of communities
(*multae civitates*) have been provided with this organization, the ministers may meet and elect from among
themselves one or more who shall act as superintendents
or visitors, until the country finally returns to "the
legitimate and evangelical archiepiscopate."[64]   Thus
a church polity is to be shaped on the principle of delegated power, the Christian people in their congregational council being the original earthly source of
authority.

The faith of Luther in the people, however, was
shaken by the fanaticism revealed in the Peasant
War, and by his growing impression of their ignorant
condition. The situation at the close of this struggle
offered a favorable opportunity for reform by co-
operation of theologians and princes. The adoption
of this plan and the postponement of popular conciliarism are indicated in the *German Mass*, 1526, in
the fateful word: "I cannot and would not order or
arrange such a community or congregation at present. I have not the requisite persons for it, nor do I
see many who are urgent for it."[65] The letter to the
Landgrave, quashing the elaborate conciliar. plan
worked out for Hesse by François Lambert at the
Synod of Homberg, is couched in similar language.
He admits that he has not the courage to sanction
the project (*denn Ich bisher und kann auch noch nicht
so kühne sein*), and advises a gradual introduction of

---

[64] *Werke*, XII, 180, 189, 191, 194.
[65] *Werke*, XIX, 44.

reform that will prepare the way for such legislation.[66] We may adjudge blame or praise here according to our view of the whole situation. In any case it is clear that the departure from the conciliar form and principle of church government was not the abandonment of the ideal, but a prudential and strategic postponement of action toward its fulfillment.

It is a highly significant fact that wherever Lutheranism has been, as in America, freed from state control, it has readily and naturally taken on a synodical form of conciliar polity. The synodical organization of American Lutheranism is usually attributed in some degree to the influence of Calvinism, an influence that was strongly felt on European soil by some of the Lutheran groups which migrated to America. Yet the point of view is expressed by numerous authorities, that the freedom for self-development offered in America, in contrast to the German territorial system with its state-appointed consistories, furnishes the primary explanation of this phenomenon. Dr. H. E. Jacobs notes:

The synodical form of organization, universally prevalent in the Lutheran Church of America, is in large measure derived from the Reformed Church, the Lutheran synodical organizations of the Reformation period, of which that in Pomerania may be regarded as the type, being of an entirely different character, as meetings for receiving instructions from the superintendents rather than for the decision of church questions. We believe that it can be safely affirmed that nowhere as in this country does the Lutheran Church have the opportunity to shape its church polity in accordance with its principles. The temporary scheme in Germany of regarding the rulers

[66] *Werke*, Erlangen ed., LVI, 170-71 (January 7, 1527).

124

as bishops may have been necessary under the circumstances; but it certainly caused great embarrassments, and often led to a practical denial of Lutheran principles, and even to their flagrant violation.[67]

It is far from clear to what degree association with Presbyterianism in Europe affected the Lutheran pioneers in America in their adoption of a synodical system, and how far the movement was a simple working out of Lutheran principles to which expression could not be given under territorialism. The influence of Spener's Pietism was prominent in early American Lutheranism, and H. M. Mühlenberg,[68] its chief organizer, was a disciple of Spener's most distinguished disciple, A. H. Francke. It would not, therefore, be surprising if we could trace American Lutheran synodical government to the ideas of Spener, who desired for Lutheranism the synodical organization which he favorably observed in French Calvinism.[69] This source is rendered less probable, however, by the fact that the earliest beginnings of synodical organization in America took place before Mühlenberg's arrival (at Raritan, 1733) in an association of German Lutheran ministers which, in the words of a recent investigator, "had nothing to do with Müh-

---

[67] *A History of the Evangelical Lutheran Church in the United States,* pp. 14f. R. Fortenbaugh, *The Development of the Synodical Polity of the Lutheran Church in America to 1829* (Phila., 1926), p. 30, says, "In contrast to the control of the secular ruler in Germany, it seems therefore safe to say that nowhere has the Lutheran church had the opportunity to shape its church polity in accordance with its principles as it has had in America." (Reprinted by permission of the author.) Fortenbaugh cites Jacobs, Richard, Krauth, and Schmucker in support of this statement.

[68] 1711–1787. Came to America 1747. See Mann, W. J., *Life and Times of Henry Melchior Mühlenberg.*

[69] Spener, *Consilia theologica Latina, Pars Prima,* Frankfort, 1719, p. 392.

lenberg or, indeed, with anybody who came out of Halle."[70]

Not to discount the claims of a Calvinist influence, either through Spener or through other channels, it is only fair to suggest that what happened was in some degree a revival of Luther's professed conciliarism, the development of which in Lutheranism had been retarded in the sixteenth century. This view is strongly supported by the formal statement made by the General Council of the Evangelical Lutheran Church in North America, at the time of its foundation in 1867. The council then adopted twelve articles "On Ecclesiastical Power and Church Government," of which the Sixth Article is as follows:

The representatives of congregations that convened in synod, and acting in accordance with these conditions of mutual congregational compact which are called a constitution, are for the ends and with the limitations defined in it, representatively the congregations themselves. A free scriptural general council or synod, chosen by the church, is, within the metes and bounds fixed by the church which chooses it, representatively that church itself; and in this case is applicable the language of the Appendix to the Schmalkald articles: "the judgments of synods are the judgments of the church."[71]

The framers of this statement evidently felt themselves, in adopting conciliar forms of government, in full accord with Lutheran tradition.

American Lutheranism, in its divergent groups, has remained distinctly Lutheran while its government has become characteristically synodical. Thus the synodical type of conciliar government has proved

---

[70] Fortenbaugh, *op. cit.*, p. 40.
[71] Quoted by Jacobs, *op. cit.*, p. 474.

itself a natural development in the different Continental varieties of Lutheranism organized in America. Some sections of Lutheranism, episcopally organized in the mother lands, have cast off episcopacy on migrating to this country. Lord Acton's generalization that while "Calvinism possessed the important faculty of self-government," "Lutheranism required to be sustained by the civil power"[72] may seem a true reading of the history of most Continental Lutheranism down to very recent times; but it must be rejected as a final characterization of Lutheranism as a whole.

CONCLUSION

The conciliar principle took deep root in the late medieval church, through the writings of a series of able exponents. It was brought to momentary expression in actual government in the early fifteenth century, but was combated with seeming success by the papacy in the pre-Reformation period. The widespread disruption of the monarchical church in the sixteenth century was attended by a revival of conciliarism which became the normal principle of church government in Protestantism. The leading Reformers advocated the principle, and brought it to fresh expression in the polities which they devised. While the medieval Conciliarists were concerned for its application primarily in the ecumenical affairs of the church, the Reformers, finding its ecumenical application impossible, sought meanwhile to establish it territorially. In the Reformed churches it became operative on a national scale, or in more local areas. The tendency to extend its operation to an interna-

---

[72] *Lectures on Modern History*, p. 155.

tional system was always present, and the idea of an ecumenical conciliar Protestantism was occasionally put forward. In Anglicanism conciliar government was long only weakly exhibited, partly through the monarchical character of the episcopate and partly by means of the Erastian control exercised by king or Parliament; but the last century has witnessed a remarkable revival of conciliarism. In Lutheranism the control exercised by the prince similarly hindered the development of conciliar institutions; but the principle was recognized in the Lutheran standards and advocated by the Pietists, and, probably aided in some measure by Calvinist influence, has emerged as the characteristic polity of American Lutheranism.

Protestant conciliarism differs from medieval in the detail with which it has been worked out in local and national church governments. It differs also in the growingly definite assertion of church autonomy against Erastian dictation. These differences from the medieval conception are decidedly advantageous to Protestantism. The defeat of medieval ecumenical conciliarism may have been in no small degree due to the absence of an adequate substructure of local conciliarism. The monarchical principle was then almost everywhere locally prominent; conciliarism was not fixed by psychological and governmental habit. Erastianism was early rejected, notably by Knox in Scotland, as incompatible with the corporate freedom of the organized communion. The conflict with Erastianism is largely won; and the current doctrines of the state, though legislators may in some instances be slow to learn them, tend to accord to churches, either peculiarly or in common with other corporate groups, an untrammeled autonomy. Whether we like or dislike the formula "a free church in a free state," with its nineteenth-century associations, we are, at any rate, living in an age of unprecedented church freedom so far as state relations are concerned. What will Protestantism do with "this freedom"? With the fuller adoption of the conciliar principle by all Protestant communions and the formation in them of an established habit of representative government, there arises the possibility of a conciliar world-Protestantism.

Lecky held that the "rudimentary virtue" of the Middle Ages was obedience. Obedience is the virtue of a monarchical society, and medievalism was as monarchical as the papacy could make it. If there is anything in the contention of the above chapters, the virtue of Protestantism is neither obedience nor "private judgment," but communion. Conciliarism is the constitutional principle which gives at once order and freedom to the exercise of the spirit of communion and the priesthood of the people. No principle of polity is an end in itself. The social experience of communion is the true objective of enlightened Christianity. If Protestantism is animated by a desire to attain that end, as some signs of the times at least seem to indicate, the means are at its disposal as never before.

PART II
EARLY PROTESTANT EFFORTS TOWARD CHRISTIAN REUNION

CHAPTER IV

REUNION ACTIVITIES OF LUTHER, BUCER AND MELANCHTHON

1. LUTHER AND THE BEGINNINGS OF UNITIVE EFFORT IN PROTESTANTISM

BOSSUET, in his *Variations*, pointed to the multiplicity and variety of the standards and organization of early Protestantism as proofs of the inherent perversity of the whole movement. The mischievous tendency to variation he regarded as common to all types of Protestantism, and derived from Luther, its founder, who had imparted to it his own "spirit of madness."[1] Such a view could arise only to an historian with a very limited conception of social causes. The decline and fall of the medieval church was not the work of the Reformers. Luther came at the end of a long period of disintegration. His attacks would have proved feeble and abortive against a flourishing institution. The papal monarchy had progressively lost prestige and authority; in certain areas it now broke down completely, and gave place to a new locally organized church order. We are presented not by a co-ordinated revolutionary movement, but by a series of spiritually related but organically dis-

---

[1] "Qu'ils disent après cela que les variations de Luther et des Luthériens ne les touchent pas: nous leur dirons au contraire, que selon leurs propres principes et leurs propres déclarations, montrer les variations et les inconstances de Luther et des Luthériens, c'est montrer l'esprit de vertige dans la source de la Réforme et dans la tête où elle a été premièrement conçue." *Histoire des variations des églises protestantes*, 1844 ed., I, 5.

tinct reformations. Protestantism developed without guidance from any single mind or central committee, and while marked by an underlying unity was divergent and multiple in organization and expression from the first. Luther was not its sole founder; he and the other Reformers were its representatives. They were the advocates and leaders of a reconstruction rather than the conspirators and demagogues of a revolution.

The passing of the *ancien régime* could not fail to be attended by much variety and experimentation before any new general order could be established. A familiar political parallel may be recalled. When the Western Empire ceased to function in certain provinces, local governments took shape. These exhibited great variety, and engaged in fierce competition which was prolonged through centuries of extraordinary confusion. The fact that most thinking people believed in Augustine's doctrine of human solidarity did not greatly mitigate conditions which were rendered inevitable by social causes. As in the sixteenth century, national and local powers and loyalties resisted unifying effort. But, in fact, the similar crisis of the sixteenth century was passed with decidedly less confusion. All the forces making for disintegration were again present, but they were in considerable degree held in restraint by the leaders, often with a rigor that has been called inhuman. Roman authority was manifestly perishing. It was their task, while entertaining the hope of a general reform by conciliar agency, to restore the church meanwhile in such local areas as they could control. There need be no surprise that these local efforts should exhibit peculiarities. The "variations" of Protestantism are not to be accounted for by the perversity of any leader, but are reflections of the unplanned variety of an age in which time-honored authority had been relaxed.

If we are to find cause of wonder here, it should rather be in the fact that the pre-Lutheran Protestantism of Bohemia, the Protestantism of Wittenberg, and the emergent parallel movements of Zurich, of Strassburg, of Geneva, of England and of Scotland, all exhibited a close affinity, regarded their fundamental principles as identical, their objectives as common, and early sought co-operation and union. For, in fact, all these movements were, in a sense, independent. There is no reason to suppose that either Switzerland or England would not have had its own reformation, even if Luther had remained a loyal Romanist. Conditions in Scotland too were shaping toward an ecclesiastical transformation apart from the various foreign strains that stimulated the Protestant movement in that country.

How may the pronounced resemblances of the Reformation churches be accounted for? Only in part by the transmission of influences from Luther to the other leaders. The common elements were, after all, great underlying principles which had been expressed before Luther, had captured him and made him a prophet, and now in turn, as environmental conditions forced them to think matters through, captured Zwingli, Calvin, and the rest. The Reformers were the continuators, under the stimuli of their own transition age, of the opposition party—in principle a constructive and not a disruptionist party—of the late Middle Ages, who asserted the headship of Christ and the sovereignty of the people as against the monarchy of the Pope, and supported their claims from Scripture and early church practice as against papal decretals. Under Popes who were libertines and tyrants these ideas became irresistibly attractive to earnest minds. In adherence to the traditional demand for a scriptural and anti-monarchical reform of the church, Protestantism was one. The judgments it made on the Pope and the Bible, and on the character of the "true church," were common to all its parts.

Unitive effort in Protestantism, in fact, begins at the beginning of Luther's public work of reform. At Leipzig Eck succeeded in identifying Luther's cause with that of the Bohemians, and apparently aroused in Luther a concern for the Bohemian "heretics." The Bohemians, both Brethren and Utraquists, reciprocated Luther's interest. In October, 1519, Luther received letters from Lukas of Prague; but his wish was to deal not with the Brethren alone, but with both parties. In his *Address to the Nobility* (1520) he says frankly:

It is high time that we should earnestly and honestly take up the Bohemian business in order to unite them with us and us with them, so that on both sides the dreadful accusations, hatred, and envy may cease.

An embassy of pious bishops and doctors, he thinks, should be sent to the Bohemians, to inquire concerning their faith with a view to uniting their sects into one church; and the Pope should allow them to choose their own ecclesiastics.[2] In the years 1522–24 he re-

---

[2] *Werke*, VI, 454-55.

ceived no less than five delegations from the Brethren. He was also in close touch with leaders of the Utraquists. Deep-seated prejudices between the Bohemian parties, and certain differences on the Lord's Supper and other points of theology and discipline between the Lutherans, and both, together with Luther's absorption in German affairs, prevented these exchanges from bearing tangible fruit.[3] They did not result, however, in controversy; and the efforts of the liberal leader of the Brethren, John Augusta (d. 1572), to establish a united national Protestant church of Bohemia,[4] are best regarded as a continuation of these negotiations.

Dutch followers of Wessel Gansfort likewise early acknowledged kinship with the new leaders. Hinne Rode, a disciple of Wessel and an associate of Cornelius Hendrix Hoen, brought a copy of the latter's *Epistle on the Eucharist* to Wittenberg, c. 1521, and subsequently visited Basel, Zurich, and Strassburg. The treatise was not accepted by Luther, but was warmly received by Œcolampadius, Zwingli, and Bucer. Zwingli had it printed in 1525, adding a few paragraphs of his own. The point at which Hoen's language gives place to Zwingli's is a matter of disagreement between two recent editors.[5] This well-

[3] Luther's *Letter to the Estates of Bohemia* (1523) has been noticed above. The whole subject is examined by J. Th. Müller, *Geschichte der böhmischen Brüder*, I, 389-435.

[4] The labors and sufferings of Augusta are set forth at some length by A. Gindely, *Geschichte der böhmischen Brüder*, I, 233ff. An up-to-date monograph on Augusta is much needed. In intrinsic qualities he takes rank with the great Reformers; and he is surpassed by none in his devotion to the cause of Protestant union.

[5] "Zwinglis Zusatz zu Kornelius Hendricks Hoen: Epistola Christiana ad modum ex Bathavis missa, sed spreta, longe aliter tractans coenam dominicam," etc., in *C. R.*, XCI, 505ff. On p. 508 W. Köhler credits Hoen with some paragraphs ascribed to Zwingli by A. Eekhof, *De Avondmaalsbrief van Cornelis Hoen*. Cf. Köhler, W., *Zwingli und*

intended mission of Rode convinced Bucer and confirmed Zwingli, but also served to intensify the rising differences on the Eucharist, over which Protestantism was to remain divided.

The tragedy of Protestantism was that its sections were kept apart by disagreements over the interpretation of that sacrament in which fellowship ought supremely to have been realized. The tragedy was poignantly felt at the time, and there are many parallels to the laments exchanged between Melanchthon and Cranmer that "the sacrament of unity is become, through the devil's malice, food for disagreement and, as it were, the apple of contention."[6] In subsequent years earnest efforts were made to reach a theological consensus, and many apparent difficulties vanished on discussion. Even on this matter of the Eucharist the formulæ of Protestantism were virtually reduced to two. To make of these two one was to prove the impossible task. The scandal of this division and the controversies that arose out of attempts to solve it have naturally attracted far more attention than the many other points of doctrine which occasioned no

---

Luther, Ihr Streit um das Abendmahl, I, 154f., 222; "Zu Zwinglis ältester Abendmahlsauffassung," *Zeitschrift für Kirchengeschichte*, XLV (1926), 399ff.; Hyma, A., "Hoen's Letter on the Eucharist and its Influence upon Carlstadt, Bucer and Zwingli," *Princeton Theological Review*, January, 1926, pp. 124ff.; *The Christian Renaissance*, pp. 218f., 286; Miller, E. W., and Scudder, J. W., *Wessel Gansfort, His Life and Writings*, I, 145, 164, 187, 203, II, 38, 317ff. (the last citation is a translation of Hardenberg's *Life of Wessel of Groningen*); Ullmann, C., *Reformers before the Reformation*, II, 510f.; Anrich, G., *Martin Bucer*, p. 47; Ritschl, O., *Dogmengeschichte des Protestantismus*, III, 87.

[6] "Et dolendum sane est, Sacramentum unitatis invidia Diaboli factum esse escam dissidii et veluti μῆλον ἔριδος." Cranmer, *Remains and Letters*, p. 433; *C. R.*, VII, 971 (March 27, 1552). Cf. Melanchthon's similar expressions in letters to Cranmer, 1548, *C. R.*, VI, 801, 894. On October 5, 1544, Melanchthon had written to Musculus: "O rem miseram, et omnium lacrymis deplorandam, quod illud ὅσιον σύμβολον τῆς ἀγάπης belli cogitur esse materia seu occasio." *C. R.*, V, 495.

conflict. In certain instances at least, while the
theological difficulty was the point in debate, the real
occasion of division was rather more political than
religious.

2. THE MARBURG COLLOQUY, 1529

The earliest formal conference for unity in Reformation history was the Colloquy of Marburg, 1529. The
circumstances and proceedings of this eventful meeting are among the familiar facts of the period and need
not here be reviewed.[7] It is sufficient to indicate one
or two points of interpretation. In the first place it
is clear that, despite the failure to reach complete
accord, the conference registered agreement in a remarkable degree. Of the fifteen articles drawn up
by Luther at the request of the Landgrave, all were
agreed on except that section of Article XV which
touched the special question of the corporeal presence
in the sacrament. Further, the Swiss and the Strassburgers were prepared to join hands with the Lutherans without insisting on exact uniformity of belief.
In this they may be credited with a liberal and Christian temper, but also with political acumen. Zwingli's
reforming work at Zurich was menaced by the recently
formed League of Innsbrück between Romanist cantons and the hereditary enemy, Austria. His cause
needed the political consolidation which the conference promised. Luther apparently thought this the

---

[7] Schmitt, L. J. K., *Das Religionsgespräch zu Marburg im Jahre 1529;*
von Schubert, H., *Bekenntnisbildung* und *Religionspolitik,* 1529-30
(1524-1534); Lenz, M., *Zwingli und Landgraf Philipp, Zeitschr. f.
Kirchengesch,* III (1879); three articles, pp. 28ff.; 220ff.; 429ff. Baum,
J. W., *Capito und Butzer,* pp. 453ff.; Waldburger, A., *Zwinglis Reise
nach Marburg* (1929); Köhler, W., *Das Marburger Religionsgespräch,*
1529 (1929).

full explanation of Zwingli's generosity. It was with this estimate of Zwingli's motives that he said to him, "You are of another spirit than we." The fact that it was always difficult for Luther to join policies with those whose views differed in any respect from his own does not fully explain his stand at Marburg. His utterances in this conference were marked by unusual acerbity and refusal to reciprocate, and are not to be taken as a true index of his attitude on Christian unity.

The fact is that Luther was deeply concerned over an issue that does not appear in the reports of the discussion and was not strictly theological at all. The meeting had been arranged in spite of his pronounced inclinations. He was well aware that what Philip of Hesse desired from it was something other than the establishment of intercommunion. The Landgrave's design was mainly political, though we may fairly suppose that it was promoted with some consideration for religion and that Bucer and the Swiss in adopting it were concerned primarily for religious guarantees. Philip wanted to bring about the merging of the League of Torgau with Zwingli's Christian Civic League (to which Strassburg was now attached) in order to consolidate the political interests of Protestantism. This was probably in itself good politics; but to Luther it looked like sheer rebellion against the emperor, which at that stage nothing would have induced him to sanction. He had previously warned the Elector of Saxony against the admission of the half-Zwinglian Oberland cities to the League of Torgau.[8] A month before the Marburg Colloquy (August

[8] De Wette, *Briefe*, III, 454.

29) he had written to Brentz: "Nothing good is likely
to ensue from such a hole-in-corner coming together
of the churches of God," advised Brentz not to attend
the gathering, condemned the project as the work
of the "Hessian Alexander," and wished that a few
pious papists might be present to bear witness against
the Swiss.[9]

The considerations most prominent in Luther's
mind here, apart from the Eucharistic disagreement
itself, were apparently three. In the first place he
had a deep conviction of the sin of rebellion, and
regarded the princes as under solemn obligations to
obey their emperor, at least until the imperial electors
should constitutionally depose him. In the second
place, he and Melanchthon still sincerely hoped for a
reunion with "pious papists" through the favor of
the emperor, and by means of the promised council
which would adequately reform the whole church.
And, thirdly, he was not unaware of the defects of
Philip of Hesse as a political leader. Philip was now
industriously negotiating with Francis I, and seeking
to commit the Protestants to the consequences of an
ambitious scheme of secret diplomacy. His suspicion
and credulity had been only recently exposed, to the
shame of his friends, in the Pack incident; and he was
obviously not the conservative and sagacious leader
to whom weighty matters could be safely intrusted.
Luther's intense fear of the consequences of forming
an armed league is shown in his letter to John of
Saxony, November 18, 1529. It will, he says, result
in bloodshed and mishap, and we shall wish in vain
to be rid of it, while "we would rather have ten times

---

[9] *Ibid.*, 501. Cf. Vedder, *The Reformation in Germany*, pp. 302f.

died" than be aware "that our gospel has been the cause of blood or shame."[10] For the Germans the question of resistance to the emperor was a vital issue: the Swiss, of course, had no direct concern in the matter.[11] The success of the Marburg Colloquy would have conflicted with Luther's hopes and realized his fears; it would have forced him to a highly uncongenial reorientation of his reforming ideas, the scrapping of his favorite policy for an entirely different one of which he was not the author. A more elastic mind might have been captivated by the world-opportunity of the occasion; but Luther was Luther. It should be remembered too that he was fully supported in his position by Melanchthon, who was possibly even more devoted to the emperor. The Romanist majority at the then recent Diet of Speyer had indicated a special antipathy to the Zwinglian and Oberland doctrine of the Supper, and this had made a deep impression on Melanchthon. He had returned from the Diet with a "disquieted conscience and a determination not to let the Swiss opinions affect Lutheran negotiations with the emperor.[12] The importance of the political question at Marburg is shown by the fact that Bucer regarded the disagreement as due to Melanchthon's devotion to the emperor and Ferdinand.[13]

If, then, Luther showed an unreasonable temper at Marburg and turned the conference into a debate,

[10] De Wette, *Briefe*, III, 526.

[11] Cf. von Schubert, *op. cit.*, pp. 182f. Lenz, Article in *Zeitschr. f. Kirchengesch*, III, esp. pp. 249f.

[12] Richard, J. W., *The Confessional History of the Lutheran Church*, pp. 17-18.

[13] Letter to A. Blaurer, October 18, 1529. Schiess, T., *Briefwechsel der Brüder Ambrosius u. Thomas Blaurer*, I, 148,

the explanation may in large part be found in the fact that by a psychological transference he took out on the Swiss leaders his antipathy toward the political aspects of the scheme to which they had, in good conscience, lent themselves. Indeed, the conjecture thrusts itself forcibly upon us that his tenacious religious imperialism may from the first have predisposed him against the Swiss theology. Lenz has clearly pointed out the close relationship between his attachment to the emperor and his rigor on the Eucharistic question:

> The orthodoxy of the Saxons (if we may so designate their tenacity in maintaining their conception of the sacrament) stands—we can by no means close our eyes to the fact—in a quite definite reciprocal relation with their attachment to the emperor. The more secure they felt themselves in face of the Catholic reaction, all the more Lutheran did they appear; the more Lutheran, the more disinclined to soil the purity of the gospel with acts of force; the more defensive, the more submissive toward the Emperor Charles; the more submissive toward the emperor, the harsher toward the Zwinglians.[14]

The problem of Marburg, then, lay deeply rooted in the socio-political situation. Luther and Melanchthon had always been accustomed to a conception of reform method which was now in danger of being completely superseded. Their way, as well as Zwingli's, contemplated the unity of the church; but the first and all-important reunion for the Saxons was the restoration of communion with the "pious" who still adhered to the Roman Church, to whom the teachings of Zwingli were exceedingly offensive. While they

[14] "Zwingli und Landgraf Philipp," in *Zeitschr. f. Kirchengesch,* III (1879), 249.

entertained this view all conciliation with the Swiss or their South German allies was excluded.

Nevertheless, from the standpoint of understanding and union the Marburg Colloquy was far from being a total failure. Von Schubert reaches the conclusion that it had high significance as the beginning of accord on the Lord's Supper, and especially as leading to the Wittenberg Concord of 1536.[15]

3. The Unitive Effort of Bucer to 1531

The men chiefly responsible for the promotion of unitive Protestantism in the German-speaking area during the next two decades were Martin Bucer and Philip Melanchthon. Of the two the former was the more active advocate of Protestant union, the latter the more concerned for the *rapprochement* of Lutherans and Roman Catholics; but for both Christian reunion, wherever a possibility of it appeared, was irresistibly attractive.

No adequate biography of Bucer (1500–1551) has appeared, but recent studies have shown his central and influential place in the Reformation as a whole.[16] He was the most zealous exponent of the ideal of church unity of his age. Although he made mistakes of judgment, and did a disservice to the moral prestige of Protestantism by his connection with the

---

[15] *Op. cit.*, pp. 96ff., especially pp. 115f.

[16] Baum, J. W., *Capito und Butzer, Strassburgs Reformatoren;* Anrich, G., *Martin Bucer;* Harvey, A. E., *Martin Bucer in England;* Lang, A., *Das Evangelienkommentar Martin Butzers;* Lenz, M., *Briefwechsel Landgraf Philipps von Hessen mit Bucer,* 3 vols.; Schiess, T., *Briefwechsel der Brüder Ambrosius und Thomas Blaurer,* 3 vols.; Eells, H., *The Attitude of Martin Bucer toward the Bigamy of Philip of Hesse;* Hyma, A., *The Christian Renaissance;* Pauck, W., *Das Reich Gottes auf Erden, Utopie und Wirklichkeit.*

bigamy of Philip of Hesse,[17] his total contribution to the Reformation cause deserves in a high degree the gratitude of posterity. Bucer, like Luther, emerged from the cloister to become a reformer. He owed his conversion largely, indeed, to Luther, whom he heard at Heidelberg in 1518; but partly also to Erasmus. His wide personal acquaintance included Reuchlin, and the Humanist strain in him was not inconsiderable. His early radicalism is shown by his connection with Sickingen and Hutten in the period of the Knights' War. He always exhibited the qualities of an aggressive personality. In close accord with Wolfgang Capito and Jacob and John Sturm he was instrumental in the Strassburg Reformation, which, in its features of discipline as well as in its theological emphasis, anticipated much that is usually associated with Calvin's Geneva.[18] In 1524 he entered into correspondence with Zwingli; and in the same year he was visited by Carlstadt, who was opposing Luther's doctrine of the sacrament, and by Hinne Rode. Bucer was deeply impressed by Rode, and, indeed, convinced in an interview with him of the spiritual as opposed to the corporeal presence. To Zwingli the Dutch teaching was only confirmatory of positions he had independently reached.[19]

As the controversy over the sacrament gained in

---

[17] Rockwell, W. W. (*Die Doppelehe des Landgraffen Philipps von Hessen*), and especially Eells, have shown that Bucer was far less guilty in this matter than was formerly supposed. He was not the author of the *Dialogus Neobuli*, which Philip caused to be published in defense of his conduct. Eells criticizes Bucer's judgment but completely exonerates him on the moral issue. *Op. cit.*, pp. 235f.

[18] Pauck, W., "Calvin and Butzer," in *Journal of Religion*, IX, 237ff. (April, 1929).

[19] Köhler, W., "Zu Zwinglis ältester Abendmahlsauffassung," *Zeitschr. f. Kirchengesch*, XLV (1926), 405.

intensity Bucer found himself occupying a particularly warm sector of the strife. He had something in common with both the Wittenberg and Zurich partisans. His theological position was essentially that of Zwingli. Eells calls him, at this stage, "a strong Zwinglian."[20] But he had a sense of the mystical which enabled him to appreciate Luther's position. He was too, in some degree, spiritually indebted to Luther and felt toward him the relation of a disciple who would gladly agree with his master if he could. Strassburg was within the empire and politically bound up with the cause of Protestantism in Germany. Bucer's mind was more liberal than that of Luther. He was concerned for theology as something purely subordinate to communion; his fundamental interest was in the security, unity, and expansion of the true church, "Regnum Christi."[21] He was, indeed, more conciliatory even than Zwingli. Anrich states this fact strongly when he says, "Zwingli, accustomed to mastery and victory, desired primarily the triumph of his own views; the Strassburgers primarily the peace of the church."[22] Zwingli, too, gave evidence of a desire for the peace of the church, but he could not make such concessions to the Saxons as Bucer unhesitatingly made. Bucer was the very incarnation of the irenical spirit. For the sake of union he was indifferent to phraseology, and by his frequent invention of new formulæ constantly exposed

---

[20] *Op. cit.,* p. 12.

[21] "Es war eine protestantische Idealpolitik grossen Stils, der er das Wort redete," says Anrich, who further indicates Bucer's interest in the international progress and co-ordination of the Protestant movement, and quotes his "equidem hoc unum contendo, ut regnum Christi quam latissime obtineat." Anrich, *op. cit.,* p. 98.

[22] *Ibid.,* p. 49.

himself to the charge of timeserving. A century later John Dury defended himself from the epithet "ambidextrous divine" by the boast that he was a "single-hearted peacemaker." Both men were free from self-seeking; they need not be thought unprincipled because they put the principle of charity before that of theological rectitude.

Bucer before Marburg customarily referred to Zwingli as his "dear brother."[23] He stood by Zwingli's side at the conference and shared with him the displeasure of Luther.[24] At a late stage of the discussion, in session with Brentz and Osiander, he showed, according to the latter, a willingness to admit some Lutheran points, and rejected only the *manducatio infidelium*,[25] but subsequently drew back from this position. He avoided at Marburg a violent break with the Wittenbergers, and remained in a position to resume negotiations. To Ambrose Blaurer he wrote characteristically: "I believe them [Luther and Melanchthon] to be sons of God, but grievously captivated by temptation; for what more serious thing could happen to any mortal than that he should thus fight against the union of the church?"[26]

The next crisis was that of the Augsburg Diet of 1530. Charles in summoning the Diet proclaimed

[23] Lenz, M., *Briefwechsel Landgraf Philipps von Hessen*, pp. 3, 5, 6.

[24] Luther on meeting him went so far as to call him, though with a smile, a rogue ("Ihr aber seid ein Schalk"); Baum, *op. cit.*, p. 459; Eells, *op. cit.*, p. 14. Cf. Hedio's *Itinerarium*, edited by Erichson, A., in "Strassburger Beiträge zur Gesch. des Marburger Religionsgesprächs: Hedio's *Itinerarium*." *Zeitschr. f. Kirchengesch*, IV, 416. Hedio's statement is: "Ad Bucerum autem inquit subridens ac digito minitans: tu es nequam."

[25] Von Schubert, *op. cit.*, p. 98.

[26] "Nam quid gravius possit ulli mortalium accidere quam sic oppugnare ecclesiae unionem?" Schiess, *op. cit.*, I, 205 (January 26, 1530).

the most pacific intentions. "All opinions," he announced, "are to be heard, understood, and compared between us in love and kindness." This fair promise completely enlisted the Saxons. The Elector himself notified the theologians (March 14) of the summons, suggesting that the Diet would take the place of the proposed national council. For this council the Lutherans had repeatedly made demands; at last their hopes seemed in large measure to be nearing realization. Melanchthon in particular came to Augsburg with high hopes. In politics he was, as Richard points out, "an absolute imperialist" who "reverenced the emperor with a veneration that bordered on idolatry and hated the democratic principles of the Swiss with a perfect hatred."[27] He had just advised the Elector against any armed resistance to the emperor in a "judicium," in which he attacks Zwingli for the contrary advice, blames Bucer for his relations with Franz von Sickingen (1522), and alludes to Philip of Hesse as Antiochus.[28] Accordingly, the Diet witnessed the supreme effort of the Lutherans to reach agreement with the emperor and the Romanist party. The policy required complete dissociation from the Zwinglians, and from the semi-Zwinglian south German cities; and this plan was rigidly followed. But, in fact, the Lutherans at Augsburg found themselves in a position similar to that of the Zwinglians at Marburg. Their opponents held the whip hand. The "soft stepping"[29] confession which Melanchthon prepared was, after prolonged negotiation, rejected by the

[27] Richard, *op. cit.*, pp. 47-48, citing numerous authorities.

[28] See text in von Schubert, *op. cit.*, pp. 233f.

[29] On Luther's use of the term *leisetreterin* see Richard, *op. cit.*, pp. 200f.

Diet, and its signatories were threatened with coercion.

In course of these proceedings the Strassburgers
asked and were refused permission to sign the Augsburg confession with the omission of the article on the
Eucharist (Art. X.). Bucer had now emerged as the
outstanding theologian of the Oberland, and he was
deputed to draw up a confession for the four cities of
Strassburg, Constance, Memingen, and Lindau. This
mediating statement, the *Tetrapolitana*,[30] met the
same fate as the Lutheran confession before the Diet;
as did also the *Fidei Ratio*[31] sent by Zwingli.

Thus in 1530 Protestantism in Germany and Switzerland exhibited a threefold division. Of the two
leaders who were chiefly concerned for Christian
union Melanchthon was vainly seeking to restore
communion with the Roman Catholics (together with
the reform of the church) while Bucer was preparing
to devote himself to the task of bringing together the
three Protestant churches. Bucer's dissociation from
the Swiss at Augsburg was necessitated by the rigor-
ous position of the Wittenbergers. He was in no
sense abandoning hope of a future concord with the
Zwinglians. Throughout the period he exchanged
frequent friendly letters with Zwingli. He freely
informed Zwingli of the *Tetrapolitana* and complained
to him of the implacable hatred of the Lutherans.[32]
But for future union he felt that he must remain on
terms of negotiation with the Saxons. His party

---

[30] For the text see Müller, E. F. K., *Die Bekenntnisschriften der
reformierten Kirche*, pp. 55-78.

[31] *Ibid.*, pp. 79-94.

[32] Zwingli, *Opera completa editio prima*, VIII, 452f.; 484; 473.

refused to satisfy the emperor by classifying themselves as either Zwinglian or Lutheran, because they
hoped to form the nucleus of a unified church which
would include both. He could for the moment make
no impression on Melanchthon, who was intent upon
his own union policy. The tenacity of Melanchthon
in this is seen by a letter of Bucer's to the Landgrave
dated August 27, when every expedient in the negotiations with the Romanists had been tried. Bucer
had dined on the 25th with Melanchthon, and broached
the subject of an understanding, but received little encouragement. "Nothing could be done without
Luther," Melanchthon had said.[33] On the 26th
Luther sent from Coburg letters that gave the
quietus to Melanchthon's fruitless compromises with
Eck.[34]

Seeing the end of the Augsburg negotiations, Bucer
promptly made approaches to both Lutherans and
Zwinglians. He turned from Melanchthon to Luther
himself, and visited him at Coburg on September 25.
Luther proved not unfriendly and was led to say that
a future agreement was not impossible.[35] Bucer then

[33] Lenz, op. cit., I, 24. "There is, alas, no emperor on our side" is
Bucer's explanation of Melanchthon's coolness.

[34] Luther sent three hot letters to Augsburg, to the Elector, Spalatin,
and Melanchthon. To Spalatin he says: "I learn that you have somewhat reluctantly begun a marvelous work, the reconciliation of the
Pope and Luther. But the Pope refuses and Luther begs to be excused." To Melanchthon he wrote that concord was impossible "unless the Pope is willing to put away his popery." De Wette, Briefe,
IV, 144, 147. Even in seeking reunion with the German adherents of
Rome, Luther never weakened in his condemnation of the claims of
papal monarchy.

[35] Koestlin, J., Life of Luther, Engl. ed., pp. 425f. De Wette, Briefe,
IV, 216f. Capito to Zwingli (September 27), rejoicing that the Lutheran princes have come to a more friendly mind, refers to Bucer's
departure on the 19th to visit Luther, and subsequent hopeful report. Zwingli, Opera Completa, VIII, 521.

hurriedly visited Zwingli, with whom Capito had been in discussion at Zurich early in September,[36] and came away hopeful.[37] He next prepared a formula for the consideration of a convention of the evangelical cities which was to meet in November at Basel, and sent a copy of it to Zwingli. Zwingli on November 20 finds fault with Bucer's inclusion of the expression "true body and true blood," not as it ought to be understood (*recte intellectum*), but as it would be understood in the vernacular by the masses.[38] The correspondence continued hopefully on Bucer's side. On January 22 Luther wrote Bucer a friendly letter, but expressed his surprise to learn that Zwingli and Ecolampadius had admitted *corpus et sanguis Christi vere in coena adesse*.[39] He still has hope of a concord with Bucer, however. Zwingli finally saw no possibility of safeguarding his "spiritual" idea under Bucer's compromise formulation, and on February 12 brought the negotiations to an end with a vigorous reassertion of his favorite view. The body and blood of Christ, he says, are present in the supper not naturally or corporally, but sacramentally and only to religious minds, that is, by contemplation, faith. He will have no more of negotiation: *"Summa summarum: perstamus perpetuo; . . . parce hac in re labori et chartae."*[40] The League of Schmalkald was formed without the participation of the Swiss, and Zwingli's death a few months later (October 11) was the cost of his isolation. Bucer maintained to the last a friendly

[36] Zwingli, *Opera Completa*, VIII, 506-07.
[37] *Ibid.*, 530.
[38] *Ibid.*, 549.
[39] De Wette, *Briefe*, IV, 216.
[40] Zwingli, *Opera Completa*, VIII, 579, 581.

correspondence with Zwingli and remained no less zealous than before to aid in the union of the Swiss with the Lutherans.

4. BUCER AND MELANCHTHON AND THE FORMATION OF THE WITTENBERG CONCORD

It was increasingly plain that the first step was to be taken within Germany itself. A contributing factor of the greatest importance here was Melanchthon's increased favor toward the Reformed doctrine. Melanchthon had always hesitated at Luther's high doctrine of corporeal presence and oral manducation; and the statement in the Augsburg Confession[41] was far from being specific on the matter. In the year of Augsburg, Ecolampadius, for whom Melanchthon always felt a high personal regard, published his *Dialogue on the Teaching of the Ancients* which gave him a new appreciation of the support given by the fathers to the figurative interpretation.[42] The failure of his own favorite plan of reunion effort at Augsburg combined with this fresh inclination toward the Swiss to make Melanchthon willing to co-operate with Bucer in the cause of Protestant union. Bucer, on his part, showed in subsequent crises an almost equal interest in negotiations for peace with the Romanists. So these two irenic spirits—who seem never to have been great personal friends—engaged in a fruitful cooperation which lasted till the *Interim* of 1548.

The chief result of this co-operation was the *Witten-*

[41] "Quod corpus et sanguis Christi vere adsint et distribuantur vescentibus." Art. X.

[42] Richard, J. W., *Philip Melanchthon*, p. 243.

berg Concord of 1536.[43] It was preceded by the Stuttgart Concord of August 2, 1534, in which Bucer with
great energy secured a settlement for Würtemburg, a
newly reformed state claimed by both the Lutherans
and the Swiss.[44] The correspondence of Bucer and
Melanchthon when the Wittenberg agreement was in
preparation shows that it was not political, but religious in motivation. Yet it is probable that the situation of the League of Schmalkald rendered it the more
desirable. Luther had finally found it possible to
sanction the league as a legitimate defense of the
gospel.[45] A theological cleavage within the League,
when it needed to be able to display undivided strength
against a possible stroke by the emperor, was a source
of great uneasiness, and the removal of every element
of division was an obvious need. Melanchthon came
to value the efforts of Philip of Hesse, and sought his
assistance in bringing about the union.

On August 1, 1534, Melanchthon wrote Bucer, "I
agree with you that accord with the Roman pontiff
is hopeless." He had already taken up with the
Elector and the Landgrave Bucer's suggestion of an
agreement; he desired nothing more than that the
gross scandal of disunion should be removed.[46] In a
letter of September 16, 1534, he refers to the project

[43] The whole subject has been dealt with in some detail chiefly in its
theological bearings and with reference to Luther by Koestlin in his
Theology of Luther, Engl. ed. II, 154-196. Ellinger, G., *Philipp Melanchthon*, pp. 530ff., and Richard, *op. cit.*, pp. 250ff., have explained the
formation of the Concord from the side of Melanchthon.

[44] Anrich, *op. cit.*, pp. 58f.

[45] See his interesting rationalization in his letter to L. Spengler of
February 15, 1531. De Wette, *Briefe*, IV., 221f. He was persuaded
by jurists at Torgau that resistance to a notoriously unjust imperial
government was authorized by imperial law. Cf. P. Smith, *Life and
Letters of Martin Luther*, p. 217.

[46] *C. R.*, II, 775f.

as "concordia Buceri."[47] He subsequently sent a
"judicium" on the Lord's Supper to Philip.[48] The
Landgrave now invited the two negotiators to a conference at Cassel, and to this place, over a bad road
in bitter weather, Bucer came to visit Melanchthon,
December 27, 1534.

Despite the fact that Luther had not wholly discouraged Bucer at the Coburg in 1530, he was now less
inclined than Melanchthon to promote an agreement
and appeared distrustful of Bucer. When the Landgrave urged on him the need of "permanent harmony"
with the Oberlanders, he replied that he feared that
Bucer had made a following among them and that
any agreement would prove impermanent. In advance of the Cassel colloquy Luther gave his col-
league an *Instruction* of an uncompromising character, in which while asserting his willingness to yield
his life on behalf of unity, he stated in conclusion that
"the body of Christ is truly broken, eaten, and torn
with the teeth."[49] On such a basis no progress was
possible. Melanchthon acted on the more irenical
suggestion of the body of the *Instruction*, and taking
up the question in a conciliatory spirit, Bucer and
he soon arrived at a joint statement. This formula
was sent by Philip of Hesse to Luther, and although
its phraseology ("the bread and wine are signs, *signa
exhibitiva*, which being given and received, the body
of Christ is at the same time given and received.")[50]
was not without ambiguity, it was viewed by him in a
favorable light, and called forth from him definite ex-

---

[47] *C. R.*, II, 788.
[48] *Ibid.*, 800-02.
[49] De Wette, *Briefe*, IV, 572.
[50] *C. R.*, II, 808.

pressions of the hope of union.[51]   Melanchthon was
enthusiastic, though not highly optimistic.   "If I
could purchase union with my death, gladly would I
pour out my life for it," he exclaimed in a letter to
Bucer.[52]

The formula of Cassel was widely circulated, and
opinions were gathered from both Saxon and Oberland theologians.   Luther himself "during the following summer . . . frequently sent kind, encouraging,
and hopeful letters to Strassburg, Augsburg, Ulm and
Esslingen."[53]   He and the other leaders felt the time
ripe for a more representative meeting.   On October
5, 1535, Luther sent, to the ministers of the above
mentioned four cities, letters proposing a convention
of delegates from all sections.[54]   The date and place
of this were left with Luther to arrange.   On March
25, 1536, from a sick bed and "scarcely able to breathe,"
he notified Bucer that he and his associates had decided to propose that the conference should meet at
Eisenach on May 14.[55]   Luther's ill health necessitated
two postponements of the meeting.   Finally the Oberland delegates came to Wittenberg on May 21, and
on the following day proceeded to their momentous
task with Luther present.

---

[51] De Wette, *Briefe*, IV, 588, 589.   Luther only cautioned against
haste, and urged the need of certainty as to the pure intent of the
Strassburgers—"ob ihre Meinung rein und recht wäre, oder etwas
dahinten hätten, damit solche Concordia hernach ärger Discordia
mocht werden."   Melanchthon explained this fact to Bucer somewhat
apologetically: "Respondit, se eam probare, addens (nihil enim dis-
simulatio apud amicum) modo ut hoc sentiamus."   *C. R.*, II, 837
(February 1, 1535).

[52] *Ibid.*

[53] Koestlin, *op. cit.*, II, 165.

[54] De Wette, *Briefe*, IV, 636-40.

[55] De Wette, *Briefe*, IV, 682.

When the conference met,[56] Luther had been freshly roused against the Swiss. Bucer had recently come from Basel, where he had with deep interest attended the birth of the *First Helvetic Confession*, the work of Bullinger. Returning to Strassburg thereafter, he had written Ambrose Blaurer that he hoped Luther would accept the new confession.[57] He had also lent his name to the publication of certain letters of Zwingli and Ecolampadius which contained statements at which Luther took offense. He now demanded a recantation of Bucer's former teaching, and the recognition that the sacrament is received by the unworthy and the ungodly. Bucer's recantation was merely a general desire to recall anything he had wrongly taught. He explained his former teaching to show as far as possible that it had always been equivalent to the views he now held. He could not admit the reception of the body by the ungodly in the sense of the unbelieving (*infideles*); he admitted it as respects the unworthy (*indignos*) on the basis of 1 Cor. 11. This point had long been in discussion, and Bucer apparently remained true to his old position.[58] Those who come without faith receive only bread and wine; though, by the act of the church in administering the elements, the true body and blood are *set before* them.[59]

Luther was finally persuaded of the honest intent

---

[56] The Reports printed in Walch, *Sämtliche Schriften*, XVII, 25326, are summarized by Koestlin, II, 167f.

[57] Basileae fui cum Elueticis ministris, et cessit res bene. Consensum est in confessionem, quam spero admittet Lutherus (February 18). Schiess, *Briefwechsel der Brüder A. and T. Blaurer*, I, 784. S. Gyrnaeus had already informed A. Blaurer of the event (February 7), and attributed the pro-Lutheran tendency of the confession to the influence of Bucer and Capito. *Ibid.*, 779.

[58] See for instance Walch, *Sämtliche Schriften*, XVII, 2413.

[59] Koestlin, *op. cit.*, II, 168.

of the Oberlanders and said regarding the remaining difference, "Upon this point we will not quarrel." Emotional expressions of brotherhood followed. Melanchthon was commissioned to draw up a statement embodying the results of the Colloquy. On the 28th (Sunday) sermons were preached by Bugenhagen, Luther and Bucer, and the delegates received the communion together. On the 26th the Articles of Concord were presented and on the 29th they were agreed to and signed by the delegates without opposition. The first article states that the body and blood of Christ are truly and substantially present, presented and received with the bread and wine.[60] The third article asserts the validity of the institution of the sacraments in the church, irrespective of the worthiness of the ministers or the receivers, and on Paul's authority affirms the participation of the unworthy. Koestlin points out the possibility of a "spiritual" interpretation of the document: "The question may here be naturally raised, whether the doctrine of the theologians of Upper Germany might not still be interpreted as being simply that the true presence of the essential body is merely a presence for the spirit or for the devout exaltation of the individual."[61] It is quite possible that Bucer remained as "Suvermerian"[62] as ever. If there was, as Koestlin suggests,[63] a mental reservation here, it must be re-

---

[60] "Itaque sentiunt et docent, cum pane et vino vere et substantialiter adesse, exhiberi et sumi corpus Christi et sanguinem." *C. R.*, III, 75.

[61] He adds that Bucer's distinction between "unworthy" and "unbelieving" does not preclude this, as the former might feel some "exaltation." Koestlin, *op. cit.*, II, 170f.

[62] This adjective had been applied by the Lutherans to Bucer and his party.

[63] *Ibid.*

membered that Luther did not finally insist on absolute identity of teaching. He recognized a remaining difference on which "we will not quarrel." It
would appear that the great leader was at the time
almost as eager for peace and union as Bucer had
always shown himself. Melanchthon, in the same
spirit, skillfully framed the instrument of accord.
Bucer, having played a leading part in the Wittenberg Concord, had now to busy himself as its champion. The ratification of the agreement by the cities
was not a foregone conclusion. Almost everywhere
there was hesitation and opposition. Gradually, by
exertions that undermined his health, Bucer was
able to swing the cities into the union, with the single
exception of Constance. Among the Lutherans opposition was also voiced; but the weight of Luther's and
Melanchthon's judgment rendered it ineffective. So
far as Germany was concerned union had actually
been accomplished. The results were of no slight
importance for Protestantism, especially as the Roman
Church was now, under Paul III, astir with new energy,
and seeking to recover lost ground in Germany. The
relatively united state of German Protestantism during the early period of the Council of Trent, and the
strength it showed in the Schmalkald wars, may be attributed in no small degree to the Concord of Wittenberg and to the two theologians who had chiefly
brought it about.

But the Concord was not thought of, even at the
beginning, as a purely German affair. The conferees
at Wittenberg discussed ways and means of extending it to foreign churches, particularly the Swiss. The
Swiss were never, indeed, out of Bucer's mind in his

dealings with the Lutherans. As an apostle of the Concord he now visited them, and at the Synod of Basel, September 24, 1536, explained the terms of the agreement.[64] On November 12 it was accepted in a convention at Basel, which sent a letter to Luther. Luther put his seal upon these negotiations by his cordial reply to the Burgomaster of Basel, February 17, 1537,[65] which acknowledges receipt of numerous letters from Switzerland conveyed to him by Bucer. Bucer interviewed him at Gotha, and found him most cordial, but apparently under the impression that the Swiss signatories were acknowledging a conversion, of which they themselves were quite unconscious. Luther appears in this letter a warm-hearted exponent of union and speaks in the most brotherly terms. A longer letter from Luther to the Swiss cities, written on December 1, 1537,[66] in response to further communications, is equally fraternal. He explains away some of their misapprehensions, and commends an attitude of kindliness and good will even where complete mutual understanding is not possible.[67] On June 9, 1538, he again explains his position in a moderate and friendly way.[68]

Bucer had had his opponents in Switzerland since the dismissal of his formula by Zwingli in 1531. From first to last the Swiss were in general willing to live in peace and union with the Lutherans, but felt little inclined to strain after identity of formulation.[69]

---

[64] *C. R.*, III, 88f.
[65] De Wette, *Briefe*, V, 54.
[66] *Sämtliche Schriften*, XVII, 2593.
[67] De Wette, *Briefe*, V, 83-86.
[68] *Ibid.*, V, 20-1.
[69] Cf. Pestalozzi, C., *Heinrich Bullinger, Leben und ausgewählte Schriften* (1858), p. 197.

Bullinger, their outstanding leader, was of this mind. He exhibited a growing impatience with Bucer's methods, and resisted any suggestion of the substitution of the Wittenberg Concord for the Swiss Confession. Such, in general, was the attitude of the Swiss. Bucer was called at Bern "Luther's Cardinal legate" and the prohibition of his writings was proposed. Bullinger condemned the proposal, but wrote sharply of Bucer's endless confession-making.[70] The remarkable thing was that Luther's letters encouraged this attitude. Thus it was Bucer's plight after having been the means of a *rapprochement* between Luther and the Swiss to be personally rejected by the latter, and regarded by them with great distrust. Probably Bucer is to be blamed for making too much of the language of the Wittenberg Concord and his own explanations of it. Bullinger definitely said that he preferred Luther to Bucer, since the latter offered unity only on the basis of the Bucerian phraseology.[71] For a period Luther showed himself toward the Swiss the most gracious of Christians, magnanimous even to the point of meekness.[72] He seemed unoffended by Bullinger's frank loyalty to Zwingli and adherence to the Swiss statements. His letter of December 1, 1537, called forth from Myconius the happy certainty that the breach was ended.[73] Bucer and Capito, however, were unfavorably received in the Zurich convention of April 29 to May 4, 1538, and it was evident

[70] His letters of the period are quoted extensively by Pestalozzi, pp. 201ff.

[71] Pestalozzi, *op. cit.*, p. 206.

[72] Luther's letters of the period indicate a constant expectation of death. This may possibly in part account for his unusually pacific and generous attitude.

[73] Pestalozzi, *op. cit.*, p. 206.

that Bucer's usefulness in Switzerland was at an end.
Bullinger was disappointed over Luther's letter of
May 12, 1538 (in which, however, he spoke of Zwingli
as *optimus vir*), probably because he had expected
some definite recognition of the Swiss Confession.
But on September 1 of that year Bullinger wrote in
the friendliest terms to Luther and Melanchthon. He
does not qualify his adherence to "our confession,"
but urges love and friendship. Bullinger confessed
that he had from his boyhood felt love for Melanchthon; and with him he continued on friendly terms
during the later strife with Luther.[74]

It is impossible to say how far Luther and Bullinger
were brought to understanding. Certainly, they did
not reach theological agreement. The Swiss position
as stated by Bullinger was: The Swiss Confession remains; anything that does not conflict with it we
accept.[75] Luther still steadfastly withheld his approval of the Swiss Confession. What was achieved
was not in the realm of theology. While the authority of the Wittenberg Concord was a factor in the
unification of German Christianity, the temporary
peace of the Germans and Swiss was attained on no
strictly documentary basis. Nevertheless, the *entente*
which was indicated in the correspondence of 1536–38
was in no small measure due to the efforts of Bucer, who
was well content to be personally humiliated *pro unitate
ecclesiae*. If that high-souled zealot of union sometimes exhibited a pathetic faith in formulæ, he never
thought of his formulæ as other than instrumental
toward the one end to which he was supremely devoted.

---

[74] Pestalozzi, *op. cit.*, pp. 210f., 215f.
[75] *Ibid.*, 202.

As for Melanchthon, he seems to have regarded the Wittenberg Concord as the best expression of his own personal belief. In his *Testament* written in November, 1539, when he felt himself in prospect of death, it is to this statement that he turns, not to the Augsburg Confession: "In regard to the Lord's Supper I embrace the Form of Concord which was made here. Therefore I united myself with our churches, and I believe that they profess the doctrine of the Catholic Church of Christ and that they truly are churches of Christ."[76] His *variata* edition of the Augsburg Confession, published in 1540, alters the text of the controverted Article X to resemble closely the wording of the Concord.[77]

5. MELANCHTHON AND FRANCIS I

The rôle of Bucer as a unifier was henceforth to be a less prominent one, while Melanchthon was to be more and more recognized as an interconfessional and international mediator. Melanchthon was far from possessing the buoyant optimism and insistent aggressiveness of Bucer, but he did possess as profound a desire for church unity on the widest scale attainable, while his great eminence as a scholar and his place as the most intimate associate of Luther gave him an influence far wider than the Strassburger's. His liberality of thought and conciliatory disposition fitted him for the work of unity; from the defects of these virtues, a certain pusillanimity and lack of initiative, he cannot be exonerated. He had not the fighting energy of men who win in their own lifetime.

---

[76] *C. R.*, III, 826.

[77] Cf. Richard, *Melanchthon*, pp. 287-88, and his *Confessional History*, pp. 224ff.

His place in Lutheranism should not obscure for us
his place in Europe. When Erasmus ceased to be
the master and guide of the scholarly youth of Europe
Melanchthon became in some degree his successor.
The humanist in him was admired where his theology was unacceptable: the theologian was acclaimed
where his humanism was suspect. He thus became a
center of attraction to elements in themselves incompatible or, at any rate, so diverse that a man
of his limitations of personality was powerless to fuse
them.

It is probable that few men in all history declined
so many flattering invitations as Melanchthon. One
of the kings to seek his aid, and that with great persistence, was Francis I of France. In France a spirit
of religious revolution was active. The impression
made by Erasmus and Lefèvre had been deepened by
the influence of Luther's books. Out of this atmosphere came forth John Calvin, the sober leader of
the Reformed Church. About the time of Calvin's
conversion to Protestantism the policies of King Francis
I reached a crisis in which the whole Reformation
movement was concerned. The king had no big-
oted devotion to the old system, and was troubled
by the fact that his Hapsburg rival, the emperor, was
now in close alliance with the Pope. He might have
followed the lead of Henry VIII if he had been politically as confident. The object of Francis at this time
was to effect a moderate reform of the church that
would if possible satisfy the religious parties and
allay agitation. He desired a constitutional settlement of religion rather than a religious revival, with
a degree of recognition of the new learning and the

163

new opinions. Bishops would be retained, and the Pope, whose powers in France were already greatly limited by the Concordat of Bologna, would not be entirely cast off. He was in touch, through members of the University of Paris, with the religious movement in Germany, and was aware that both Bucer and Melanchthon held opinions that could be harmonized with his aims. They both regarded some characteristic Roman practices as indifferent or desirable. They both allowed the possibility of the retention of government by bishops, though *jure humano* only; and Melanchthon at Augsburg had labored for a union which would not only have retained bishops, but have given the Pope a function, though not an absolute monarchy, in the church.[78] The plan was probably not of his own devising. Bucer attributed its origin to certain approved Christians at the Royal Court.[79]

Paul III was inaugurating an era of reform which it was then expected would take the lines of conciliarism.[80] What was there to hinder Melanchthon and Bucer from co-operating in this movement? Francis at least would invite their aid.

---

[78] The Protestant negotiators on August 15, 1530, had presented an *Opinion* in which they actually stated: "If the Pope be antichrist, yet may we be subject to him as the Jews were subject to Pharaoh. . . . But the pure doctrine must be allowed." Brück, however, marginally protested against any admission of papal power *jure divino. C. R.*, II, 284. Richard, *Confessional History*, p. 148. Cf. Melanchthon's view expressed at Schmalkald in 1537: "Of the Pope I hold that if he will permit the gospel, the government of bishops which he now has from others may be *jure humano* also conceded to him by us." Richard, *op. cit.*, p. 261.

[79] "Optimi quidem et veris probati testimoniis Christiani in aula regis." Letter to T. Blaurer, beginning of February, 1535. Schiess, *op. cit.*, I, 641.

[80] Imbart de la Tour, *Les origines de la réforme*, III, 520ff.; 587ff.

in the effort to win them the king had the assistance of John Sturm, then in Paris, and of the brothers du Bellay, of whom William was a lay noble, and John was Bishop of Paris. William du Bellay, a man of most attractive personality, visited Germany in 1534 to advance the king's scheme. He dealt with Philip of Hesse, met Bucer, and corresponded with Melanchthon. He also visited Switzerland and discussed religious union with Bullinger, Conrad Pellican and Myconius. On his return he wrote to Bucer and induced the king to send a messenger to Melanchthon.[81] Sturm sent a stream of ardent letters to both Bucer and Melanchthon. Bucer was enthusiastic: he could not hear of a reunion movement without the excitement of a noble hound on the scent. Melanchthon prepared and sent, August 1, 1534, to the French ambassador his *consilium ad Gallos*, or advice on union, addressed to King Francis.[82] This document was an irenical response to the king's project. It laid down conciliatory terms in matters of worship and entered into the project of a conference of theologians for the settlement of doctrine. While the Lutheran theological positions are moderately reaffirmed, the attitude of frank hopefulness of union, and the concession of papal authority (*superioritas pontifica*)[83] are striking. But it is also a striking fact that his letter to Bucer of the same date expressed agreement with the latter that no concord with the Pope could be hoped for. His real desire and hope did not go further than an

[81] Imbart de la Tour, *op. cit.*, III, 538ff.

[82] *C. R.*, II, 741ff. Three variant texts are given, including that of the copy sent to Du Bellay by the hand of Ulrich Chelius, the French emissary. A fourth text varies widely from these three and is thought to be a French revision. *Ibid.*, 742.

[83] *Ibid.*, 746.

understanding with the French moderates.[84] Bucer
prepared a similar statement which Bishop John du
Bellay circulated in the Oberland, and which called
forth a remarkably favorable response.[85] Even Farel,
now in Geneva, frankly approved the project and fully
shared the hopes which John Sturm and the Strassburg theologians placed in the projected conference.[86]

Fanaticism in the religious movement in France
now played a disturbing part. Amid these hopeful
preparations occurred the alarming incident of the
Placards (October 18, 1534). If violent propaganda
sheets could be hung on the king's bedchamber door
and stuck in the receptacle in which he kept his hand-
kerchief, well might Francis tremble for his kingdom
and for his life. His anxiety found vent in severe
persecution (January, 1535)[87] which in turn sent a
shock through Protestantism everywhere. The Swiss
were confirmed in their hostile attitude. Melanchthon
wrote gloomily to Camerarius of the "savage cruelty
against wise and pious men" that had broken out in
France.[88] The du Bellay brothers and Sturm renewed their efforts at reconciliation and the king
sought to allay the anti-French reaction among his
allies of the Schmalkald League by a letter to the

---

[84] Assentior tibi, mi Bucere, desperandum esse concordiam cum
pontifice Romano . . . spero eam moderationem doctis placituram
esse. *C. R.*, II, 775-6.

[85] Imbart de la Tour, *op. cit.*, III, 540, 574. This author thinks Farel
wanted a conference as an opportunity merely for vigorous declama-
tion against Rome. His ideas were, in fact, more constructive.

[86] Herminjard, A. L., *Correspondance des Réformateurs*, III, 358,
footnote 7, on a passage in Farel's long and cordial letter to du Bellay,
late September, 1535.

[87] Viénot, John, *Histoire de la Réforme française*, pp. 121f.; Imbart
de la Tour, *op. cit.*, III, 533f.

[88] *C. R.*, II, 822, 866.

Evangelical Princes assuring them of his friendliness
to Germans and to all but treasonable agitators (February 1, 1535).[89]

Preparations for the conference were now actively
renewed. The king sought the consent of the new
Pope, Paul III, who adopted a favorable attitude and
prepared to co-operate.[90] Melanchthon was approached, at first through Sturm, and then by means
of a new envoy, Barnabas de Vere, Seigneur de la
Fosse; and Sturm besought Bucer, in the most urgent
language, to come to France.[91] Francis wrote a personal invitation to Melanchthon (June 23); the two Du
Bellays supported the invitation with fresh letters.[92]

It was clear, however, that the project would meet
with opposition. The effort to enlist the Swiss called
forth from Bullinger an irrelevant memorandum
which has been described as a "confession of faith
much more than a business proposal."[93] Myconius
was equally noncommittal. The attitude of the Swiss
to Francis was, in fact, one of total distrust—"that
impure, profane, ambitious man," wrote Bullinger
to Myconius. They warned Bucer that thousands of
Protestants would die rather than be reunited with
the Pope.[94] A large number of the Reformed in France
proved totally intractable Equally hostile, on the
other hand, was the attitude of the ever-reactionary

---

[89] *C. R.*, II, 828ff.

[90] Imbart de la Tour, *op. cit.*, III, 560. Herminjard shows evidence
that the Pope counselled Francis to modify his severities toward the
Lutherans. *Op. cit.* III., 311f.

[91] Herminjard, *op. cit.*, III, 266ff.; 271ff.

[92] *C. R.*, II, 879ff.; 886ff.

[93] Imbart de la Tour, *op. cit.*, III, 541, 572. Cf. Herminjard, *op. cit.*,
III, 181ff.

[94] D'Aubigné, M., *Reformation in Europe*, IV, 353.

Sorbonne. On August 30, 1535, the theologians presented to the king a memoir roundly condemning Melanchthon's advice.[95] Melanchthon had finally resolved to go to France, and had secured the complete acquiescence of Luther. But his prince, the Elector of Saxony, who at the moment was seeking concessions from the Hapsburgs, and was always desirous of keeping Melanchthon by his side, declined to allow him to make the journey. On August 18 he wrote to King Francis that Melanchthon could not be spared,[96] and on August 28, two days before the action of the Sorbonne, Melanchthon himself wrote the king, declining with regret.[97]

The incident was ended. The abandonment of the project for a conference was not due to Melanchthon or Bucer. Even Luther had in the end supported it. It was blocked by the Sorbonne theologians on the one hand and by the Elector of Saxony on the other. On the side of Germany it seemed a small concern, but for French Protestantism it was a momentous *dénouement*. Henceforth the Protestants of France could hope for no concessions from their sovereign.

6. THE ENGLISH-LUTHERAN NEGOTIATIONS

Brief notice must also be accorded to the English-Lutheran negotiations in which both Bucer and Melanchthon were with others concerned. In 1531 Melanchthon had given an "opinion" on the annulment of Henry VIII's marriage.[98] A year after the

---

[95] Imbart de la Tour, *op. cit.*, III, 574, 576f.

[96] *C. R.*, II, 905ff.

[97] *C. R.*, II, 913f.

[98] He excludes divorce, but advises "in this emergency" a bigamous marriage. *C. R.*, II, 520ff.

assertion of ecclesiastical headship by Henry, Melanchthon, at the suggestion of Robert Barnes, an English Lutheran, wrote the king a letter mingling flattery and counsel, and suggesting that Henry should set forth a form of doctrine with the aid of "the deliberation of learned men."[99] A few months later, just when the French negotiations were breaking down, he dedicated to Henry, as "the most learned of all kings," an edition of the *Loci Communes* (August, 1535).[100] That useful Scot, Alexander Alesius, took the book to Henry and a letter to Cranmer.[101] Henry, in acknowledgment, presented Melanchthon with two hundred crowns.

Barnes now became the representative of Henry and Cromwell in an effort to bring agreement between England and the Lutheran states on the basis of a theological consensus. The plan was probably, on Henry's side, purely political, designed both to counter the activities of Francis I and to place Henry within and at the leadership of the Schmalkald League. The proposals which Barnes brought to Wittenberg in September, 1535, included the release of Melanchthon for a conference in England. Here, as in the French incident, it was not Luther, but the Elector who refused to let Melanchthon go. He also virtually notified Henry that entrance to the League would involve acceptance of the Augsburg Confession.[102] Barnes was joined in Wittenberg by Nicholas Heath

---

[99] March 3, 1535. *C. R.*, II, 861ff.

[100] *C. R.*, II, 921-30. The phrase quoted in column 927.

[101] Jacobs, H. E., *The Lutheran Movement in England*, p. 57. This careful study gives the most adequate examination of the events of the English-Lutheran negotiations of 1535–39 (Chaps. IV and V).

[102] *C. R.*, II, 941f.

and the scholarly and able Edward Fox, who eloquently addressed the Convention of the League on December 24, 1535.[103] On the following (Christmas) day Melanchthon presented to the Convention a memorial of thirteen articles.[104] The first article lays down the Augsburg Confession as the basis of negotiation, though admitting the possibility that some things in it may require correction. The third article demands the rejection of a papal council, but any opportunity of "a Christian free and general council" is not to be refused. The three English representatives signed this document, and remained in Wittenberg, but, handicapped by the lack of any specific instructions, were forced to play a time-wasting diplomatic game. Substantial agreement was apparent in the discussions; but Henry delayed the formulation of a concord. In a communication received on March 12, 1536, he raised objections to some of the articles and asked for "a man of excellent learning" to go to England with other delegates, for conference.[105] Further negotiation in Germany was useless, and on April 22 the Elector dismissed the English delegates with a reaffirmation of the Christmas articles and a courteous letter to the king.[106] The judicial murder, May 19, of Anne Boleyn, who had been a factor in the advance of Lutheranism, left the Germans more than ever suspicious of Henry,[107] and the indeterminate

---

[103] The speech is given in *C. R.*, II, 1028-32, from Spalatin's record.

[104] *C. R.*, II, 1032-36. Jacobs gives a translation, *op. cit.*, pp. 63-67.

[105] *C. R.*, III, 46-50.

[106] *C. R.*, III, 60ff., 63f.

[107] Sergeant, R. W., *Life of Anne Boleyn*, p. 274, notes the gleeful report of Chapuys, Charles V's ambassador. Cf. Melanchthon to Camerarius, June 9, 1536, referring to information of the death of Anne, "magis accusata quam convicta adulterii." *C. R.*, III, 89.

character of the *Ten Articles*, June, 1536, which, as H. M. Gwatkin remarks, merely represent "the old doctrine everywhere loosened,"[108] was not calculated to create confidence, although the statement flattered Melanchthon by repeating much of his phraseology.[109]

It was not until January, 1538, that Henry resumed negotiations. Meanwhile his relations with the League remained undefined, and his reform policy in England cautious and compromising. The influence of Cromwell was now at its height, and Henry seemed prepared to carry through the pro-Lutheran policy of his minister. He sent Christopher Mount to a League convention in February, and at his request a commission of three was dispatched to England in March. The commission included only one theologian; and that one not Melanchthon, whom Henry wanted, hoping to find him more indulgent to medieval practices than the rigid Myconius of Gotha. Their departure was followed by a gracious letter from Luther to Bishop Edward Fox, who, in fact, had died four days before it was written.[110] The delegates engaged in conference with seven English commissioners, under Cranmer's chairmanship, from April to September. The basis of discussion was the Augsburg Confession, which has two parts, doctrinal and "concerning abuses." Agreement was completely reached on the doctrinal issues. Cranmer's papers disclosed to Doctor Jenkyns a century ago the thirteen Articles then drawn up, and apparently jointly approved by the

[108] *Church and State in England*, p. 171.

[109] Jacobs, *op. cit.*, pp. 90ff., shows the parallels.

[110] Jacobs, *op. cit.*, 130ff. Jacobs translates the letter from De Wette, *Briefe*, V, 110ff.

negotiators.[111] The document bears a close relation to the Anglican *Articles* of 1543; and in their final form the *Thirty-nine Articles* preserve a Lutheran phraseology. The Anglican delegates now proposed to take up the seven sacraments, instead of proceeding, as the Lutherans demanded, with the "articles of abuses." This has commonly been interpreted as due to prompting from the king, who no longer desired— if he ever had desired—a close alliance with the Lutherans. The fact that the delegates were, as Cranmer complained to Cromwell, August 23, "very evill lodged," and distressed both by "a multitude of Ratts" and by nauseating odors from the kitchen adjacent to their "parlar,"[112] gave proof that Henry's friendliness had its limitations. Myconius became ill, and at the same time was convinced that the king was merely trifling, and desired nothing more in the way of reform than "that King Harry be Pope."[113] Finally the Germans were dismissed with honorable gifts. No definite rupture had taken place, and Henry accepted about the same time the dedication of the translation

[111] The document is contained in the Parker Society *Remains and Letters of Cranmer*, pp. 472ff. (App. XIII, "A Book Containing Divers Articles *de unitate Dei*," etc.). Strype, John, *Ecclesiastical Memorials . . . of the Church of England . . .* , 1822 ed., II, 384f. gives a letter from Myconius to Cromwell which indicates that agreement has been reached in the principal matters. Myconius complains that he is ill and cannot, even if he wished, continue his labors. Strype adds other documents, including an English summary of the Lutheran objections regarding certain abuses, pp. 386ff.

[112] Parker Society, *Remains and Letters of Cranmer*, pp. 379f. Cranmer asks for them a "commodious house."

[113] Jacobs, *op. cit.*, p. 134. Cranmer's letter just cited indicates that he held the same opinion. He desires to follow the plan proposed by the Germans. The bishops in declining claim the king's authority although they "know certainly that the Germans will not agree." Dixon, *History of the Church of England*, II, 3, explains the English attitude on the ground that they were following the outlines of the "Institution of a Christian Man."

of a Lutheran treatise by Sarcerius which Cromwell had induced Richard Travener to translate.

After the return of the delegates, and fearing a *rapprochement* between Charles and the League through the fresh negotiations mooted in 1539, Henry showed a disposition to renew the discussion of terms. His envoy, Mount, reopened the issue at the Convention of Frankfort (March, 1539), and lay commissioners were sent to England.[114] Melanchthon again by letters applauded Henry and urged him to further reform. But in England reaction had set in, and with the favor of the king the *Six Articles Statute*[115] passed the Lords in spite of Cranmer's opposition and Cromwell's desire. Henry still played for Lutheran favor, and the Anne of Cleves incident marks a striking phase of his shifting policy. Bucer urged the sending of Melanchthon to England, but the Elector flatly declined to permit this. Melanchthon himself lost all faith in the negotiation, and on November 1 wrote Henry a long, reproachful, and admonitory letter.[116] The executions of late July, 1540, in which Cromwell and Barnes and other leaders, including papists and Protestants, perished under the Six Articles, made further conference unthinkable.

Enough attention has been given to these abortive negotiations. They exhibit the difficulties of international unitive effort in the sixteenth century. The Augsburg Confession, as the standard of the

[114] The negotiations of this period have been fully examined by Singer, P.: *Beziehungen des schmalkaldischen Bundes zu England im Jahre 1539.*

[115] See Gee and Hardy, *Documents illustrative of English Church History,* pp. 303ff. Gairdner, J., *The English Church in the Sixteenth Century,* pp. 207ff.

[116] *C. R.,* III, 805-19. Jacobs, *op. cit.,* pp. 148ff.

Schmalkald League, had already become for Lutherans virtually the indispensable basis of any wider agreement; yet Melanchthon had shown a willingness to see it amended in detail, and Luther had supported the policy of negotiation. The Thirteen Articles show some measure of elasticity on the part of the League's delegates. They exhibit also the readiness of the English theologians of the reforming party to unite with the Lutherans. While some responsibility for the failure of the negotiations may perhaps be laid upon the shoulders of the Elector and the Lutherans, the fundamental reason for it is to be found in the timeserving political policy of Henry. England was, in fact, not yet converted to Protestantism, and Henry was not inclined to promote its conversion. It was in politics rather than in Protestantism that the obstacles to union lay.

The Lutheran-Romanist conferences held at Hagenau, Worms, and Regensburg in 1540 and 1541 have been made familiar in many works,[117] and the reader may well be spared the narrative of this belated effort at a recovery of general unity. In these conferences Calvin stood by the side of Bucer and Melanchthon, and while he differed from them in the method by which they sought the end of union, and condemned the "ambiguous formulas"[118] which they devised, he felt no difference from them in belief. Janssen's

[117] See, for example, Richard, *Confessional History*, pp. 246ff., where much of the literature is cited. Janssen, in his review of the negotiations, declares that the cause of their failure "lay not in the influence of this or that personality, but in the nature of the business itself, in the effort to unite irreconcilable opposites." *History of the German People*, Engl. ed., VI, 148. Cardauns, L., *Zur Gesch. der Kirchlichen Unions- und Reformsbestrebungen von 1538 bis 1542*, examines the subject from Roman sources.

[118] *C. R.*, XXX, 217.

opinion that the result was advantageous to Protestantism[119] is probably justified.

Conclusion

It would be a mistake to regard the efforts reviewed in the above chapter as significant only for their immediate results in the achievement of unity. Yet merely on that count their significance is not slight. Though the Marburg Colloquy showed something of the character of a disputation, it set forth a joint document which exhibited a large measure of unity in Protestant ranks, and furnished the basis for later approaches. The Wittenberg Concord was a pact of high historical importance as a definite act of union for German Protestantism. Luther's correspondence with Bullinger marks a triumph of good will. The negotiations with France were unproductive; those with England only served to promote a theological influence which was perpetuated in the Thirty-nine Articles.

But as an exhibition of the spirit of unity these facts have a deeper significance. They indicate that the greater minds of the Reformation really desired Christian concord and intercommunion. Zwingli was zealous for the unity of Protestantism. As for Luther, his antagonistic attitude at Marburg is no index of his conduct in other crises. In the *Wittenberg Concord*, the French exchanges, the English negotiations, as well as his correspondence with Bullinger, Luther, while anxious for what he thinks essential, appears conciliatory and desirous of understanding. Melanchthon almost invariably gave proof of his zeal for

---

[119] *History of the German People*, VI., 148.

peace and union; and Bucer's simple-hearted devotion to the same cause is written large on the documentary records of the Reformation. Calvin and Cranmer, not to mention minor leaders, were, as we shall see, hardly less than Bucer, though less exclusively than he, devoted to the unification of the church.

The sources of religious discord did not, in fact, lie primarily in the minds of the religious leaders. Whenever the Protestant theologians got together in the sixteenth century, their conferences were marked by a very large measure of agreement. This was the case even at Marburg, where we have seen reason to think that the element of discord was injected largely from the field of politics. It was in that field far more than in Protestantism as a religious movement that the occasions of disunion arose. A rash political leader like Philip of Hesse, even in espousing union, damages as much as he promotes its cause, since he conceives of it as an agency for political ends that are quite unacceptable to one party in the discussions. The over-cautious politician John Frederick restrains Melanchthon, when, supported by Luther, he would go abroad on a union mission. An ambitious and secular-minded king like Henry VIII makes the union sentiment of the men of religion a pawn in his international game, and nullifies their sincere and promising efforts. We cannot exculpate the Reformers from the charge of occasionally exhibiting a schismatic spirit; they were sometimes unduly opinionated and intolerant. But if they are looked at fairly, it will be seen that they were predominantly conciliatory and zealous for peace, concord, and communion. Luther's last

journey was taken for the purpose of making peace
between two quarreling princes. Protestantism had
much of this to do, and it was not always strong
enough to do it. The divisive forces in politics were
often too strong for the unitive forces in religion.

CHAPTER V

UNION ACTIVITIES OF CALVIN AND BEZA

1. The Genesis of Calvin's Unionism

CALVIN's conversion, or life-dedication,[1] has been variously dated from 1529 to 1534. The first Protestant writings of which his authorship is certain were written in the autumn of 1535. The first edition of the *Institutes* appeared in March, 1536. Facts observed in the previous chapter will help us to realize the critical condition of French Protestantism in this period. The Erasmian and Lutheran strains in the movement were in process of differentiation. The left wing of the followers of that ecclesiastically moderate and hesitant though theologically radical leader Jacques Lefèvre d'Étaples was tending to push his ideas to their logical conclusion of disowning the authority and denying the catholicity of Rome. Both Lutheran and Zwinglian influences enhanced this tendency. Calvin was not a personal disciple of Lefèvre, but he was much in the company of some of his more radical pupils, and was later to be associated with the most vigorously Protestant of them all, Guillaume Farel. Calvin was deeply indebted to both Erasmus and Luther. Humanist teachers had polished and refined his intellectual powers. But his conversion involved a public alignment with the fighting, and in France suffering, Reformers rather than with

---

[1] "Animum meum, qui pro aetate nimis obduerat subita conversione ad docilitatem subegit." *C. R.*, LIX, 21.

ecclesiastically patient and cautious humanism. He himself connects his conversion closely with sympathy for the persecuted Protestants, in whom he came to see the "true church."

We have seen evidence of his emphatic catholicity and detestation of schism. From the beginning of his work he was powerfully motivated by a great zeal for "the Church of God," but this devotion had its negative side in an unqualified opposition to the alleged but ungenuine Church of Rome. Accordingly, for him separation from Rome was not schism. Christian unity for him must be a unity of Christians, the visible unity of the "true church," not of a nominal church which has departed from the truth. In his brilliant reply to Sadoleto (1539) he expressed the relation in his mind of unity and truth. He puts in the mouth of the reforming preacher the claim that he has been faithful in denouncing those who "were wasting the church with a tyranny worse than impious." "For I was fully conscious how great was the zeal with which I burned for the unity of the church, provided only that thy truth should be the bond of concord."[2] In the section following, a layman is made to say that the reforming teachers had instructed him in the difference between schism and reform, and that "they spake nobly (*præclare*) of the church, and gave themselves with the greatest zeal to the cultivation of its unity," but they have also inveighed against the Roman pontiff.[3] Calvin does not deny the existence of particular congregations of

[2] "Eram enim mihi optime conscius, quanto uniendae ecclesiae tuae studio flagrarem modo concordiae eius vinculum esset tua veritas." *C. R.,* XXXIII, 410.

[3] *Ibid.,* p. 412.

Christians under good pastors here and there in the Roman Church; he admits, for instance, that the churches over which Sadoleto himself presides are churches of Christ.[4] But for him that church as a whole is in error, and its pastors ravening wolves. It is not to be expected, then, that Calvin should look forward seriously to any unification which would include the papacy. His union effort is primarily directed toward the consolidation of Protestantism. Projects of compromise with Rome make him suspicious and impatient. His desire for the visible unity of the Church of God did not lead him to concede a place in that church to official Rome. The modern reader may think this attitude unjustifiably harsh. It is not intended here to advocate or oppose the views of Calvin, but to expound them. Certainly, these views were sincerely held and clearly thought out. Nobody ever condemned schism from the true church more vigorously than Calvin; and nobody ever felt logically and emotionally more certainty in rejecting the obedience of Rome.

Early in his career as a Reformer, Calvin began to make proposals of Protestant union. It is possible that we should assign his union interest partly to the influence of Bucer. Bucer's correspondence with French Protestants goes back to the beginning of the year 1525.[5] In the late twenties he was a fairly frequent correspondent with Farel.[6] In August, 1530, he reported to Luther the progress of French Protestantism, and lamented its dissensions.[7] As Strass-

---

[4] *C. R.*, XXXIII, p. 403.

[5] Herminjard, *Correspondance des Réformateurs*, I, 318ff.

[6] *Ibid.*, II, 51ff. (1527), 112ff., 127ff., 131ff., 173ff.

[7] *Ibid.*, II, 272.

burg became a place of retreat for French sufferers under Francis I, Bucer and Capito were thought of in France with special regard. Calvin first wrote to Bucer on September 4, 1534(?), commending to him in deep sympathy an endangered evangelical wrongly accused of being an Anabaptist.[8] Almost immediately after the beginning of Calvin's work in Geneva, Bucer wrote to him seeking a conference with a view to "a consensus of God's churches and ministers."[9] Calvin, however, was not wholly favorable to Bucer's union methods. In 1538 he freely criticized Bucer's Swiss activities, which had resulted in a deplorable situation in Bern.[10] Bucer was not downright enough, but instead of seeking "a sincere concord in the pure Word of God," had yielded too much to Luther, who mingled ambition with his piety.[11] Eells has stressed Calvin's difference from Bucer at this point. But it is a difference rather in the degree of concession held

---

[8] *Ibid.*, III, 208ff.

[9] *Ibid.*, IV, 115. The date is probably November 1, 1536, as indicated by Eells, H., "Martin Butzer and the Conversion of John Calvin," *Princeton Theological Review*, XXII (1924), 402. Cf. Pauck, W., "Calvin and Butzer," *Journal of Religion*, IX (1929), 242. Eells thinks Calvin had been in Strassburg during the previous month when Bucer was absent.

[10] Bucer's overintense propaganda for the *Wittenberg Concord* occasioned much disturbance in Bern, where Megander's decidedly Zwinglian *Catechism* of 1536 stood in the way of the acceptance of the Concord. Bucer altered the *Catechism* and succeeded in having his new version of it accepted by the Council, November, 1537. Megander soon afterward left for Zurich. In February, 1538, both *Catechisms* were ambiguously sanctioned. An anti-Lutheran reaction set in in 1541, and Bern finally moved to the Calvinist position. Good, J. I., *History of the Swiss Reformed Church Since the Reformation*, pp. 38–46, following Hundeshagen, *Die Conflikte des Zwinglianismus, Lutheranismus, und Calvinismus in der bernischen Landeskirche von 1532–1538* (Bern, 1842).

[11] In a letter to Bucer, of January 12, 1538, *C. R.*, XXXVIII, 137-144. Pauck remarks on the liberty taken in this letter from the junior to the senior theologian. *Op. cit.*, p. 243.

possible than in theological belief. Three months after the above-mentioned letter Calvin and Farel were exiled from Geneva, and at Bucer's earnest and repeated invitation, Calvin in September made his home in Strassburg for the period of his exile.[12]

Calvin was now to be intimately associated with Bucer for a period of nearly three years; but it is not clear in what degree he became Bucer's follower. Pauck has concluded that as a result of this association Calvin's "views on predestination and on the Lord's Supper became more precise. In regard to these doctrines he was when he left Strassburg a pupil or follower of Butzer. Furthermore, there can hardly be any doubt that, in Strassburg, Calvin was introduced to the idea of a universal Protestantism, for the cause of which he worked so enthusiastically and ceaselessly during the last years of his life."[13] This is putting the case for Bucer's influence strongly. So far as Calvin's thought is concerned, the principle of unity can be discerned in it from the first. In the first edition of the *Institutes* it is not stressed, but it is at least embraced;[14] and it is implied in the doctrine of the church therein briefly set forth.[15] But apparently it required the experience of the Strassburg years to bring the principle to activity as a part of his reforming program.

It is possible, indeed, that Calvin's first active interest in union was confined to the Swiss field. In

---

[12] The circumstances and correspondence are fully examined by Doumergue, *op. cit.*, II, 293ff. Originals in Herminjard, *op. cit.*, V, 43ff.

[13] Pauck, *op. cit.*, p. 244.

[14] *C. R.*, XXXIX, 120f. Cf. Doumergue, *op. cit.*, V, 368.

[15] *C. R.* XXXIX, 210ff.

connection with the Bern affair, in February, 1537, before the forced retirement of Megander (Grossmann) from the pastorate which called forth his disapproving letter to Bucer, Calvin wrote to Megander and his associates earnestly voicing the desire for a synod (*fratrum conventus*) to settle the issues in dispute in Swiss circles.[16] Similarly, he asked Bullinger, February, 1538, within six weeks after the letter to Bucer, why there might not take place a "public synod," where individuals might propose anything they thought beneficial to the churches, with a view to mutual (apparently Swiss) agreement (*inter nos concordia*).[17]

It can hardly be taken as a certainty, however, that Bucer "introduced" Calvin to the idea of universal Protestantism. It should be remembered that Farel, with whom Calvin had labored for a year and a half, was as ardent, if not as prominent, a unionist as Bucer himself, and carried his enthusiasm for the cause so far as heartily to have supported the French proposals of 1534.[18] It is not unlikely, moreover, that his contacts with Melanchthon, whom he met only a few months after his removal to Strassburg, strongly impelled Calvin in the same direction. His friendship with Melanchthon, and their discourses together on frequent occasions during the years 1539–41, remained among Calvin's most vivid memories, and his references to these associations show that he valued particularly the consciousness that the Lutheran theologian and he were in full accord.[19] This fact

[16] *C. R.*, XXXVIII, 84.
[17] *Ibid.*, p. 154.
[18] See above, p. 165.
[19] See below, pp. 212f., and Doumergue, *op. cit.*, II, 538ff.

must have encouraged in his mind the idea of a united Protestantism.

Another factor worth considering here is Calvin's experience in the exercise of discipline in the French church at Strassburg. The difficulties he met with in this task led him to desire a generally authorized plan of discipline backed by "the consent of the churches," and to seek a general conference to provide this.[20]

It seems likely that all these experiences, together with the natural ripening of his thought, led Calvin to the increased emphasis upon Christian union which marks his Strassburg years. It is a safe conjecture that the influence of Bucer was among the most potent factors in deepening his concern for union. In Bucer he saw an active, constant and indomitable devotion to the cause; and for him it now became, as it was for the Strassburg apostle, a definite aim rather than merely a congenial idea.

His resolve constantly to promote the peace of the Reformation churches is strongly affirmed in a letter to Bullinger of March, 1540, in which he says:

What, my dear Bullinger, should more concern us in writing at this time, than to keep up and strengthen brotherly friendship between us by all possible means? We see how much it concerns not our church alone but all Christianity that all to whom the Lord has intrusted any charge in his church should agree in true concord. . . . We must therefore purposefully and carefully cherish association and friendship with all true ministers of Christ (*ut cum omni-*

---

[20] "De disciplina bene facis quod urges. Sed quum omnia diligentius, expendo, nescio an constitui queat nisi consentientibus ecclesiis. Optandum ergo imprimis est, ut aliquando ea de re in deliberatione conveniant ecclesiae." Letter to Farel, December 31, 1539. *C. R.,* XXXVIII, 440.

bus Christi ministris societatem amicitiamque colamus). . .
in order that the churches to which we minister the Word
of God may faithfully agree together. [Their personal
friendship, he is assured, will continue.] As for me, as far
as in me lies, I will always labor to this end.

He puts in a word for Bucer and Capito, to allay
unwarranted suspicion; and he desires that occasion
might arise for him to see Bullinger, that they may
talk matters over face to face and come to complete
agreement.[21]

In this letter Calvin is pledging himself to and
entering upon the mediating task in which, among
other labors, he was to be active for the remainder
of his life. By the bonds of friendship with his
Strassburg associates and Melanchthon he was becoming more sympathetic with Lutheranism. He now
justified their acceptance of the Lutheran "ceremonies," and urged Farel and the Swiss to avoid making these a cause of dissension.[22] In such utterances
we see the beginnings of Calvin's activity as a promoter of Protestant union. He faithfully abode by the
resolution gravely taken in the letter to Bullinger just
quoted, and never lost hope that the several Protestant
groups would yet realize that corporate unity which
entered into his definition of the catholic church.[23]

2. CALVIN'S MEDIATING POSITION ON THE EUCHARIST

On the question of the Lord's Supper, in which
dissent between Wittenberg and Zurich was most
marked, Calvin, as he gained acquaintance with

---

[21] *C. R.*, XXXIX, 28f.

[22] *C. R.*, XXXIX, 341.

[23] See above, p. 69, footnote 16.

both viewpoints, realized that he shared some of the ideas of each of the contending parties. He was anxious to do justice to the religious significance of the Lord's Supper in the experience of the church, and could not be satisfied with the conception of it as a mere sign, or a mere aid to the memory, factors which entered so largely into—if they did not (as the Lutherans supposed) exhaust—the Zwinglian interpretation. Calvin, like Luther, desired to give a weighty content to the idea of the sacrament, a fact which leads G. Reichel to remark, a little misleadingly, that his teaching here is rather a modification of Luther's than of Zwingli's.[24] On the other hand, he could not accept the materialistic terms of corporeal presence in which the Lutheran position was often stated, nor the literal view of *Hoc est corpus meum* for which Luther had contended at Marburg. He supposed, however, that both groups of reformers had been led to extremes by the heat of controversy, and that both had the root of the matter in them, however distorted the upgrowth appeared. He believed too that the two parties in some degree misunderstood each other, and that by conferences they might be reconciled. In short, he hoped to follow the thesis and antithesis of Luther and Zwingli with a synthesis in which all the values would be comprehended and the disputants reconciled.

Not that his doctrine was deliberately shaped as a conciliatory one. It took shape before he realized his calling as a moderator of extremes. Beckmann has indicated that he formulated it with the help of Augustine, independently of any contemporary writer.[25]

---

[24] *Calvin als Unionsmann*, p. 7.
[25] Beckmann, J., *Vom Sakrament bei Calvin*, pp. 4ff.

He was resolutely determined not to sacrifice truth to peace. But on this matter he felt that no conflict between truth and charity was involved. Kolfhaus[26] agrees with Lang that Calvin "united the exegetical clarity of Zwingli with the religious depth and inwardness of Luther." In broad comparison he admired Luther more highly than Zwingli,[27] yet he sincerely revered both. He naturally sought to unite parties which represented elements already fused in his own thinking.

In course of time he became the self-conscious mediator. His position on the Lord's Supper in the second edition of the *Institutes* (1539) bears the mark of reflection on the sacramentarian controversy. His *Little Treatise on the Lord's Supper* (1540) is notably irenic in purpose.

"The recent contention," he remarks, "is an unhappy business, the devil having stirred it up to impede, nay, completely to interrupt the work of the Gospel." [Luther in denying transubstantiation] "said the bread was the body of Christ, and . . . added similitudes that were somewhat harsh and rude; but he did this, as it were, by constraint, since he could not otherwise explain his meaning, for it is difficult to give an explanation of so high a matter without impropriety. Zwingli and Ecolampadius were intent on removing the idea of the carnal Presence. While they interested

---

[26] *Calvinstudien*, p. 47.

[27] "If the two men are compared," he writes to Farel, February 26, 1540, "you yourself know how much Luther has the preference": "Si inter se comparantur scis ipse quanto intervallo Lutherus excellat" (*C. R.*, XXXIX, 24). Doumergue remarks: "If he put Luther above Zwingli, much more did he put the Zwinglians above the Lutherans. The former had modified, the latter had exaggerated, their master." *Op. cit.*, II, 569.

themselves in this point they forgot to show what presence of Jesus Christ ought to be believed in the Supper and what communion of his body and blood is there received. Luther thought they meant to leave nothing but the bare signs and began to call them heretics. Both parties failed in not having the patience to listen to each other in order to follow the truth without passion. Still, they should be reverenced for their holiness, knowledge, and zeal. God has ended, or silenced, the strife, preparatory to its final settlement. No formulary is yet agreed upon, but this will be when God will be pleased to assemble in one place those who are to frame it."[28]

In his relations to Lutheranism Calvin built his hopes upon Melanchthon's *Augustana Variata* of 1540. This edition of the great Lutheran Confession was Melanchthon's boldest move for reconciliation with the South Germans and the Swiss. It appeared a year and a half after Calvin's first personal intercourse with its author at Frankfort in February, 1539, when their enduring friendship was begun. It is, therefore, possible that Calvin's influence should be recognized in the modification of the Lutheran doctrine of the Lord's Supper, for which it is remarkable.[29] The resemblance of the phraseology to that

---

[28] *Petit traicte de la saincte cene, C. R.*, XXXIII, 458-60 (condensed).

[29] The Tenth Article, which originally read, "De coena Domini docent quod corpus et sanguis (wahrer Leib und Blut) Christi vere adsint (unter Gestalt des Brods und Weins) et distribuantur vescentibus in coena Domini; et improbant secus docentes," was materially altered to read, "De Coena Domini docent quod cum pane et vino vere exhibeantur corpus et sanguis Christi vescentibus in Coena Domini" (*C. R.*, XXVI, 278, 357, 559). Grisar (*Luther*, Engl. ed., II, 445) thinks Philip of Hesse made the suggestion of this revision to Melanchthon. On the view that the *Variata* was written in 1538 see J. W. Richards, *The Confessional History of the Lutheran Church*, p. 225.

of the *Wittenberg Concord* of 1536, however, largely
offsets the suggestion of such an influence. It was
this version, to Eck's displeasure, that was presented
in the negotiations with the Romanists at Worms and
Ratisbon. There is no evidence that Luther ever ex-
pressly disapproved of the alteration. The *Variata*
was warmly and repeatedly approved by Calvin. His
later strictures on the Confession were on the original
edition, and were mainly on points on which it differed
from the revised version. He was in close association with Bucer and Melanchthon during the period
of the conferences of Hagenau, Worms, and Ratisbon
(June, 1540–April, 1541). If he differed from them
on certain issues of the negotiations with the Romanists in these conferences, he remained conscious of substantial accord with them on the sacramental question.[30]

3. The Situation Before the Zurich Consensus

The significance of the Zurich *Consensus* (1549) can
be seen only in relation to the renewed sacramental
controversy of the forties. Zwingli's *Exposition of the
Christian Faith*, published by Bullinger in 1536, with
its consideration for certain unbaptized pagans, had
displeased Luther. To his chagrin the Swiss had also
published a new German Bible in 1543. He was
further annoyed by the discords of the right and left
wings of his followers, men like Amsdorf and Westphal
opposing the liberalism of Melanchthon. He reopened the battle with his *Short Confession of the
Lord's Supper* (September, 1544),[31] which contained

---

[30] For details, see Doumergue, *op. cit.*, II, 580ff., and Calvin's informing letters of the period in *C. R.*, Vol. XXXIX.

[31] *Kurzes Bekenntnis vom Heiligen Sakrament.* *Werke*, LIV, 141ff.

an attack upon Zwingli and Ecolampadius that out-Luthered Luther in vehemence. This inexcusable outburst crushed Melanchthon's, but not Calvin's hopes of peace. Melanchthon wrote Bullinger (August 30, 1544) regretting "this most atrocious book of Luther's." "I cease to hope," he laments, "for the peace of the churches. . . . Our enemies who defend the idols of the monks, raise their crests, and once more our churches are put asunder, for which I take great sorrow."[32]

Calvin, though deeply distressed by the renewal of the controversy, found in it an opportunity to seek peace and understanding anew. He now "devoted time and strength to the program of bridging over the chasm between Zwingli and Luther, and by setting aside their particularities to produce a true unity."[33]

---

[32] "Fortassis priusquam hae meae literae ad te perferentur, accipies atrocissimum Lutheri scriptum, in quo bellum περὶ δείπνου κυριακοῦ instaurat. . . . Desino igitur sperare Ecclesiarum pacem. Tollent cristas inimici nostri, qui defendunt ἴδωλα monachorum: Ac rursus Ecclesiae nostrae magis distrahentur, qua ex re ingentem capio dolorem" (*C. R.*, V, 475). Melanchthon's correspondence of the period of the incubation and publication of Luther's manifesto is informing. It shows him in a mood of depression and abounds with ejaculatory prayers for the peace of the church. To Bucer (August 28), *ibid.*, p. 474, he writes of the "fierce book in which you and I are beaten black and blue": "atrocem librum . . . in quo ego et tu sugillamur." As for himself, he is a tranquil bird, and would not unwillingly escape from his house of correction if his troubler should press him hard: "Ego sum tranquilla avis, nec invitus ex hoc ergastulo discedam si infestus me urgebit." Cf. a letter to Jonas, September 27, *ibid.*, p. 484. At this stage he was much more distressed to see the hope of Protestant union dashed than concerned to reopen the discussions with the Romanists, with whom negotiations were now again mooted in anticipation of the Council of Trent. See his letters to Camerarius and to V. Theodorus, both of August 11. To the latter he writes: "Nunc jussi sumus componere παρασκευὴν futuri conventus. Quid dicam consilii esse nostris? Instituere volunt conciliationes cum Pontificiis, et nostrarum ecclesiarum concordiam non fovent" (*C. R.*, V, 461). To Camerarius: "Odi haec fucosa consilia, et liberari me opto" (*ibid.*, p. 462).

[33] Kolfhaus, W., *Calvinstudien*, p. 45.

Though not named in Luther's attack, he felt himself by implication condemned; but his first concern was to calm the indignation of the Zurichers. He declined an imprudent suggestion of Farel which amounted to asking the injured party to seek forgiveness,[34] and wrote to Bullinger a letter of advice that does him credit. "I learn," he says, "that Luther in his insolent petulance attacks us all together." Thus first identifying himself with the victims of the wrong that Luther has done, he asks Bullinger to consider how great a man Luther is, by what extraordinary gifts he is dintinguished, and with what energy of soul, perseverance, ability, and success he has continued to overthrow the kingdom of antichrist. "I have already often said," Calvin adds, "that were he to call me a devil, I should still continue to venerate him as a distinguished servant of God, who, while excelling in extraordinary virtues, also labors under some great faults."[35]

There is no record that Luther ever called Calvin "a devil." Doumergue gives the impression, indeed, that Luther's praise of Calvin's work, in 1539 and subsequently, disposed the latter to think more favorably of the former than he had done previously. Luther had been shown a criticism of himself by Calvin, and had generously remarked, "I hope Calvin will one day think better of us." Calvin, on learning this, wrote to Farel (November 20, 1539), "I am completely vanquished (*fractus*) by such moderation."[36]

---

[34] Calvin to Farel, October 10, 1544. *C. R.*, XXXIX, 755.

[35] "Etiam si me diabolum vocaret, me tamen hoc illi honoris habiturum, ut insignem Dei servum agnoscam: qui tamen ut pollet eximiis virtutibus, ita magnis vitiis laboret." *C. R.*, XXXIX, 774.

[36] *C. R.*, XXXVIII, 432. Doumergue, *op. cit.*, II, 572f. De Wette, *Briefe*, V, 411.

But Calvin was deeply conscious of his debt to the Saxon reformer. His lasting reverence for Luther is attested by many passages, including his spirited defense of Luther against Pighius on the doctrine of predestination,[37] and the letter he wrote to his "honored father" (January 20, 1545) to ask an opinion on his exhortations to undeclared Protestants of France. Says Calvin here: "Would to God that I could take flight to you, were it but to enjoy a few hours of your conversation. . . . I hope that that which is not given us on earth will soon be granted us in the kingdom of heaven. Farewell, man of high renown and faithful servant of Jesus Christ and at all times my most revered father. May the Lord continue to guide you by his Spirit to the end, for the common good of his church."[38] Melanchthon, in whose care this letter was sent, wisely or unwisely withheld it from Luther on the ground that "Doctor Martin looks at things with suspicion, and does not wish to have his sentiments . . . published abroad."[39]

Apparently in January, 1545, to a correspondent who cannot be identified, Calvin wrote to discount the expectation of any results from a possible conference with the Romanists. In case any attempt at this is made, unacceptable demands will be presented on both sides, and the Pope will know how "to throw all into disorder." But as for divisions among the reformed: "In the midst of these hostile prepara-

---

[37] "Defensio sanae et orthodoxae doctrinae de servitute et liberatione humani arbitrii adversus calumnias Alberti Pighii, Campensis" (Geneva, 1543). *C. R.*, XXXV, 225ff.

[38] The letter was sent by the hand of Claude de Senarclens, with one for Melanchthon in which Calvin alludes judiciously to the controversy and laments Osiander's fresh attacks. *C. R.*, XXXX, 8.

[39] *C. R.*, XXXX, 61.

tions, that certain persons should find leisure enough
for senseless quarreling with one another looks rather
portentous. . . . We seem to have hired ourselves
both hand and tongue to the ungodly, that we may
afford them sport and pastime by tearing one another to pieces." But with God's aid, "the church
will at length surmount these perils." The letter too
suggests some difficulties in the way of union that it
is easy for us nowadays to overlook. His correspondent has proposed that he should go to Wittenberg.
The journey would require twenty days. He has no
money; he is in debt and cannot turn to the merchants
of Geneva, who, after two years of dearth, are themselves "almost starving." "Add to this what I have
already said, that the time is unseasonable for consult-
ing Luther because his anger has scarcely settled down
from the heat of contention." He has sent a messenger, Claude de Senarclens, with a letter to Melanchthon.[40]

About the time of this correspondence appeared the
reply of the Zurichers to Luther's tirade. It was
entitled "A truthful Confession of the Servants of the
Church at Zurich as to what they from the Word of
God and in common with the holy universal Christian
Church believe and teach especially concerning the
Lord's Supper, in answer to the Slanders, Condemnation and Jests of Dr. Martin Luther."[41] Calvin had
no praise for this work. On June 28 he wrote Melanchthon, "The Zurichers have the better cause, but their

---

[40] *C. R.*, XXXX, 23-26.

[41] *Wahrhaftes Bekenntniss der Diener der Kirche zu Zürich, was sie
aus Gottes Wort mit der heiligen, allgemeinen, christlichen Kirche glauben und lehren, insbesondere aber von dem Abendmahl unseres Herrn
Jesu Christi, mit gebührliche Antwort auf das unbegründete, ärgerliche
Schmähen D. Martin Luthers* . . .

book is jejune and puerile." Again he expresses his admiration with his criticism of Luther. "From my heart I reverence him, but I am thoroughly ashamed of him." The calamity of the church resulting from Luther's example of tyranny is not to be deplored merely in silence. Melanchthon ought to take the opportunity to declare his own mind. Nevertheless, he writes not so much to arouse as to console him.[42]

Luther contributed nothing further to the controversy, but remained unrepentant. It is doubtful, indeed, whether any friend frankly expostulated with him. A few weeks before his death he wrote facetiously to Probst of Bremen (January 17, 1546): "This one beatitude of the psalm is enough for me, the most unhappy of men: Blessed is the man who hath not walked in the council of the Sacramentarians, nor stood in the way of the Zwinglians, nor sat in the seat of the Zurichers."[43] Luther's, however, was a mind of many facets; and some probability attaches to certain anecdotes of a different color, told by Christopher Pezel.[44] Pezel narrates that Luther, before setting out on his last journey, remarked to Melanchthon: "In the matter of the sacraments we have gone much too far" (*viel zu viel gethan*). Melanchthon suggested the preparation of a new statement, that the churches might be united again. "I've often thought of that," said Luther, "but in that case all the doctrine will become doubtful. I will commend the thing to the Lord. You," he added, "do some-

[42] *C. R.*, XXXX, 98f.
[43] De Wette, *Briefe*, IV, 778.
[44] *Ausführliche wahrhafte und bestandige Erzählung vom Sacramentstreit* (Bremen, 1600), pp. 125f., cited by Doumergue, *op. cit.*, II, 572.

thing after my death." Pezel's informant, Hardenberg, vouched for the story with the remark, "This
is true, as God is God."[45]   Another story of Pezel's is
to the effect that Luther, in 1545, praised Calvin's
De coena Domini to the bookseller, Moritz Golsch,
saying: "I might have intrusted the whole affair of
this controversy to him from the beginning. If my opponents had done the like, we should soon have been
reconciled."[46]

After the opening of the Council of Trent, Calvin's
activity in the cause of Protestant union increased.[47]
The death of Luther, and his own growing success
in Geneva, placed him clearly in the leadership of
the Protestant forces.   Melanchthon, surrounded by
tumults and depressed by many griefs, proved unable
at this stage to contribute in any appreciable degree
to the union effort.   Bucer had met with a repulse from
the Zurichers in the spring of 1538, and, for some time
afterward at least, felt a grievance against Bullinger
for his part on that occasion.   Calvin advanced evidence that Bullinger had not intended to wound
Bucer personally,[48] assured Bullinger of Bucer's sincerity,[49] and sought to restore mutual confidence.
But the Zurichers would hardly receive favorably
suggestions of union from Bucer.   In any case Bucer
was now living amid increasing trouble at Strassburg,
and yielding at last to the wishes of his friends and

[45] Hardenberg was the friend and correspondent of Bucer, à Lasco,
and Cranmer; Cranmer regarded him as very influential with Melanchthon (Cranmer, *Remains and Letters,* p. 422).

[46] Pezel, *op. cit.*, p. 137; Doumergue, *loc. cit.*

[47] His *Acts of the Council of Trent with the Antidote* appeared in November, 1547.   *C. R.*, XXXV, 365f.

[48] Calvin to Farel, February 28, 1540.   *C. R.*, XXXIX, 24.

[49] See above, p. 185.

the invitations of Cranmer, he departed to England in May, 1549, never to return.

4. FORMATION AND OUTCOME OF THE ZURICH CONSENSUS

Calvin's plan was to make the unification of Geneva and Zurich the first stage in a general agreement.[50] He had maintained occasional correspondence with Bullinger since 1537, and they had become friends. He had always believed that no vital issue divided them and that complete accord could be reached between them. On November 25, 1544, after Luther's attack, he wrote to Bullinger: "If we could only talk together for half a day, we would agree without difficulty, not only concerning the matter itself, but concerning the form of stating it. Meanwhile the present occasion of offense must not hinder us from bearing in our hearts brotherly friendship in the Lord."[51]

He now deliberately wooed Bullinger and led him to discuss a formal consensus. In November, 1548, he sent him twenty-four propositions on the sacraments. Bullinger commented on these with general approval, and Calvin replied.[52] In March, at a Synod in Bern, Calvin presented twenty similar articles.[53] These were not accepted by the Bernese, but he did not lose hope of a later agreement. In May, 1549, while privately depressed by the recent death of his wife, on Bullinger's invitation and accompanied by Farel he made a flying visit to Zurich, and with Bullinger

[50] Cr. Reichel, *op. cit.*, pp. 11f.
[51] *C. R.*, XXXIX, 775.
[52] *C. R.*, XXXV, 689f.
[53] *C. R.*, XXXV, 717f.

completed the twenty-six articles of the *Consensus*. So far had agreement already been reached that the final shaping of the document required only two hours.[54] Conference was had and agreement secured with the ministers and the civic council. In August a signed copy of the *Consensus* was sent by Bullinger to Calvin.

These articles of agreement,[55] if somewhat repetitious. are unambiguous and full of nervous thought. The sacraments are described as "marks and badges of Christian profession and fellowship or fraternity, to be incitements to gratitude and exercises of faith and a godly life" (7). But beyond this Zwinglian conception "he undoubtedly truly performs inwardly by the Spirit that which the sacraments figure to our eyes and senses; in other words, we obtain possession of Christ as the fountain of all blessings" (8). They are effective, however, only for the elect (16-18). "For as he enlightens unto faith none but those whom he has foreordained to life, so by the secret agency of the Spirit he makes the elect receive what the sacraments offer." "The signs are administered alike to reprobate and elect, but the reality reaches the latter only." Those who hold the literal view of the words of institution are "repudiated as preposterous interpreters" (22). The phrases about "eating His flesh" and "drinking His blood" are explained as not involving any "transfusion of substance," but in the sense that "we draw life from the flesh once offered in sacrifice and the blood shed in expiation" (23).

---

[54] Calvin to Myconius, November 26, 1549. *C. R.*, XLI, 457.
[55] *C. R.*, XXXV, 733f.

The sharply Zwinglian phraseology of some of these clauses, and especially the reference to "preposterous interpreters," strikes the reader at once, and Dorner's remark that Calvin had employed the language of the *Variata*[56] is hardly borne out. Why did Calvin, if he desired to conciliate the Lutherans, accept language which was not adapted to win them? Something must be ascribed here to Bullinger's habitual disinclination to move in the direction of Lutheranism. It is possible also that Calvin and Bullinger had in view as their immediate aim obtaining the assent of Bern, where the majority party was now extreme Zwinglian. If so, the object was only partially attained. Bern had taken offense at Calvin's theocratic scheme, by which Geneva had assumed a place of secure independence of her ambitious neighbor; and for many of the Bernese no good thing could come out of Geneva. They objected to the publication of the document, and finally consented to this, giving only verbal, because not unanimous, assent to its contents.[57] The other Swiss Protestant communities gave their adherence to the *Consensus;* and its adoption marked the virtual unification of French and German Swiss Protestantism and prevented all further danger of a split over the Lord's Supper in the reformed churches of Europe.[58] Through Calvin's efforts there were now "two Protestantisms" instead of three.[59]

It is clear that from the first Calvin hoped to use the

---

[56] *History of Protestant Theology* (Engl. ed., 1871), I, 410.

[57] *C. R.*, XLI, 391 (Ministri Bernenses Turicensibus, anno 1549), and *ibid.*, p. 397 (Calvinus Vireto, September 23, 1549).

[58] Doumergue, *op. cit.*, V, 368, quoting A. Witz-Oberlin, *Calvin der Unionsmann*, p. 10.

[59] Doumergue, *op. cit.*, VI, 527.

Consensus in order to accredit, not Geneva, with which
the Lutherans had then no controversy, but the German Swiss, to the German Lutherans. "Those who
had formed an unworthy opinion of us," he writes,
"will see that we proposed nothing but what was good
and right. . . . Those in distant lands who differ from
us in opinion will soon, we hope, offer us the
hand."[60] Here he may have had reference to England
as well as Germany. But his main design was to ele-
vate the Swiss theology to a plane on which the Germans would feel free to recognize it. How could he
have expected so much from the *Consensus*, which
nobody could possibly mistake for a Lutheran document? In order to answer this question it is necessary to remember, in the first place, that the document was an unequivocal assertion on the part of the
Swiss that the sacraments were not bare signs, and
this was calculated to overcome Lutheran assumptions
about the Zwinglians.[61] Again it was clearly Calvin's
opinion that the essential, as distinct from the acci-
dental, elements of the Lutheran view were comprised in the doctrine of spiritual presence as forcibly
stated and reiterated in the *Consensus*, and that moderate Lutherans would regard the positive sections of
the document with no disfavor. It is not to be supposed, either, that he intended to make the *Consensus*
a *sine qua non* of negotiation with the Lutherans.
Beza, during Calvin's lifetime and with his support,
made greater concessions. The *Consensus* would

[60] Quoted by Henry, *Life and Times of John Calvin* (tr. by Stebbins,
1852), II, 82.
[61] Henry quotes Planck to the effect that the *Consensus* "accomplished, or at least declared," the union of the Swiss with the Lutheran
system, and that by it all doubt as to whether the Swiss recognized the
actual presence was completely removed (*ibid.*).

serve, however, to introduce the Zurichers to the Wittenbergers. In point of fact it did serve that purpose. Melanchthon, on reading it, said he had never before understood the Swiss position.[62] Dorner says, "Many Germans, especially at Strassburg and Wittenberg, shared Calvin's hope."[63] Never before had there seemed so fair a prospect of Protestant peace and intercommunion. Bucer and à Lasco sent congratulations from England, where the idea of a general consensus of Protestantism was now being canvassed from another angle.

The success of Calvin's project depended on the ascendancy in Germany of the conciliatory wing of the Lutherans. After the Schmalkald Wars, however, the strict confessionalists bestirred themselves to oppose the concord. They were reactionaries protesting against the growing liberalism in Lutheran circles. Their movement began, not with an assault upon the *Variata* (which seems not to have been in controversy till 1560), but by a violent attack upon the Tigurine agreement. In this controversy Calvin's most prominent antagonist was Joachim Westphal (1510–74, pastor at Hamburg since 1541). There is some truth in Doumergue's remark: "Calvin and Westphal were not simply individuals; they were spirits—Westphal the spirit of division, Calvin the spirit of union."[64] Beginning in 1552 Westphal issued a series of five tracts, vigorously denouncing Calvin, Bullinger, à

---

[62] Henry, *op. cit.*, II, 83, citing Lavater. See, however, *C. R.*, XLII, 417, where Calvin writes Melanchthon (November 29, 1552) that he has been informed that his friend had stricken out a sentence of the *Consensus* on election.

[63] Dorner, *op. cit.*, I, 410.

[64] *Op. cit.*, VI, 527.

Lasco,[65] Peter Martyr, and the Swiss *Consensus*. Learning that he was canvassing lower Germany for pledges against the doctrine of the *Consensus*, Calvin entered the lists in reply, and issued in 1554 the text of the *Consensus* with an exposition (*Mutual Consent in Regard to the Sacraments*), and in 1556 his *Second Defense of the Sound and Orthodox Faith Concerning the Sacraments, in Answer to the Calumnies of Joachim Westphal*. This was followed in 1557 by a *Final Admonition* to Westphal.[66] In these vigorous pamphlets Calvin sometimes resorted to bitter invective. But they are remarkable for his insistent claim that he has always approved of the *Augustana* as it was presented in the conferences with the Romanists (that is, the *Variata*), and for a bold appeal to Melanchthon, its "most distinguished author." For the sake of illustration some paragraphs from the *Final Admonition* may here be quoted in Beveridge's flowing English:

To free ourselves from the prejudice thus craftily sought to be excited, I appealed, I admit, to the author of the Confession, and I do not repent having done so. What does Westphal do? With his gross barbarism he represents me as making the victory to depend upon Philip's subscribing to us. Let not my readers wait till he himself becomes ashamed of this falsehood; there is too much brass in his brow; let them only judge what such vile talk deserves.

My words are: in regard to the Confession of Augsburg my answer is, that (as it was published at Ratisbon) it does not contain a word contrary to our doctrine. If there is any ambiguity in its meaning, there cannot be a more

---

[65] Westphal made the disaster to à Lasco and his followers on the coast of Denmark, in their flight from Mary of England (1553), the occasion of bitter insults. He called the victims "martyrs of the Devil." Doumergue, *op. cit.*, VI, 505.

[66] Doumergue has described the whole controversy, with copious references to the literature. *Op. cit.*, VI, 503ff.

competent interpreter than its author, to whom, as his due, all pious and learned men will readily pay this honor. To him I boldly appeal; and thus Westphal with his vile garrulity lies prostrate.

Let him extract from these words, if he can, that I made the victory to depend on the subscription of any single man. No less sordid is the vanity which makes him wonder exceedingly that such a stigma was fastened on his master, though, from Philip's answer, he has learned the fact of our agreement more clearly than I ventured to declare it. But what need is there of words? If Joachim wishes once for all to rid himself of all trouble and put an end to the controversy, let him extract one word in his favor from Philip's lips. The means of access are open, and the journey is not so very laborious, to visit one whose consent he boasts so loftily, and with whom he may thus have familiar intercourse. If I shall be found to have used Philip's name rashly, there is no stamp of ignominy to which I am not willing to submit.

The passage which Westphal quotes, it is not mine to refute, nor do I regard what, during the first conflict, before the matter was clearly and lucidly explained, the importunity of some may have extorted from one who was then too backward in giving a denial. It were too harsh to lay it down as a law on literary men, that after they have given a specimen of their talent and learning they are never after to go beyond it in the course of their lives. Assuredly, whosoever shall say that Philip has added nothing by the labor of forty years, does great wrong to him individually, and to the whole church. The only thing I said, and, if need be, a hundred times repeat, is, that in this matter Philip can no more be torn from me than he can from his own bowels. But although fearing the thunder which threatened to burst from violent men (those who know the boisterous blasts of Luther understand what I mean), he did not always speak out so openly as I could have wished, there is no reason why Westphal, while pretending differently, should indirectly charge him with having begun to incline to us only after Luther was dead.

For when more than seventeen years ago we conferred together on this point of doctrine, at our first meeting not a syllable required to be changed. Nor should I omit to mention Gasper Cruciger, who, from his excellent talents and learning, stood next after Philip highest in Luther's estimation, and far beyond all others. He so cordially embraced what Westphal now impugns, that nothing can be imagined more perfectly accordant than our opinions. But if there is still any doubt as to Philip, do I not make a sufficient offer when I wait silent and confident for his answer, assured that it will make manifest the dishonesty which has falsely sheltered itself under the venerable name of that most excellent man?[67]

Melanchthon, who had already suffered from the venom of Westphal's pen,[68] now, as Moeller says, "wrapped himself in silence." But his silence gave assent to Calvin's claim, and the extremists are soon found accusing him of a secret understanding with Calvin. Thus the promising effort for the peace and consolidation of Protestantism issued in the violent Crypto-Calvinist controversy, in which the exclusive party finally triumphed and the possibility of a general agreement was rendered exceedingly remote.

Calvin did not live to learn of the expulsion of the Philippists from Wittenberg or to read the *Formula of Concord,* and he never despaired of the ultimate success of the consensus project. Kolfhaus ascribes his undimmed hope to his sense of unity with Melanchthon.[69] It is to be remembered, however, that he always insisted on his essential agreement with Luther.

---

[67] Calvin, *Tracts,* II, 355f.; original in *C. R.,* XXXVII, 148f.

[68] *Historia vituli aurei Aaronis ad nostra tempora accommodata* (1549). Cf. Kawerau, "Westphal," in *Realencyklopädie,* 3rd ed., XXI, 186.

[69] *Calvinstudien,* p. 111.

Thus he wrote to Marbach, a Lutheran minister of Strassburg, in 1554:

> If that excellent servant of the Lord and faithful Doctor of the Church, Martin Luther, were still alive, he would not be so severe and implacable as to refuse his ready assent to this Confession, namely, that that is truly afforded us which the sacraments figure, and we are therefore partakers in the Lord's Supper of the body and blood of Christ. How often did he say that he contended for nothing but that it might be clearly understood that the Lord does not mock us with empty signs. . . . Greatly would it trouble me if a doctrine should now be rejected which I so many years ago taught freely and openly at Strassburg, both in the schools and in the churches.[70]

5. Union Activities of Beza and Farel

Doumergue regards the years 1556–58 as those of Calvin's main effort to make "of the two Protestant-isms one."[71] In his sixth volume he has furnished a full narrative of the conferences of that period. But while Calvin is still seen to be hopeful and active, his figure now largely recedes behind that of his stalwart lieutenant, Beza. It is Beza's hand that shapes the documents of negotiation, and it is Beza who goes (four times) to confer with the Germans. This appears clearly in the extended treatment of the subject in Baum's old work on Beza.[72]

Theodore Beza (1519–1605) became in Calvin's own lifetime an international figure, and after Calvin's death maintained for forty years a personal ascendancy in Calvinism. His only modifications of Calvin's teaching

---

[70] *C. R.*, XLIII, 212f.

[71] *Op. cit.*, VI, 527ff.

[72] Baum, J. W., *Theodor Beza nach handschriftlichen Quellen dargestellt* (1853), I, 275ff.

lay in his refinement and heightening of the doctrine
of predestination (supralapsarianism) and in his extension of Calvin's political ideas to the justification
of resistance to tyrants.[73] In nothing was he more
Calvinist than in his unionism. His activity in the
cause of union is first marked in this period. The distress of the Waldenses in territory recently acquired by
France from the Duke of Savoy, where persecution
began in 1555, offered the occasion and opportunity for
a union mission. It is of interest to see that the
Vaudois were at once recognized as kindred by Calvin and Bullinger. Beza toured the Swiss cantons,
Strassburg and Heidelberg (1557). He was accompanied by Farel, aged now, but with undimmed enthusiasm both for Protestantism and for union. Bullinger aided in their efforts to secure the sending of
delegates to the French king to intercede not only for
the Waldenses but for the Calvinists of France. Beza
and Farel, however, went further than to propose
merely the sending of delegates. Their object was a
not less ambitious one than the negotiation of a consensus with the Lutherans.

Conversations on this project had already been initiated by John à Lasco, the Polish scholar and reformer, one of the most irenical and constructive minds
of the age, despite misfortunes that largely nullified his
efforts. Forced to remain for some time in western
Europe after the disaster that has attended his attempt to reach Poland in the fall of 1553, à Lasco,
seeking Lutheran recognition of his followers, in May,

---

[73] Chartier, A. "Les idées politiques de Théodore de Béze d'après le
traité du droit des magistrats sur leur sujets," in *Bulletin de la société
d'histoire et d'archeologie de Genève*, II (1900), 187-206, shows Beza's
authorship of the treatise *Du Droit des magistrats sur leurs sujets*, 1574.

1556, held a two-day conference with Brenz at Stuttgart. A Lasco professed agreement with the *Augustana*, but could not fully accept the interpretation put upon it by Brenz and by him laid down as the condition of an understanding. The discussion was without result.[74] Beza and Farel now engaged in conversations with Marbach of Strassburg and Diller of Heidelberg, and addressed to the Duke of Württemburg a confession which Beza framed and to which Farel subscribed with him (May 10, 1557).[75] The language of this confession is ambiguous, but in the expression "true flesh" (*veram carnem*) it is, to say the least, not a natural formulation of Calvinism. This action was taken without consultation with either Calvin or Bullinger, nor were they directly informed of it by the author.[76] Calvin heard of it with surprise some weeks later, but on obtaining the text from Beza, commended it, with reservations, to Bullinger.[77] But Bullinger was displeased and apprehensive. Since the incidents of 1544 Bullinger had not favored any effort to put on a confessional basis the relations of Swiss and Lutherans. Both à Lasco and Beza, as well as Calvin, fully stated their acceptance of the *Augustana* in its then current version of the *Variata* of 1540. This Bullinger, proudly loyal to the Helvetic formula which he had helped to frame in 1536, would never do. "Before God and all the churches we cannot recognize that confession," he wrote. Moreover, the proposal for a general convention would, he thought, only

---

[74] À Lasco's report of the colloquy is in *C. R.*, XLIV, 163ff.

[75] Text in Baum, *op. cit.*, I, 406-09. Baird, H. M., *Theodore Beza*, p. 92, has translated a paragraph.

[76] The news came to Calvin by way of the Elector Palatine, Sturm, and François Hotman. Hotman wrote from Strassburg, May 28.

[77] *C. R.*, XLIX, 501-02.

bring trouble, and Westphal would shout: "They are out of accord among themselves."[78] Haller shared these views, and wrote from Bern that the negotiators had imbibed (*sugerunt*) the spirit of Bucer,[79] a word of reproach in German Switzerland. In the Zwinglian area disapproval was general.

The Genevans were disappointed but not discouraged. The news of fresh persecution in France stirred up Beza and Farel to renewed effort. In October they attended a gathering of German theologians at Worms, Melanchthon being present. Here Beza, on the 8th, presented, in the name of the Protestants of France, a new confession.[80] In this carefully phrased document the definition of the Lord's Supper is left inexplicit, but pains are taken to differentiate the French Protestant teaching from that of the Anabaptists and of Schwenkfeld that the sacrament is a "mere sign." A conference on the question is proposed. On all other points full agreement with the Lutherans is asserted. Reformed and Lutheran indeed "form one true church of the Son of God."[81] It is more modest in its claims than the previous confession, and is also, we may say, more religious; for example, in the quotation: "The bread is the communion (Κοινωνία) of the body of Christ."[82] Beza claimed with Farel the authorship of this document, but Calvin thought he saw in it the master hand of Melanchthon. Perhaps Beza prepared it with a view

---

[78] *C. R.*, XLIV, 568.

[79] Baum, *op. cit.*, I, 280f.

[80] Text in Baum, *op. cit.*, I, 409-11.

[81] "Sentimus et nos et vos unam veram Ecclesiam filii Dei esse et damnamus vobiscum Idola papistica," p. 411.

[82] *Ibid.*

to making an appeal to Melanchthon, whose sentiments it admirably expresses. At the conference Melanchthon seems to have felt the power of the anti-Calvinist agitators to such a degree that he appeared somewhat cool toward the delegates.[83] That Melanchthon's manner was, however, changing in this period is shown by a letter of Hubert Languet to Calvin, of March, 1558. Languet had prolonged intercourse with him after the Colloquy of Worms. He reports that Melanchthon had "openly condemned" at Frankfort certain propositions of Westphal, and that Hardenberg had prudently and effectively supported him. But Melanchthon appeared to be crushed by age, toil, and the calumnies of many foes; nothing remained of his old-time mirth.[84]

The Lutheran theologians so far accepted the confession of Beza as to recommend to their princes sending commissioners to France as Beza asked. Through information given by the Romanist secretary of the Elector Palatine to the effect that persecution had ceased, the dispatch of the commissioners was delayed. Calvin grew impatient and at his bidding Beza undertook a third mission to Germany. He secured the sending of the messengers, with vigorous demands,[85]

---

[83] "Ziemlich ceremoniell und kalt," says Baum, *op. cit.*, I, 304.

[84] "D. Philippus annis, laboribus, calumniis et sycophantiis multorum ita fractus est ut ex illa consueta hilaritate nihil prorsus in eo sit reliquum." *C. R.*, XLV, 92.

[85] The remonstrance which they bore to the king might have been written by Calvin himself. The faithfulness of the Protestants of France to "the doctrine of the Catholic Church as contained in the books of the Apostles and Prophets and the symbols of the ancient doctors," and the continuity of their principles with those of "Guillaume Paris, Jean Gerson, Wessel, and other savants" of the University of Paris in previous times, are among the claims pressed. *C. R.*, XLV, 100ff. (Is "Guillaume Paris" a mistake for John of Paris?—or for William of Nogaret?)

208

to Henry. Apparently, the embassy bore no fruit. Henry's answer to his "cousins" was that they should cease to trouble him about the matter.[86] When we realize the cordial disapproval among the "Flaccians," or exclusive Lutherans, of any recognition of the Reformed, this incident surely marks a triumph for the liberal or Melanchthonian element. Without professing a complete theological accord, the two churches were for the moment identified in the cause of the persecuted. It was likewise a triumph for the spirit of Calvin, who explained his purpose in first writing his *Institutes* as in part that of interesting Protestants abroad on behalf of those who were suffering in France.[87]

If the Reformed had been of one mind with Beza and Calvin, further progress might have been made. But Bullinger remained opposed to all negotiation, and in this he was supported by the German Swiss in general. They wanted no Augsburg Confession and no conference to interpret its one disputed article.[88] In vain did Calvin at the outset invite Bullinger to Geneva to talk over the project (March 30, 1557), moderately stating his hopes of a conference.[89] Bullinger was determined not to co-operate; he professed suspicion of the good faith of all who wished to confer, even of Calvin himself, whom he likened to Bucer

[86] Doumergue, *op. cit.*, VI, 535.

[87] *C. R.*, LIX, 22.

[88] Bullinger, says Doumergue, was "obstinément enfermé dans son sentiment: l'horreur du Colloque. Ni colloque ni Confession de foi d'Augsburg." Bullinger's correspondence shows that he is thinking of Westphal as the interpreter of the Augsburg Confession. *Op. cit.*, VI, 540. Calvin, it should be noted, always thought of Melanchthon, the author of the confession, as its rightful Lutheran interpreter. See above, p. 202.

[89] *C. R.*, XLIV, 435.

in the policy of disingenuous compromise.[90] Doumergue has treated without extenuation Bullinger's opposition to the obviously more liberal and enlightened
policy of Calvin in this business. Certainly, he must
take his share with Westphal for the shipwreck of the
larger union aims of the Genevans. But it would be
unfair to Bullinger to make no reference to the positive aspect of his own utterances on the subject of
union. In a letter to Beza of December 15, 1557, he
and his Zurich colleagues make the claim that they
too are in quest of "a holy concord with those who confess Christ with us, whether Saxons or Suevi," but it
must be a "concord that is religious, moderate, con-
flicting in nothing with the pure truth hitherto professed, introducing no obscurity," and free from all
that will occasion "fresh dissensions." Briefly the
viewpoint of the writer was that since dissension had
resulted from Bucer's attempts at a conciliatory
formula, nothing but dissension would follow renewed
attempts of the kind. While "nothing is more desirable or happy than peace and concord among
brethren," the end is not to be reached by the means
proposed.[91] Probably we are justified in the opinion
that Bullinger was not in this matter a mere obstruc-
tionist. The *First Helvetic Confession*, largely his
work, is strongly marked by concern for a catholic
Protestantism. His loyalty to that confession, later
than and in many respects superior to the Augustana,
is indeed pardonable. If the proposal had come to
him to discuss the two confessions on equal terms,

[90] So Calvin informed Farel in a letter of September 24, 1557. *Ibid.*,
639.

[91] This long letter is given in full by Baum, *op. cit.*, I, 503ff. Cf.
Baird, H. M., *op. cit.*, pp. 93f.

his refusal would have been more inexcusable than in the circumstances it was. The only document considered as a basis of discussion was the Lutheran symbol; in other words, the Helvetic statement was to be scrapped at the outset. Nevertheless, it is very doubtful if more equitable terms would have enlisted Bullinger's co-operation. His refusal to enter into any discussion even with Calvin reveals an obsession of distrust unworthy of a great leader.

In contrast to Bullinger's "horreur du colloque," Beza was an exponent of the synod and conference method of managing church affairs. In a letter to Bullinger of this period he emphasizes the function of synods in the history of the church.[92] With the (medieval) ruin of synods the whole fabric of the church has fallen, and there is no better remedy for its restoration than to revive them. In the past synods and conferences may sometimes have been disappointing. But they have not been wholly futile, and even if they had been so that should not discourage further attempts. Does anyone argue that the Reformers should cease to write because their books so often fail of their objects? Doumergue sees in this the Calvinist mentality that was about to produce the synodical system of the French Reformed Church.[93] To put the interpretation a little differently we may say that Beza was a convinced Conciliarist.

Calvin, Farel, and Beza continued to advocate a convention to discuss union, and took every occasion to promote the project. Beza made a fourth journey

---

[92] September, 1557. *C. R.*, XLIV, 615.
[93] *Op. cit.*, VI, 552.

to Germany in 1559. The project was favored by other outstanding reforming leaders, such as Viret and the political philosopher Hotman, and by the city of Strassburg, where Hotman was then residing. But the Flaccians in Germany and the German Swiss under Bullinger's leadership, in their mutual antipathies, became allies in preventing the fruition of the scheme.

6. Later Efforts of Calvin, Beza, and Salvard

At this period Calvin repeatedly besought Melanchthon to take action on behalf of peace and union. In a letter of August 3, 1557, he suggests a conference to be held at Strassburg, Tübingen, Heidelberg, or Frankfort, on invitation of the princes, whom Melanchthon is to persuade. Even if the princes refuse, the idea ought not to be abandoned. A gathering of pious, upright (*integris*) and moderate men must be brought about. If he is himself regarded as of this class, no necessity whatever will prevent his attendance.[94] After Melanchthon's death Calvin mourned for him with fraternal feeling and cherished the memory of their former intimacy, as is shown in a singularly self-revealing and emotional passage written in 1561: "O Philip Melanchthon! it is upon thee that I call. . . . A hundred times, worn out with labors and depressed with anxieties thou didst lay thy head familiarly upon my breast, and say 'Would that I might die upon this bosom!' And I a thousand times since then have earnestly desired that it should be granted us to be together. Certainly, thou wouldst have been more valiant to face danger and stronger

---

[94] *C. R.*, XLIV, 558.

to despise hatred. . . . Thus the wickedness of many would have been restrained."[95]

Near the end of 1560 Calvin tried to renew the union project and sent a memorandum to the Reformed Churches of France, then newly organized on a national basis and since Henry II's death filled with hope of liberty. He now proposed the assembling of "a free and universal council to put an end to the divisions of Christendom." Such a council must be thoroughly representative. It would determine matters of doctrine, "ceremonies," and church government. In order that it should effect the reunion of Christendom (*afin que toute la chrestiente soit reunie*), the participants in it must be prepared to abide by its decisions or be cast off as schismatics from the general body.[96] It does not appear that Calvin expected or would have tolerated any scheme of reunion with an unrepentant papacy. Yet he countenanced the Colloquy of Poissy in 1561, and stated his willingness to attend it.[97]

It was the desire of Archbishop Parker, as indicated by him in a letter to Cecil, that "Mr. Martyr, Mr. Calvin, or both" should attend the Colloquy, because they were men "able to stand in defense of a truth." In the same year Calvin, as Strype informs us, wrote to Parker, renewing the proposals that had

[95] *Dulcida Explicatio ad Discutiendas Heshusii Nebulas. C. R.,* XXXVII, 461-62.

[96] *Memoire sur le concile. C. R.,* XLVI, 285f. At this period Admiral Coligny repeatedly advocated a "free and holy council," either general or national (March and August, 1560), Baird, H. M., *Rise of the Huguenots,* I, 384, 420.

[97] That Calvin did not attend was due to the fears of his French friends for his safety, and the refusal of the Romanists to meet him in conference. Baird, *op. cit.,* I, 494; *Bulletin de la société de l'histoire du protestantisme français,* XVI (1867), 602ff.

been entertained between him and Cranmer in King Edward's reign, and suggesting "a general assembly of all the Protestant clergy wherever dispersed," with the object of forming a general communion to include "all the Reformed and Evangelic churches." Parker took the project to the royal Council, who instructed him to reply that they liked his proposals, but to stipulate the retention of Episcopacy in the English church, since it had been bestowed on England not by the Pope, but by Joseph of Arimathæa. Parker continued to entertain the suggestion favorably, but found no opportunity of action on it until Calvin's death occasioned its indefinite postponement.[98]

Beza and his associates after the death of Calvin continued to seek union, and set on foot a movement to secure a common confession for all the Protestant churches. Lutheranism was now engaged in the Crypto-Calvinist controversy, and was soon, in the *Formula of Concord*, to repudiate all Calvinist elements. The Reformed still sought to maintain communion with the Lutherans. In this period Ambrose Wolf (Christoph Hardesianus), a Palatine Calvinist, wrote his irenical *Orthodox Consensus of the Holy Scriptures and the Ancient Church*, and his *Acta Concordiae*. The latter work reviews the history of the eucharistic controversy, and especially the correspondence and negotiations of 1537, with the aim of showing that Luther was not unfriendly to the Swiss.[99]

---

[98] Strype, *Life of Mathew Parker*, I, 138ff.; Parker, *Correspondence* (Parker Society), I, 147. The reference to Joseph of Arimathæa is probably an echo of Parker's own antiquarian studies.

[99] *Consensus Orthodoxus Sacrae Scripturae et Veteris Ecclesiae*, 1573; *Acta Concordiae*, 1575.

Beza was concerned in a conference held in 1577 at Frankfort, which was attended by representatives of Queen Elizabeth and of the Reformed churches of Poland and France. This conference agreed to ask the princes to convoke a general Protestant synod.[100] Beza is credited also with participation in the compilation of the first "harmony" of the confessions of the Protestant churches.

This remarkable book was mainly the work of Jean François Sallvard or Salvard (d.1585),[101] but he was assisted in it by Beza and two others. The original Latin edition appeared in Geneva in August, 1581, under the title *Harmonia Confessionum Fidei Orthodoxarum et Reformatarum Ecclesiarum,* etc. It illustrates the chief points of Protestant doctrine from fifteen confessions, including the Augustana. But its most remarkable feature is the "Preface in the name of the churches of France and Belgia," with which it opens. This is an anti-Roman, Protestant irenicum. Regret is expressed that "the state of the times hath not suffered that a general councell of all those that professe the reformed religion, might be

---

[100] Choisy, E., *L'état chrétien calviniste à Genève au temps de Théodore de Bèze,* p. 142.

[101] Salvard was a Geneva minister whose name early passed through such confusing variations as Galluard, Palluard, Gabert, Salvar, Salnar, and Halnar. In 1887 A. Ebrard republished the *Harmony* with an introduction; certain mistakes in this edition called forth a series of critical notes in the *Bulletin,* XXXVI (1887). See the review by "L. D.," p. 387, theno te by P. Félice, "Salvar's Harmonia Confessionum Fidei," p. 443, and especially the article "Jean-François Salvard," by A. Bernus, pp. 498ff.; also a note entitled "Les Salvard," by C. Dardier, pp. 623f. of the volume cited. The English edition of 1586, published without indication of authorship (*An Harmony of the Confessions of the Faith of All Christian and Reformed Churches, which purely professe the holy doctrine of the Gospel in all the chiefe Kingdomes, Nations and Provinces of Europe*), is listed under the name "Salnar" (without Christian name) in the British Museum Catalogue.

holden." A "common councell of the churches well-nigh of all Europe," to frame a common confession, is, however, anticipated. The object of the book is to let all know of the attachment of these churches to "the holie and truelie Catholike church of God," and "to knit all the churches of Christ together with one hand of brotherlie love."[102] The work was warmly approved by the French church in the National synod of Vitre in 1583.[103]

7. Conclusion

Widely divergent views have been expressed of Calvin's advocacy of unification. The Lutheran G. Kawerau approves the remark that Calvin engaged in the conflict with Westphal from "motives of church politics."[104] The Roman Catholic J. M. V. Audin, while in general representing Calvin as a destructive radical, occasionally, and particularly in the matter of union, regards him as an ecclesiastical politician intent upon molding a vast socio-political organization.[105] On the other hand, some admirers of the reformer have held that his plan had nothing to do with organic union.[106] Neither of these theses can be exclusively maintained in the face of his known principles and practice; yet both preserve aspects of the truth. His work and letters on every page proclaim

---

[102] Preface, Engl. ed. of 1586 (pages unnumbered).

[103] Jalla, Jean, "Melanges" in *Bulletin*, L. (1901), p. 487.

[104] *Realencyklopädie*, XXI, 187.

[105] *Histoire de la vie, des ouvrages, et des doctrines de Jean Calvin* (1850), I, v, viii, 360; II, 383.

[106] See, for example, P. Vollmer, *John Calvin, Preacher, Educator, Statesman* (1909). This writer states (p. 145): "The close connection between church and state in all Protestant countries excluded all ideas of organic or absorptive union." Calvin, he thinks, was far from proposing any governmental unification.

him a man of religion; he cared for political affairs only as they related themselves to religion. On the other hand, he had a deep concern for church government that must have asserted itself in the development of any plan of union. G. Reichel concludes that the motive inspiring Calvin's union activity was his love of the church,[107] and quotes in that connection his letter to Dryander of May 18, 1547.[108] This motive stands out so clearly in all the reformer's work, that the judgment is beyond question sound.

The idea of a catholic unity dominated the church theory of Calvin. Practically too he exhibited an ecumenical outlook and combined with a strict conception of doctrine a surprising degree of ecclesiastical liberalism. Hence he not only tolerated, but commended the office of archbishop for Poland,[109] regretted Hooper's overstrained Puritan scruples about vestments,[110] and repeatedly urged the avoidance of separation even where concessions in opinion constituted the price of unity.[111] In the very midst of the conflict with Westphal, in March, 1554, he besought the English refugees in Wesel not to desert the communion of the Lutheran Church there, since the defects of the Lutheran worship were not such as to occasion a breach of communion.[112] Similar was his advice in the following year to the English at Frankfort, concerning the Book of Common Prayer, in

[107] *Calvin als Unionsmann*, p. 41.

[108] *C. R.*, XLI, 525.

[109] Letter to Sigismund Augustus, December, 1554 (*C. R.*, XLIII, 330).

[110] To Bullinger, March, 1551 (*C. R.*, XLII, 75).

[111] E. g., *Inst.*, IV, i, 12. *C. R.*, XXX, 756; XXXVII, 36.

[112] *C. R.*, XLV, 80. Hollweg, W., "Calvins Beziehungen zu den Rheinländen," in *Calvinstudien*, p. 155.

which he found *multas tolerabiles ineptias*[113]—many stupidities indeed, but they were tolerable. Again in 1557 he wrote to à Lasco to avoid the rigorism that would exclude the Bohemian Brethren from "our communion."[114]

Holl has noted that Calvin's ecumenicity took root in the churches founded under his influence, and resulted in an international bond and an active intercourse between the Calvinist countries. These contacts, he observes, "strengthened the sense of belonging together (*die Empfindung der Zusammengehörigkeit*) and the consciousness of the greatness of the *regnum Christi*." The Calvinist churches, he further points out, have never had a conflict in which national difference played a part. The idea of the universal church, "a religious imponderable of priceless value," was realized in Calvinism without resort to the compulsion employed by Rome. Indeed, in this ecumenicity of Calvin, Calvinist toleration was rooted. Calvin himself did not shrink from the word "syncretism."[115] From this attitude of Calvin there developed, according to Holl, an interconfessional toleration. Significant too in this connection he finds Calvin's irenical admission that some of the elect are in the Roman Church.[116] What was it that Calvin and his associates were seeking in these efforts? Troeltsch has acutely remarked: "Following the example of Geneva itself, the center of the strictest doctrinal

---

[113] *C. R.*, XLV, 394.

[114] *C.R.*, XLVI, 674ff. Cf. Reichel, *op. cit.*, p. 35.

[115] Quid? an non hostis quoque ipse diabolus occulos nobis ad syncretismum agendum admovere debet? *C. R.*, XXXIII, 321. Holl notes also Bucer's use of the term. Enders, *Briefwechsel Luthers*, II, 301.

[116] Holl, K., *Gesammelte Aufsätze*, III, 274-5.

unity and discipline, Calvin thought he could, by arranging all peripheric peculiarities, weld the various countries and churches into the great body of General Protestantism."[117]

Calvin approached the task in a religious spirit and sought to build a Europe-wide religious communion; but his success would probably have involved the erection of a somewhat elastic and locally adapted general church polity and, where possible, the employment of the secular power in the service of the church. To this policy Calvin's view of the function of the state committed him. For him the state is to be maintained "in order that a public form of religion may exist among Christians, and humanity be established among men."[118] It would be difficult or impossible to distinguish Calvin's opinions and aims on any of these points from those of his chief associates whose co-operation with him in the cause of church unity has here been reviewed.

Calvin played for high stakes. Had his ardent hopes been fulfilled, Protestantism would have taken the outlines of a church ecumenical and conciliar, in which the unity which was once attained on the monarchical principle of government at the cost of no little repression, under the papacy, would have been succeeded by a general communion under the government of a representative body expressive of the voluntary cohesion of the states, cities, and groups participating. Once established, this Protestant conciliar church of Europe might have chosen to employ

---

[117] "Calvin and Calvinism," *Hibbert Journal*, VIII (1909), 102.

[118] "Ut inter Christianos publica religionis facies exsistat, inter homines constet humanitas" (*Inst.*, IV, xx, 3. *C. R.*, XXX, 1094).

the weapon of political coercion and thus have brought upon itself reproach, embarrassment, or ruin. On the other hand, if the resulting system had proved true to Calvin's idea of the communion of saints, it would have given expression on a grand scale to Christian fraternity, catholicity, and democracy, reversed the process of dissolution in the church, exhibited to the distracted states of Europe an impressive pattern of spontaneous unity, and rendered the last four centuries of Western history incomparably richer and happier than they have been.

CHAPTER VI

CRANMER'S PROJECT FOR A REFORMED CONSENSUS

1. CRANMER'S PLACE IN THE REFORMATION

CRANMER stands in history as the most typical and influential, if not the most admired, of Tudor churchmen. The story of his public career is to a great degree the story of the English Reformation; and the ideas and principles which find expression in his words and acts are essentially those which underlie Tudor Anglicanism as a whole. While his admirers of later days have been mainly of the low-church party, his influence has been strongly felt by high churchmen who have repudiated his leadership. The fact that Laud was numbered among the Erastians is not unconnected with Cranmer's awe of kings; nor is it fantastic to suppose that Pusey's *Eirenicon* was rendered possible by the ecumenical range of Cranmer's churchmanship and his insistence upon the note of catholicity.

On one side of his nature Cranmer was a Hamlet for whom the native hue of resolution was sicklied o'er by the pale cast of thought. Amid pressing crises he could pause to appreciate variant opinions, with results that disqualified him for that aggressive leadership possible only to prompt natures like those of Luther, Calvin, and Knox. An element of hesitancy and indecision, quite distinct from both timidity and prudence, entered into all his actions—a feature prophetic of the temper and policies of his church in later

times. Cranmer's lack of driving power, his relative
unconcern for the triumph of his own views and plans,
exposed him to that reverse of events in which he obtained the higher success of martyrdom. It was not
Wittenberg or Geneva or Edinburgh, where downright
policies were pursued, that saw a great reformer per-
ish in the flames, but English Oxford, in the land of
illogic and compromise. Or should we rather say,
the land in which men are more intent on playing the
game than on winning it? The Israel of which he
was the Moses has like him exhibited more moderation than zeal, more breadth of view than depth of
conviction, and has often been content with tempor-
izing measures. But there is a kind of greatness in
the spirit of the Anglican communion of which these
qualities are the natural accompaniment and, we
might say, the condition. Its catholicity, comprehensiveness, and variety of spontaneous religious
expression have been made possible by the very
elasticity and indeterminatencss which are found exemplified in the psychology of its chief reformer.

But while too deliberative for a man of affairs, Cranmer, on the other hand, was not lacking in natural
vigor. He was unique among the major Reformers
in the possession of a robust physique, and was accustomed from youth "to ride rough horses; so that
when he was bishop he feared not to ride the rough-
est horses that came into his stables, which he would
do very comely."[1] There is more than a dash of the
knight-errant in the composition of his character.

[1] Strype, *Memorials of Thomas Cranmer* (London, 1853), I, 2. The
reader familiar with Tudor literature will recall a famous sentence of
Sir Thomas Eliot: "The most honorable exercise in mine opinion . . .
is to ride surely and clene on a great horse and a roughe" (*The Book
Called the Governour* [1531], I, xvii.)

His assault upon Roman teaching is as vigorous, if not so violent, as Luther's; and he fearlessly maintained his ground until temporarily overcome by the mental torture of his imprisonment and the conflict of loyalties between truth and his queen. He had, moreover, a mind extraordinarily fertile of fresh projects. Not even the responsibilities of office sapped his genius of this quality. From his proposal to Henry that the universities be consulted on the annulment of the royal marriage to the revision of the canon law and the project of a Protestant consensus, Cranmer was habitually surprising his contemporaries with constructive suggestions of real significance.

The relations of Cranmer with the persons and groups of the Continental Reformation have never been adequately investigated, but his attitudes in general to the reforming parties are not in doubt. Cranmer was six years younger than Luther and twenty years older than Calvin. His awakening came with the reading of Erasmus and Lefèvre, which he began in 1511, when he was twenty-two. During the next dozen years he was a diligent student of Scripture and theology, "seldom reading without pen in hand," and keeping copious notes which were to serve him well in later days. Luther's books began to be read in England in 1520, and Cranmer was in touch with the Cambridge group among whom they were most influential. Toward Lutheranism his attitude was, however, that of an independent inquirer. "Considering what great controversy was in matters of religion . . . he bent himself to try out the truth herein."[2] By 1525 he began praying that the Pope's

---

[2] Strype, loc. cit.

power might be abolished in England;[3] and when the royal marriage issue arose he denied the Pope's dispensing power, and hence the validity of the marriage of Henry and Katherine. His prominence in the king's matrimonial business led to his promotion to the dangerous and uncoveted post of Archbishop of Canterbury on the eve of Henry's most decisive acts affecting the church.

In 1532, during his visit to Germany in Henry's cause, his relations with Lutheranism became more intimate. At Nürnberg he had conferences with John Frederick, Elector of Saxony, and spent much time in the home and company of the reformer Andrew Osiander. The egotism of Osiander repelled the fine-mannered Calvin and the sensitive Melanchthon; Cranmer, on the other hand, formed with him a lasting friendship, took the Nürnberg reformer's niece as his second wife, and maintained occasional correspondence with him for twenty years thereafter.[4] It has been suggested by Jacobs that the preparation at this time by Brentz, Osiander, and others of the Brandenburg-Nürnberg *Kirchenordnung* directed Cranmer's attention to the need of a common order of worship.[5] It was apparently in this period too that he first made the valuable acquaintance of Bucer, who was to become the mutual friend, as Osiander was the common opponent, of Melanchthon and Calvin.

The negotiations of 1535–39 between the Lutheran and the English theologians brought Cranmer again into intimate contact with the Germans. There is

---

[3] Smyth, C. H., *Cranmer and the Reformation under Edward VI*, p. 32.
[4] Strype, *op. cit.*, I, 15.
[5] Jacobs, H. E., *The Lutheran Movement in England*, p. 48.

nothing to show, however, that he played a decisive part in these negotiations. His plea for decent housing for the German delegates in London in 1538 indicates his good will toward them and his distress at the discourtesy by which Henry shabbily indicated his intention to make of the whole incident nothing more than a by-play of his opportunist foreign policy. It would seem that he approved the formula reached by the theologians. Even if, as seems probable, he at that time retained much of the Roman doctrine of the sacrament, he might, like the Romanist delegates at Regensburg in 1541, have admitted the undoubtedly Lutheran phraseology of this formula in a sense different from that in which it was understood by the Lutherans.[6]

2. Aspects of His Doctrinal and Ecclesiastical Outlook

Certain aspects of Cranmer's doctrinal position and ecclesiastical outlook deserve brief notice at the outset on account of their relation to his interest in the consensus project. In the first place, about eight years after the Lutheran-English negotiations he was led to a view of the sacrament virtually identical with the reformed interpretation. It is the contention of Mr. C. H. Smyth's recent volume on Cranmer that he is to be credited with an intellectual consistency that has hitherto in general been denied him. Smyth stoutly maintains that in his view of the Lord's Supper Cranmer was never either a Lutheran or a Zwinglian.

---

[6] For a short account of these negotiations see above, p. 168ff. The confession prepared by the theologians is contained in the Parker Society *Remains and Letters of Cranmer*, pp. 472f. (App. XIII, "A Book Containing Divers Articles *de unitate Dei*," etc.).

Instead he held, after he had discarded transubstantiation, the residue of the Roman doctrine of the real presence till 1546, when he moved to an opinion identical with that which Bucer had earlier reached by another path. In respect to his view of the sacrament, Cranmer owed his conversion to Ridley, who had arrived at the same position through a study of Ratramnus.[7]

While the ambiguities and inconsistencies of this ninth-century monk of Corbie made it possible for both the principal sixteenth-century parties to claim him, his position gave peculiar encouragement to those reformers who favored the view which came to be known as the Reformed, in distinction from the Lutheran. He was indeed one of the few medieval authors in whom they could find aid and comfort. It helped to establish their own catholicity that they could claim as a comrade one who had run the gantlet of discussion and inquisition for seven centuries and survived uncondemned. The English reformers made frequent use of his teaching on the Eucharist, the principal elements of which were identical with those which made up the doctrine of Zwingli, of Bucer, and of Calvin. Foxe notes the decisive influence of "Bertram"[8] upon Ridley, and the latter's conferences with Cranmer over the treatise of the monk.[9] Foxe here

---

[7] *Op. cit.*, pp. 50f.

[8] From the twelfth century Ratramnus was occasionally called Bertram, and he was constantly referred to under this name in the sixteenth century. Naegle, A. *Ratramnus und die heilige Eucharistie* (Wien, 1903), pp. 4f.

[9] *Acts and Monuments* (ed. Townshend), VII, 409. At his trial Ridley advised the commissioner, Doctor Brooks, to read Bertram. *Ibid.*, p. 544. The *De Corpore et Sanguine Domini* of Ratramnus had been published by Johannes Prael at Cologne in 1532 with the doubly erroneous ascription: *Bertrami presbyteri ad Carolum Magnum Impera-*

suggests that Cranmer had anticipated Ridley in the new opinion; but Cranmer himself, and his intimate acquaintance, Sir John Cheke, both make it clear that the reverse is true.[10] Cranmer's own references to Ratramnus are expressions of warm approval.[11]

But Cranmer also repeatedly asserts his own agreement with Bucer, as well as with Peter Martyr and the Swiss. Gardiner had employed against him Bucer's similitude of the sun and the sunbeams. Cranmer convincingly shows this to be in accord with his own

---

torem. Leo Jud, that distinguished translator as well as prominent reformer of Zurich, at once produced a German version to which Bullinger contributed an introduction. Numerous editions and translations followed. An English version by William Hugh appeared in 1548: *The Book of Bertram the Priest concerning the Body and Blood of Christ in the Sacrament.* Although favorably mentioned by Trithemius (*Catalogus scriptorum ecclesiasticorum,* 1494), by John Fisher, bishop of Rochester, against Ecolampadius (1527), and by Richard Smith in defense of the mass (1546), the work was in 1559 put on the Index on the supposition that it was a Protestant forgery. Migne, *Patrol. Lat.,* CXXI, cols. 104ff.; *Realencyklopädie* (3d ed.), XVI., 467; Harnack, *History of Dogma,* V, 381f.; Parker Society, *Works of Bishop Ridley,* p. 159, footnote 3; p. 206; Naegle, *op. cit.,* pp. 84f.

[10] The date of Cranmer's conversion by Ridley, as stated by Cheke, was 1546. Parker Society, *Miscellaneous Writings and Letters,* p. 218, footnote 5. Smyth assumes, with probability, that Cheke was the editor of the Latin edition of Cranmer's *Defence, op. cit.,* p. 60.

[11] In reply to Gardiner, who had referred to Bertram in a list of those who had previously taught an erroneous doctrine of the Eucharist and had failed of acceptance, Cranmer responds: "And as for Bertram he did nothing else but, at the request of King Charles, set out the true doctrine of the holy catholic church, from Christ unto his time, concerning the sacrament." *Answer to a Sophistical Cavillation, etc.* (1550). Parker Society, *Writings and Disputations of Thomas Cranmer,* p. 14; Cf. 13, 172, 196. Against Richard Smith, who, unfortunately for his cause, had approved Ratramnus, Cranmer quotes a sample of "Bertram's doctrine" to show that it is in full agreement with his own (*ibid.,* p. 78). Cranmer found in it that insistence upon the spiritual and memorial aspects which he now strongly favored. Cf. the concluding chapters of the treatise in Migne, *P. L.* CXXI, 170, especially the phrases "*in figuram sive memoriam,*" "*spiritualis est esca et spiritualis potus,*" and the citation of John 6. 64, similarly used by Zwingli and Ecolampadius at Marburg, 1529. Köhler, W., *Das marburger Religionsgespräch 1529: Versuch einer Rekonstruktion,* pp. 65ff.; Kidd, B. J. *Documents of the Continental Reformation,* No. 109, p. 248.

teaching.[12]   In another passage he remarks: "In the place by you alleged he [Bucer] dissenteth in nothing from Ecolampadius and Zwinglius."[13]   As Gardiner had labored to show evidences of discord among the opponents of Rome, Cranmer constantly suggests their essential concord—a concord which he was already seeking to bring to formal expression.   This attitude extends to the Lutherans as well as to Bucer and the Swiss.   He was anxious to maintain an open road between Wittenberg and Canterbury.[14]   Yet he was in closer accord with the Reformed; and when he wrote his *Defensio Verae et Catholicae Doctrinae de Sacramentis* (1550), this accord was complete.[15]   Smyth can hardly be confuted when he says that Cranmer never was a Lutheran.   The statement that he never was a Zwinglian is apparently based on a misconception of Zwinglianism.[16]

[12] *Writings and Disputations*, 19, 90.   Bucer has not, he notes, taught the error that the substance of the sun is here present on the earth, to which his opponent's doctrine would be analogous.

[13] *Ibid.*, p. 78.

[14] *Writings and Disputations*, pp. 20f.; pp. 179f.

[15] See especially lib. III, cap. xi, *op. cit.*, pp. 58f.

[16] Cranmer's doctrine differed from that of Luther, as did that of Bucer and Calvin.   Smyth thinks (66) he finds a variation from the doctrine of Bucer; but Cranmer himself explicitly denies the variation alleged by Smyth, *Writings and Disputations*, p. 225.   The phrases in which Smyth also finds (p. 70) "a vigorous repudiation of Zwinglianism" are no less Zwinglian than the fifteenth article signed by Zwingli at Marburg or the eighth chapter of Zwingli's *Fidei Ratio* presented to Charles V at Augsburg.   The error here is shared by many writers. It is that of beginning with the assumption that Bucer and Zwingli were representatives of two irreconcilable types of Reformed doctrine. Smyth ignores the common influence upon them of Cornelius Henrix Hoen and Hinne Rode, disciples of Wessel Gansfort, an influence that was determinative for both.   Wessel was largely in agreement with Ratramnus and Wyclif, although apparently independent of both. Hoen and Rode developed Wessel's interpretation and gave Zwingli his *"est=significat"* argument.   Both Bucer and Zwingli held much more than what is suggested by that argument alone.   The difference between them, like that between Calvin and Bullinger, was a matter of

A second point of importance to note in approaching a consideration of Cranmer's project is that in his view of the Catholic Church he was a Conciliarist. This statement calls for a brief exposition. Intensely English though he was, Cranmer had no thought of severing the English from the universal church. It is true that his Erastianism limited his conciliarism; but both principles were employed in his resistance to the papal claims. Burnet's summary of a since lost manuscript of a long speech made by Cranmer after the legislation of November-December, 1534, on the subject of church councils, is of interest here.[17] It should be remembered that at this period, as Cranmer was aware, Paul III had just come to the papal throne pledged to call a general council. It is not surprising, then, that Cranmer, supporting the cause of the new "Supreme Head of the Church of England," should seek to guard against any recognition of the authority of a council held under the Pope's control. On the one hand he cites Gerson's *De auferibilitate Papae*, and the decrees of Constance, on the superiority of the council to the Pope; while on the other he affirms that "the power of councils does not extend to princes. . . . The standard of the council's definition should be only taken from the Scriptures, and not from men's tradition."

In 1536 Cranmer signed, and probably framed,

---

emphasis, not of substance. In Cranmer's view these reformers were in essential agreement. Hyma remarks that "Rode was more of a 'Calvinist' in 1520 than Calvin was in 1535 before he met Bucer." Hyma, A., *The Christian Renaissance*, pp. 218f. For the literature consulted see above, p. 137, Note 5. Cf. Deane, A. C., *Thomas Cranmer, Archbishop of Canterbury*, pp. 167f.

[17] Burnet, *History of the Reformation* (ed. Pocock), I, 285f.; *Miscellaneous Writings and Letters*, pp. 76f.

the Judgment of Convocation concerning General Councils. This official document of Convocation emphatically approves general councils, when properly representative, in the following terms:

As concerning general councils, like as all (taught by long experience) so perfectly know, there never was, ne is, any thing devised, invented, nor instituted by our forefathers more expedient, or more necessary to the establishment of our faith, for the extirpation of heresies and the abolishing of sects and schisms, and finally for the reducing of Christ's people unto one perfect unity and concord in his religion, than by the having of general councils, so that the same be lawfully had, and congregated in *Spiritu Sancto*, and be also conform and agreeable, as well concerning the surety and indifferency of the places, as all other points requisite and necessary to the same unto that wholesome and godly institution and usage for which they were at first devised and used in the primitive church.

Christian princes, he continues, should provide that they be not perverted to wicked ends; considering (1) "who hath authority to call a general council"; (2) whether the causes alleged for a council are adequate; (3) who ought to be the judges in a council; (4) the order of procedure in the council; and (5) "what doctrines are to be allowed or defended." No general council should be called by the Pope or any one prince without the express consent of "the residue of Christian princes."[18]

This is obviously designed to exclude both a merely papal and a merely imperial council, or one called by agreement only of the emperor and the Pope. About the same time, presumably in reference to the proposed council at Mantua, Cranmer, with twelve

[18] Burnet, *op. cit.*, I, 284f.; *Miscellaneous Writings and Letters*, pp. 463f.

other bishops and clergy, signed an "Opinion" in which
it is explained that conditions are changed, since the
Roman emperors, by virtue of their general rule,
authoritatively called councils of the whole church:

"Yet now, forasmuch that the Empire of Rome and the
monarchy of the same hath no such general dominion,
but many princes have absolute power in their own realms,
and an whole and entire monarchy, no one prince may by
his authority call any general council."

One prince may propose it, but it is to be assembled
on the free consent of all.[19]

In the course of Cranmer's trial, and on the occasion
of his degradation in February, 1556, he presented a
carefully worded appeal from the authority of the
Pope to that of "a free general council." He here
asserts that: "it is openly enough confessed, that a
holy general council, lawfully gathered together in
the Holy Ghost, and representing the holy Catholic
Church, is above the Pope, especially in matters concerning faith; that he cannot make decrees that men
shall not appeal from him to a general council. . . ."
and states in the essential clause: "Therefore I do
challenge and appeal in these writings from the Pope
. . . as well for myself as for every one that cleaveth
to me or will hereafter be on my side, unto a free
general council, that shall hereafter lawful be, and
in a sure place, to which place I or a proctor, deputed
by me, may freely and with safety come."[20]

---

[19] *Miscellaneous Writings and Letters*, p. 467. Cf. the "Protestation
of the King, Council, and Clergy, 1537, against the Council of Mantua," quoted by Jenkyns, *Remains of Thomas Cranmer*, I, x, footnote u.

[20] Jenkyns, H. *Remains of Thomas Cranmer*, IV, 121f.; *Miscellaneous Writings and Letters*, pp. 224f.; Foxe, *Acts and Monuments*, VIII
73. Jenkyns remarks (p. 121) that Cranmer probably received help
from a lawyer in drawing up this appeal.

In all these utterances Cranmer was a typical Conciliarist. For him the General Council was not infallible: but within the limits set by the standards of Scripture and the inalienable rights of temporal sovereigns, it was authoritative. Since for him the Roman papacy had deserted the true church, and that church was now to be sought in the still uncemented sections of Protestantism, he would seek to secure the assembling of a conference of Protestant leaders who would prepare a basis of union for the groups they represented and thus effect the consolidation of Protestantism.

3. HIS PROJECT FOR A CONFERENCE, 1547-50

At what date the consensus idea emerged as a distinct plan in Cranmer's mind it is impossible to say. Its genesis may have owed something to Melanchthon, who in 1535, just when he was regretfully declining the invitations of Francis I and Henry VIII to undertake unification missions to their respective kingdoms,[21] wrote a laudatory letter to Cranmer in which he remarked that if there were bishops like him elsewhere, there would be no difficulty in establishing general concord and reform.[22] Melanchthon had already begun to exhibit that inclination toward the Reformed teaching on the sacrament which was later to cost him the loss of much Lutheran support.[23] Whether it was these words of Melanchthon's that led Cranmer to realize the possibilities of his position for instituting a unification conference or not, it was

[21] See above, p.

[22] "*Non difficulter et concordia orbis terrarum constitui et sanari ecclesia posset.*" *Corpus Reformatorum*, II, 93.

[23] J. W. Richard indicates Melanchthon's response to a work of Ecolampadius (1530), which convinced him that many ancient fathers held the figurative interpretation. *Philip Melanchthon*, pp. 242f.

apparently to Melanchthon that he first turned for foreign co-operation in the project. More than twelve years had since passed. The English-Lutheran negotiations had broken down. The Council of Trent had held its first series of sessions. Luther had died, and the first Schmalkald War had left the German Protestants in a weak and distressful state. The death of Henry VIII and the succession of Edward VI, at the end of January, 1547, had given Cranmer once more his freedom of action as archbishop. Within the first eight months of Edward's reign Cranmer began to prepare the way for his consensus project. It appears from the correspondence of à Lasco that both he and Melanchthon were invited to England before October 11, 1547. On that date à Lasco wrote from Emden to Albert Hardenberg of Bremen that he was sending a messenger with a letter to Melanchthon "in regard to the call to England."[24] On October 26 Melanchthon, in a letter to Nicholas Medler, noted the receipt of letters by which he was called into England.[25] This is our first intimation that Melanchthon had become informed of the proposal. It was not, apparently, till January, 1548, that he wrote Cranmer in reply. This letter, hastily written while messengers waited, consists of vague commendations of the proposal. He himself had "always desired that a summary of necessary doctrine should be publicly set forth." He warns against ambiguities that would

---

[24] *"Nuntium mittimus Witebergam ad Philippum aut ubi is sit, scribimusque ad illum de vocatione in Angliam de qua hodie ad te scripsi."* Kuyper, *Johannis à Lasco Opera*, II, 61; Jenkyns, *Remains of Thomas Cranmer*, I, 329. It is barely possible that à Lasco does not mean to suggest that Melanchthon shares the invitation.

[25] *"Hic tabellarius literas mihi attulit, quibus in Angliam vocor."* C. R., VI, 715.

prove occasions of dispute to posterity.[26] On January 20, in a letter to Camerarius, he alludes to the offers of hospitality which he has received from Denmark and England; he prefers to remain where he is.[27] On May 1, possibly in response to a further communication, he wrote more at length to Cranmer, but was still disappointingly indefinite as to his own participation. Once more he emphasizes the importance of reaching unambiguous terms in the proposed consensus. The confession to be drawn up will, he expects, not differ greatly from the *Augustana;* but some additional articles should be included for the sake of clearness.

"In the church it is better to call a spade a spade than to cast ambiguous utterances before posterity as the apple of discord is said in fables to have been offered to the goddesses seated at the feast." In one sentence he seems to hope to be present: "I will gladly listen to other learned men and declare my opinion in turn, . . . as is fitting in a conference of pious men."[28]

But he says nothing of the prospect of the journey, and gives no indication of a definite decision to go.

Cranmer pressed the invitation, writing at least four letters in series to Melanchthon, and seeking to influence him also through mutual friends. On July 4, 1548, he wrote to à Lasco: "I am now sending a third letter to Melanchthon, in which I exhort him to come to us." He had already at least once invited à Lasco

---

[26] "Ne reliqui posteris ambiguitates tanquam μῆλον ἔριδος." *C. R.,* VI, 801.

[27] Since the word "principes" in the text is doubtful, the passage may or may not mean that Cranmer's invitation has been followed by one in the king's name. *C. R.,* VI, 790-91.

[28] *Ibid.,* col. 894.

himself, and the latter had indicated his intention to come, but had been prevented through some unexpected business. He now urges à Lasco to come and to direct all his care and planning to the one end of securing Melanchthon's presence.[29] À Lasco himself did his utmost to further Cranmer's wish. What we may suppose to have been the second of Cranmer's letters to Melanchthon over the matter had been sent in care of à Lasco, who intrusted it to Aepinus for delivery. À Lasco now wrote Hardenberg on July 28 asking him to inquire of Melanchthon whether he had received this letter, and to request a reply. On August 4 à Lasco received Cranmer's letter of July 4, and understood from it that no reply had come from Melanchthon. He immediately wrote to Melanchthon, expressing doubt about the delivery of the former letter, inclosing a copy of Cranmer's letter to himself, and laying the matter upon Melanchthon's conscience.[30] This letter indicates that the writer had himself written Melanchthon in "April or May," and recalls the fact that he had written Hardenberg, as just noted.[31]

In order to strengthen his plea with Melanchthon, Cranmer seems to have induced a number of leading men to write to him. On May 26, 1548, Melanchthon informed Camerarius, *Ego in Angliam multorum et*

---

[29] "*Ut omnem curam cogitationemque tuam in hoc unice convertas, ut Philippum nostrum plane nostrum facias.*" *Miscellaneous Writings and Letters*, p. 421.

[30] "*Nescio qua conscientia vocationem hanc negligere possis.*"

[31] *C. R.*, II, 92-95; Kuyper, *Johannis à Lasco Opera*, II, 618-19. The Parker Society editor, Doctor Cox (*Miscellaneous Writings and Letters*, p. 421, note 7), mistakenly supposes that the letter of à Lasco to Hardenberg had reference to the *tertia epistola* of Cranmer; the letter of August 4 shows that à Lasco had not learned of the *tertia epistola* when he wrote.

praecipuorum literis vocor. Sed nondum ex Germania discedam. He hopes the English will move wisely in the beginning of so great a change. He has lovingly warned them, he says, to set forth after grave deliberation a pious confession, lest they later become divided into sects.[32] Apparently he was thinking of Cranmer's proposal as primarily an English concern. Two months after this letter Cranmer was seeking the good offices of Hardenberg to persuade Melanchthon. On July 28, 1548, he wrote what is only incidentally an invitation to the Bremen pastor himself and primarily a request to him to join in the appeal to Melanchthon. He explains that he has called to his side "many pious and learned men," some of whom have already arrived: of Melanchthon, however, he has "no certain intelligence." "For which cause we most earnestly entreat of you, if by any means you can accomplish it, that you will endeavor to induce him to take the journey hither." Ample assurances are given of personal safety, of traveling expenses, and of the greatness of the opportunity—one much greater, he observes, than that which drew Melanchthon to Cologne in 1543.[33] There is no indication of Hardenberg's response.

Still unsuccessful, Cranmer wrote a fourth letter to Melanchthon on February 10, 1549. Here he prays God, who has "rescued our Island from the waves" of trouble which churches elsewhere are suffering, that he will gather a perpetual church, not only there, but in other nations. "For many pious and learned men have come over to us, some from Italy and some from

---

[32] *C. R.*, VI, 918.
[33] *Miscellaneous Writings and Letters*, p. 422.

Germany, and we are daily expecting other." Will
not Melanchthon consent to adorn their society with
his presence? "I am well aware," he adds, "that
you have often desired that pious and wise men taking counsel together, and comparing their judgments,
should set forth with the weight of their authority
some work that would embrace the chief matters of
ecclesiastical doctrine, and transmit the truth uncor-
rupted to posterity," and he warns Melanchthon
against inconsistency, and against resisting the manifest calling of God.

The letter was to be delivered in person by à Lasco,
who had resided with the writer on intimate terms
for some months past.[34] About a year later a fresh
invitation was dispatched, receipt of which Melanchthon laconically notes in a letter to Camerarius,
April 15, 1550.[35] There is no specific evidence that
Cranmer was the author of this invitation, though
that is not unlikely.

As for Melanchthon, so far as records show, he met
with silence the whole bombardment of invitation. His
letter to Cranmer of March 1, 1549, is not a reply to
Cranmer's letter of three weeks earlier, and contains
no reference to the proposal. It is clear, of course,
that the correspondence between Cranmer and Melanchthon is not completely preserved. Two, at least,
of Cranmer's letters are lost; and it is possible that
some communication from Melanchthon was sent
between the dubious acceptance of May 1, 1548, and

[34] *Op. cit.*, p. 425. A number of authorities have been searched in
vain for information as to whether à Lasco met Melanchthon during
his Continental visit of this period; I find no record of the delivery of
the letter.

[35] *"Ego rursus in Angliam vocor."* *C. R.*, VII, 573.

the irrelevant but friendly letter of March 1, 1549. Nevertheless, everything goes to show that Melanchthon finally "did not choose" to join the conference in person.

Meanwhile Bucer had also been invited to England. On September 3, 1548, he writes to Cranmer describing the troubles that have fallen upon Strassburg: "Wherefore," he says, "we are daily expecting the termination of our ministry. And as we would prefer to undergo any suffering rather than dwell in the tents of Kedar, how very acceptably does your reverend fatherhood offer yourself to our relief."[36] Cranmer now (October 2) sent Bucer a further urgent and cordial invitation. The letter contains a suggestion, though no clear indication, of the plan for a consensus. "You will not," he assures Bucer, "be of less benefit to the universal church of God while you are with us than if you retain your former position. . . . We will make it manifest that nothing will be more gratifying or delightful to us than the presence of Bucer."[37] Bucer, however, stuck to his now dangerous post for half a year more. On December 23 he thanked Cranmer for having "called us from death to life," but did not indicate a decision.[38] On the following day he wrote Peter Martyr, now at Canterbury, suggesting that the invitation might be extended to three of his colleagues. Of these, Paul Fagius (whose son was already in school at Canterbury) was also invited, and on March 24 Peter Alexander wrote on Cranmer's behalf urging them to

---

[36] *Original Letters*, II, 532.
[37] *Miscellaneous Writings and Letters*, pp. 423f.
[38] *Original Letters*, II, 533.

come at once. They had already been dismissed by the Senate on March 1.[39] They arrived in England some days before April 26, 1549, when they wrote a joint letter to the ministers at Strassburg.[40]

It was apparently due to Melanchthon's nonparticipation that the plan was halted. Cranmer evidently felt that Melanchthon was the key man, without whose co-operation no general consensus could be arrived at. The scholars at his side were men of a different class. For the most part they were men who lacked any Continental influence, or had lost it, and could not speak for imposing groups. Capable and moderate men they might be, but to proceed with them alone would be to present a consensus of exiles, not of representatives. Indeed, Cranmer seems not to have opened any serious discussion of the matter with them. His invitations to Bucer contain no explicit reference to the subject. If he discussed the matter with Bucer while they were together at Lambeth, Bucer's published correspondence does not reflect such conference. Neither Bucer's letters to Calvin in 1549, when he had occasion to refer to the *Consensus Tigurinus*,[41] nor Calvin's letters to him and to Somerset[42] contain any references to the matter. None of the brilliant company of foreign divines in England seems to have been initiated into the plan. The talents of the visitors were employed in teaching, in ministering to foreign congregations in England, and on the English Prayer Book. Yet all effort did

[39] *Ibid.*, p. 538. Cf. Strype, *Memorials of Cranmer*, I, 238; Smyth *op. cit.*, pp. 157f.

[40] *Original Letters*, II, 544.

[41] August 14. *C. R.*, XIV, 350-58.

[42] *C. R.*, XIV, 437; XIII, 64f., 531f.

not cease on account of Melanchthon's lack of response.

4. ACTIVITIES OF THE ROYAL COUNCIL

While between Cranmer and his invited guests the proposal was left in abeyance, the same project, or one very like it, was being canvassed in Switzerland on behalf of the royal Council. Christopher Mount (or Mont), a talented German who had been in Henry VIII's employ on important missions—he had conveyed an invitation to Melanchthon in 1535[43]—was now posted at Strassburg. His letters to the Council at this period[44] are valuable for their information on the moving drama of Continental affairs. On June 13, 1549, he sent the information that Zurich and Bern would not join a Swiss-French league and that they would not fight against the English.[45] On October 20 a letter was dispatched to the Senate of Zurich, in the name of the boy king, cementing good will in these terms: "We cannot but hold you in special affection (*non possumus et nos quoque non vehementer vos amare*), and the more because we have understood from the frequent letters of our faithful and beloved servant, Christopher Mont, both your friendly disposition toward us and ready will to deserve well of us. In addition to which there is a certain mutual agreement (*consensus*) concerning the Christian re-

---

[43] "Mont, Christopher," *Dictionary of National Biography.* "Though he could not induce him to come to England, he induced him to abstain from visiting France." This is, of course, a misleading explanation of Melanchthon's decision, which was taken in obedience to his prince. See above, p. 168.

[44] *Calendar of State Papers, Foreign, 1547–1553; Camden Society,* 2d Series, XXXVII, 110f.

[45] *Calendar of State Papers, 1547–1553,* p. 38.

ligion and true piety, which ought to render this our friendship the closer."[46]

A similar letter was sent to Bern, as is evident from the reply of the Bernese Council to King Edward on December 14. From this letter it appears that Mount had conveyed the king's letter in person. Whether from Mount's conversation or from the letter which he conveyed to the Bernese, the latter had become aware that a "council" was projected. "With respect to a future council," they state their determination to continue in their own religious settlement of 1528; they will not, however, refuse to participate in a "general or national council" if it is held in the spirit of the Lord, its members given safe conduct, and the Scriptures taken as the standard.[47] Dixon, without explanation, connects the activities of Mount in Switzerland with Cranmer's project.[48] The suggestion is supported by the apparent identity of the plan with his own.

With these diplomatic approaches we cannot leave unmentioned the proposal submitted by Doctor Bruno, a Lutheran in the pay of the Council, and indorsed by Cecil in October, 1550. The *Discursus D. Brunonis* was printed by Dixon, in all its "brutal Latinity," as a footnote. It crowds the text out of four pages of his *History*.[49] It is framed in anticipation of a renewal of the Council of Trent. It contains an extended list of most serene kings, German princes, counts and cities, and Swiss Evangelical cantons favorable to the

---

[46] *Epistolae Tigurinae*, p. 1.
[47] *Original Letters*, II, 718.
[48] *History of the Church of England*, III, 98.
[49] *Op. cit.*, III, 345f.

Protestant cause, and advocates joint action of them all in sending "some of our bishops" with Bucer, Melanchthon, Brentz, and other leading theologians to the forthcoming meeting of the Council. If they effect nothing at the Council, it will be necessary to form a "defensive league" of the Protestant powers. Some negotiations had taken place, in which an unnamed "messenger from the princes of Germany," possibly Bruno himself, had informed Cecil that the princes consulted "desire and propose a mutual conjunction with the King's Majesty, who is raised up by God for the beautifying of the Church of Christ." They further suggest that in case war is declared against either themselves or England the alliance is to be so dissembled as to appear other than religious, while between themselves it is to be understood that they are "one body in Christ." This ambitious but unethical scheme did not get beyond the sanction of Cecil.[50] The Bruno proposal, at least in the advice of the "messenger," recommends à Lasco as special counselor of the government, but bears no evidence of any reference to Cranmer. It is quite possible that Cranmer, now since the fall of Somerset less closely in touch with the Council than formerly, knew nothing of it, and even that à Lasco had not been consulted. If it was not solely the product of Bruno's own scheming, its genesis may with some probability be ascribed to the artful brain of Cecil.

5. RESUMPTION OF CRANMER'S PROPOSAL

Nothing came of these political maneuvers. But Cranmer's proposal for a meeting to frame a consensus

---

[50] *Op. cit.*, III, 349-50.

was yet to be vigorously renewed. Somerset was executed January 22, 1552; Northumberland, whom Cranmer consistently opposed, was now in the saddle. Trent had resumed May 1, 1551. The emperor was seeking to impose the compromise of the *Interim*, and Melanchthon had adopted a modification of it. Maurice of Saxony, who held the balance of power in Germany, had secured the attendance of Protestant representatives at Trent (Autumn, 1551), to divert attention while he formed a pact (January 15, 1552) with Henry II which presently made possible a Protestant attack upon the emperor. Charles was soon defeated in the Second Schmalkald War (April, 1552), and the Truce of Passau (August 2, 1552) prepared the way for the Peace of Augsburg three years later. These events were closely watched in England.[51] While in Germany the turn of the tide against Charles dashed the imperial projects for a Lutheran-Roman reunion, Cranmer apparently felt the time opportune for a resumption of his effort. He may also have felt peculiarly at this time the need of an authoritative general Protestant pronouncement as a stabilizing influence on the English situation. The Hooper incident had been decided in his favor, but it had given expression to a strain of radical puritanism far more extreme than that of Geneva. Northumberland, a shabby adventurer, was simulating Protestant zeal as a cloak for his rapacity. Something might be hoped for from the precocious wisdom and piety of the king; but his tenure of life was precarious.

Cranmer's works of 1550–51 on the Eucharist

---

[51] See the correspondence of Mount, Moryson, and Wotton, *Calendar of State Papers, Foreign, 1547–53*.

showed clearly his fundamental agreement with à Lasco and Calvin, and with Bucer, whose death, February 28, 1551, had deeply bereaved many English as well as Continental associates. The *Consensus Tigurinus*, framed by Calvin and Bullinger (1549), was hailed by both Bucer and à Lasco; the latter, with Calvin himself, saw in it the promise of a wider union, and issued an edition of the text in London (1552).[52] Bucer had stated that he believed he would agree with à Lasco if they should confer.[53] The points of difference in theology represented by these leaders and their followers were so slight as to make it seem probable that they would vanish, like those of Calvin and Bullinger, on adequate mutual explanation. Melanchthon, too, it was known, was not far from the Reformed doctrine, especially on its most controverted point of the Eucharist. He had disappointed Cranmer before; would he do so again?

Bullinger, as inheriting the leadership of the left wing of the Reformed, desired to see the English Reformation move more rapidly in a Puritan direction. He held Cranmer in some degree of suspicion, and offered him unsolicited advice. On February 24, 1551, he wrote to Cranmer urging him to advise the king against sending delegates to the approaching meeting of the Council of Trent, and interceding on Hooper's behalf. Cranmer's reply to this letter, over a year later (March 20, 1552), marks the resumption of his plan. The Hooper incident was now closed, and Hooper was Cranmer's guest at Lambeth. The

---

[52] Kuyper, *op. cit.*, I, lxv; II, 646, 650; Kruske, *Johannes à Lasco*, p. 79.

[53] Micronius to Bullinger, August 28, 1550. *Epistolae Tigurinae*, p. 369.

advice regarding Trent was also, he explains, super-
fluous, as the king had never considered the course
suggested. But Cranmer had decided to recommend
to him the plan of a "synod of most learned and excellent men" to be convoked "in England or elsewhere."
The king had indicated his approval of this plan, as
being most profitable to the Christian common-
wealth (*reipublicae Christianae utilissimum*). It is
not for us to fail the Church of God in a matter so important. He is writing "Dr. Philip" and "Dr. Calvin"
on the matter; and he asks Bullinger to "consider how
the synod may most conveniently be assembled either
in England or elsewhere."[54]

The letter to Calvin is of the same date. He desires
a harmony of doctrine in order to unite the churches
of God. To this end he has often wished for a meeting
of learned and godly men, that, having deliberated
together, they might hand down to posterity an authoritative statement. The doctrine of the sacrament
especially should be defined, in answer to the decrees
of Trent on the subject, thus ending the dissensions
over the sacrament of unity by which the Church of
God has been so grievously injured. He is writing
Melanchthon and Bullinger: "I beg," he says (for-
getful of distances), "that you will deliberate among
yourselves how this synod may most conveniently be
assembled."[55]

To Melanchthon he wrote a week later (March
27). In the early church, he observes, differences
were composed by councils of the apostles and elders.
Had the differences between reformed groups been so

[54] *Miscellaneous Writings and Letters,* p. 430.
[55] *Ibid.,* pp. 431-32.

settled, the emperor would not have made war on them. "It is truly grievous that the sacrament of unity is made by the devil food for disagreement, and, as it were, the apple of contention." He therefore proposes a conference of those who excel in erudition and judgment. If Melanchthon objects that the matter cannot be settled without the aid of princes, Cranmer answers that he has consulted the king, who "places his kingdom at your disposal," and promises security and assistance. He has written Calvin and Bullinger, exhorting them not to fail in a matter so necessary to the *respublica Christiana*. Melanchthon had recently written him[56] of the Tridentine decrees on the worship of the host; let this diligence of ungodliness be answered by a corresponding zeal in setting forth the doctrine of godliness.[57]

What response did these letters elicit? Calvin replied promptly, in a letter of some length. He laments the license and confusion that prevail, not sparing to single out Cranmer's wife's uncle, Osiander, as a trouble-maker. He has learned with joy of the success of the gospel in England, where Cranmer, he knows, has had a hard battle to fight. "I know," he says, "that your purpose is not confined to England alone, but together with her you take consideration for the whole world. The generous disposition of the most serene king, and his rare piety are deservedly to be admired, since the pious plan of holding such a gathering [*conventu*] is accompanied by his favor, and he offers a meeting place in his kingdom." The lack of intercourse and of holy communion

---

[56] This letter is not extant.
[57] *Ibid.*, p. 434.

between Christians is one of the evils of the day. This is chiefly the fault of princes, who consult only their own security. "Thus it comes to pass that the members being scattered, the body of the church lies mangled." As far as he is personally concerned he will not shrink from crossing ten seas for the purpose, if he can be of any service. He would find reason enough for this if it were only to serve England. But since there is proposed a weighty consensus of learned men, properly composed according to the standard of Scripture, by which churches otherwise far separated may be brought to unity, he would adjudge it wicked on his part to decline any labors or annoyances. Nevertheless, he hopes that the smallness of his capacity (*tenuitatem*) will cause him to be excused. If so, he will perform his part by prayer. He reminds Cranmer that Melanchthon is too far off for ready communication. Bullinger will probably have answered already. "I wish," he adds, "that my ability were equal to the ardor of my zeal. But what I at first declined, I perceive the difficulty of the business compels me to attempt; not that I should merely exhort you, but that I should implore you to go forward, until at least something be effected, if all does not turn out as you wish. Farewell, most accomplished leader, sincerely revered by me. May the Lord continue to guide you by his Spirit, and bless your holy labors."[58]

This characteristic letter shows Calvin to have been fully sympathetic with Cranmer's proposal, and to have regarded it with moderate hopefulness. His

---

[58] *C. R.*, XLI, 312-14. The editors remark: "*Vix dubium esse potest hanc ad finem Aprilis vel initium Maii referendam esse.*"

language constitutes a promise to go to England if his services are needed. Perhaps the depreciation of his own abilities may be due to the fact that Cranmer's letter did not convey an explicit personal invitation, but only proposed in a general way the holding of a conference. He may have been a little puzzled or a little piqued by the rather brief and casual way in which Cranmer had opened up so important a project. Cranmer, in his part, undoubtedly desired the presence as well as the approval of his correspondents, and thought to show them respect by presenting only a shadowy plan which they were invited to complete.

Cranmer, awaiting word from Melanchthon and Bullinger, did not reply till October 4. He was now persuaded that the plan would have to be at least temporarily abandoned. He had had, so far, no word from Melanchthon; Bullinger, he says, has answered that he fears it is vain to discuss a council while Germany is so disturbed by war that neither he nor Melanchthon can leave his own church. Consequently the project must be relinquished either completely or until a more convenient season. "As for us, we are again vigorously engaged in reforming the English Church."[59]

There exists an undated reply of Calvin to this decision to postpone the matter indefinitely. Since a general gathering to set forth our common teaching is excluded, he warmly approves (*vehementer laudo*) the new plan to carry forward the Reformation in England itself. Here Calvin animadverts upon certain defects in the English reform hitherto, and admon-

[59] *C. R.*, XLI, 370.

ishes Cranmer not through negligence to leave the task of reform unfinished.[60]

Melanchthon seems never to have replied to Cranmer's letter of March 27, 1552. Whether at Cranmer's request or not, he was, however, once more invited to England in the following May. On August 10, 1553, he informed Camerarius that he had been called once again to England by royal letters sent the previous May; and that in the meantime the pious king had died.[61]

To what cause are we to attribute the failure of Cranmer's project? Strype, without particularizing, remarks, "The troubles at home and abroad frustrated this excellent purpose."[62] Smyth unhesitatingly lays the blame at Melanchthon's door. Melanchthon, he says, "preferred the ignominy of submitting to the Interim to the inconvenience and possible danger of a journey to London."[63] In this judgment no consideration is given to the question of whether Melanchthon could honorably have absented himself from Germany during the troublous times of the Schmalkald Wars. His alleged "ignominy" was not at any rate the ignominy of ease. He complained to Cranmer[64] of the "miseries" and "tumults" amid which he was placed. To Calvin he wrote October 1, 1552, three days before Cranmer's letter abandoning the pro-

---

[60] Calvin, *Epistolae* (Geneva, 1616), pp. 134–35, quoted by Jenkyns, *Remains of Thomas Cranmer*, I, 347; Beza, *Life of John Calvin*, tr. F. Sibson (Philadelphia, 1836), pp. 298f.

[61] *C. R.*, VIII, 135.

[62] *Memorials*, II, 159.

[63] Smyth, *op. cit.*, p. 40. On p. 48 he quotes Dalton's *John à Lasco*, tr. Evans, in condemnation of Melanchthon's failure to aid Cranmer "in the most decisive hour."

[64] May 1, 1548, *C. R.*, VI, 894f.; July 4, 1553, *C. R.*, VIII, 119.

ject, "I am living as in a wasp's nest." If exile comes, he adds, "I am determined to turn to you."[65] He was, in fact, striving, perhaps mistakenly, for a consensus within Germany; and he regarded that as his first task. Until the internal Lutheran tumults were composed he must have felt that he could not negotiate as a representative. To have gone to England would have been to flee from Germany. It would have been of little advantage to Cranmer's aim for him to have joined the discussions as an *émigré*. Nor should it be forgotten that the treatment accorded by Henry VIII to the Lutheran delegates in England in 1538 had justified considerable hesitancy about attending further conferences there. Melanchthon may have prejudged the conference to failure and felt it a waste of time to take any concern for it. His failure to reply to Cranmer is in that case discourtesy, but it is nothing more.

The assumption that Melanchthon's aloofness was the sole cause of the relinquishment of the project is also open to objection. It is due, *inter alia*, to oversight of the letter of Cranmer of October 4, which mentions Bullinger's advice, with Melanchthon's silence, among "many things" (*multa*) which have led him to postpone action. It is probable, from his language, that he would have renewed the proposal at the first favorable opportunity, as he had already once done after an interval. But he had staked success upon the aid of the young king, on whom now lay the hand of death. The royal invitation to Melanchthon sent two months before Edward's death may indeed represent a renewal of Cranmer's purpose.

[65] *C. R.*, XIV, 415.

Before Melanchthon received it, he had learned the news of the king's decease. This is the real terminus. Other factors in the situation might have nullified the effort; the change of sovereigns at once put its success out of the question.

6. CONCLUSION

The foregoing brief survey of the documentary history of Cranmer's proposal has afforded the reader little definite indication of the content of the plan. There is no evidence that he ever drew up a *schema* of the projected conference. The evidence for the fact that he had such a plan at all rests upon the correspondence that has just been examined, and from his brief letters it is difficult to guess how far he had shaped in his imagination the details of procedure. We may be sure, indeed, that, whatever outlines the matter had assumed in his own mind, all was left so elastic as to be readily modified at the suggestion of others. In the letter to Bullinger of February 20, 1552, he is not even determined to have the meeting in England, though that is assumed in the letter to Melanchthon of the twenty-seventh. In the letter to Calvin of October 4, 1552, he refers to the project as *consilium meum de conventu doctissimorum et optimorum virorum in Anglia habendo*. Obviously, the presumption is that the conference is to meet in England, and the personal interest and favor of the king have been enlisted with that end in view. The phrase just quoted, indeed, may be taken as containing Cranmer's plan in a nutshell. Possibly it is the entire plan. If he could assemble under protection a meeting of the *doctissimi et optimi* of Protestantism, he was confident that the consensus issue would take care of itself.

Smyth regards the proposal as "an echo of the Conciliar Movement," and adds: "To convene a general council of Protestantism . . . to discover a formula that would unite all the divergent forces of the Reformation . . .—that was the dominant aim of Cranmer's statesmanship."[66] But the conciliar movement aimed at more than formulas; it aimed to establish a supernational representative form of church government. From evidence presented in previous paragraphs it is clear that Cranmer favored, in broad lines at least, a conciliar government of the church catholic, the true church which in his mind was now to be sought among those who had severed connection with Rome. We are justified, then, in supposing that the consensus of the wise and good for which he immediately planned was thought of as initiating some conciliar means of securing that intercommunion which dissension over "the sacrament of unity" had prevented. Such traditional phrases in the correspondence we have cited as "the church of God," "the universal church of God," "*respublica Christiana*," may be taken as significant of Cranmer's ideal, which is that of a general reintegration of living Christianity by conciliar means. He must have seen, however, beyond the difficulty of securing the presence in a conference of those qualified, grave obstacles in the way of the erection of a conciliar system. For the accomplishment of this end his plan, so far as revealed, was entirely inadequate. For his conception of a general council, as we have seen, was

---

[66] Smyth, *op. cit.*, p. 36.

that it required not only the favor of one, but the concurrence of all Christian princes. Calvin at times attributed the general disunion primarily to the discords of self-seeking princes; and Cranmer was equally aware of the seriousness of this factor. Any insistence upon Cranmer's conception of the valid council would necessitate its indefinite postponement. Cranmer was not, however, the man to insist upon definitions, and he probably hoped, as Calvin did, for the co-operation of enough princes to make possible some steps toward the goal of comprehensive conciliar union.

This project of Cranmer was seriously put forward and, although void of visible results, it should not be dismissed as fantastic, but taken seriously as a chapter in the history of the ideals of the Reformation. From Cranmer's point of view in that movement it was reasonable to expect of the proposed conference some useful outcome. If he had succeeded in gathering about him at one discussion table Melanchthon, Calvin, Bullinger, and a select number of the troop of foreign scholars who were his guests in England, the fathers of Trent would have trembled and Protestantism would have taken on new vitality. From all that we know of the temper and opinions of these men, they would hardly have found cause for serious disagreement. They would in all probability have reached a consensus; and a statement put forth on their authority could not have failed to prove of epochal significance.[67]

---

[67] Dr. Philip Schaff delivered an address before the General Presbyterian Council at Edinburgh in 1877, entitled "The Consensus of the Reformed Confessions." It is concerned with the proof of harmony of doctrine among the standards of all the Reformed groups, not with

projects of agreement or union. But it opens with an allusion to Cranmer's proposal, in which Doctor Schaff uses the following words: "Cranmer, the moderate and cautious reformer and martyr of the Church of England, the chief framer of its liturgy and Articles of Religion; Melanchthon, the preceptor of Germany, the gentle companion of the heroic Luther, the author of the Augsburg Confession, and the surviving patriarch of the German Reformation; Bullinger, the friend and successor of Zwingli, the teacher and benefactor of the Marian exiles, and the author of the most ecumenical among the Reformed Confessions; Bucer, the indefatigable, though unsuccessful, peacemaker between the Lutherans and Zwinglians, and the mediator between the Anglican and the Continental Reformation; Calvin, the master theologian, commentator, legislator, and disciplinarian, who was then just in the prime of his power, and (in the language of John Knox) at the head of "the most flourishing school of Christ since the days of the apostles"—these representative men, assembled in Lambeth Palace or the Jerusalem Chamber, would have filled an important chapter in church history, and challenged the assent of the Reformed Churches for a common confession of faith that embodied their learning, wisdom, and experience" (*The Consensus of the Reformed Confessions*, p. 2). (There is, of course, no proof that Calvin was consulted till after the death of Bucer.)

PART III
THE SURVIVAL AND REVIVAL OF THE
UNITIVE PRINCIPLE

CHAPTER VII

THE SURVIVAL OF THE UNITIVE PRINCIPLE IN PROTESTANTISM THROUGH THE SEVENTEENTH AND EIGHTEENTH CENTURIES

1. THE POST-REFORMATION SITUATION

THE present chapter has for its object not to record the detailed history of unitive effort in post-Reformation Protestantism, but to illustrate the survival of the unitive principle and exhibit the continuity in this respect between the sixteenth and the nineteenth century.

The Reformers undertook a fundamental restatement of the faith by which their contemporaries lived. Confidence in the older expression of Christianity had become so shaken that in many places the Protestant revival of faith entered what was almost a vacuum. But the decadent system had both inert sympathizers and active defenders, and the period as a whole bears the character of a vast and not ignoble intellectual battle, of which the Schmalkald Wars, the Huguenot Wars, and the Thirty Years' War are the less significant physical concomitants. For twenty years or more Protestantism met with little effective opposition except the hindrances of habit and inertia. But with the coming of the Jesuits, the situation changed. This powerful force, placing itself unreservedly under obedience to the Pope, stabilized the monarchical principle in the Roman Church and checked the advance of Protestantism. On the Protestant side there was a large measure of unity of sentiment, but the general recognition of the headship of Christ and the authority of Scripture offered no real unity of command; since claims of specific direction from Christ or the Scripture could always be disputed. The effective authorities set up in Protestantism lay in the confessions and organizations of the different churches. Some of the principal Protestant efforts to bring harmony and unity between its groups have engaged our attention. These efforts have been viewed as serious phases of Reformation history, and not without important positive results. But every reader is already familiar with the fact that they failed of their ultimate objective of Christian union. After the Reformation, there followed a period characterized by religious nationalism and confessionalism.

The confessional period should itself be regarded as marking a considerable degree of Protestant unity. Indeed, it is not improbable that there was less actual sectarianism in Western Christianity in the seventeenth than in the fourteenth century. Anyone who has tried to unravel the tangled skein of the heretical movements of the late Middle Ages knows how far the papal government was from securing a complete religious unity. And if one looks a little more closely at the late medieval centuries, he comes to recognize the partial validity of the charge of sectarianism made by many writers from Wyclif[1] to Calvin[2] against

[1] Wyclif's "main argument against monasticism" follows from his doctrine of "the church as one Body. . . . Hence his usual nickname is that of 'Sects.'" Workman, H. B., *John Wyclif*, II, 93.

[2] In *Inst.* IV, xiii, 14–16. *C. R.* XXX, 935–37, Calvin accuses the monastic orders of "destroying the communion of the church." They are "schismatics" who have "excommunicated themselves."

the multiplicity of rival monastic orders and fraternities. The religious bond between Lutheran and Reformed at the time of the Thirty Years' War was at least as close as that between Dominicans and Franciscans at the time of the Hundred Years' War.

The number of Protestant confessions is a highly misleading index of the degree of Protestant divergence. The *Augsburg Confession* and the *Formula of Concord* formed the uniting symbol of a large number of state churches which maintained active intercourse with each other. The fifty-eight documents of the Reformed churches, given by K. Müller in his valuable collection,[3] largely repeat each other's ideas. Apart from the Arminian controversy, there has been no essential divergence in belief between the churches of the Reformed.[4] Divergences in polity were generally due simply to local adjustments in which no principle was involved. When conflicts over polity arose, the question was usually one of how far the state's interference, unwelcome to all, was to be tolerated and how far resisted. In all Reformed churches the principle of Catholic unity was sincerely cherished at the opening of the seventeenth century. In the words of Professor John Dickie:

Each church regarded itself and all others as being the local representative of the one Holy Catholic and Apostolic Church of Christ. The whole Reformed Church laid great stress upon unity and Catholicity as notes of the true visible Church of Christ on earth. Never has there been a stronger sense of the unity of the church than that which knit together the Reformed of the latter half of the six-

[3] *Die Bekenntnisschriften der reformierten Kirche.*
[4] They have of course responded in variant degree to present-day liberalism.

teenth century and the earlier half of the seventeenth. Never has theology or church fellowship been more truly and fully international.[5]

This picture is offset by certain manifest defects in the expression of unity. While each confession was a unifying symbol for the group adhering to it, and the demonstrable consensus of confessions gave a degree of unity to the whole series of Reformed churches, there was a tendency to overstress the function of confessions in the church and so to hamper the freedom of thought and the expression of fresh experience. In the Netherlands the Arminians were treated with a harshness that was injurious to communion and disruptive of unity. It is, to say the least, very doubtful whether Calvin, who allowed Bullinger to differ from him considerably on predestination, would have wished the Remonstrants excommunicated. Though Richard Hooker had already written the famous words, "There will come a time when three words uttered with charity and meekness shall receive a far more blessed reward than three thousand volumes written with disdainful sharpness of wit,"[6] Calvinism had not learned the lesson of toleration. The only unity ultimately compatible with the Protestant conception of communion and priesthood is a voluntary unity; but this fact was not generally realized by the first or second generation of Protestants. The prevalence of a spirit of intolerance was an occasion of division. While the Reformed churches were

---

[5] "The Reformed Conception of the Church," *Quarterly Register,* xii, (1924), 745. Quoted in United Church of Canada, *A Statement Concerning Ordination,* p. 22.

[6] *Laws of Ecclesiastical Polity,* ed. Keble, 1888, Preface, I, 142.

racked by the Arminian controversy, Lutheranism,
with but one fundamental confession, was disturbed
by many intense conflicts, a number of which were
related to the influence of Calvinism in Lutheran
lands. But the most obvious failure of Protestant
union effort lay in the continued separation of the
Lutheran from the Reformed communion. As on
both sides the churches became interlocked with political and social organization, the prospect of union here
became more and more dim. The prevalence of Erastianism rendered vain any dreams of a church unity
that would traverse political boundaries and alliances.
The seventeenth century was to see vigorous and in-
cessant efforts to put recognized principles into practice and establish an international Protestantism; but
these efforts met with little encouragement.

Erastianism sometimes appears as corrective of
Protestant sectarianism and conducive to religious
unification. Such instances as the efforts of Olden-
barneveldt in 1613 to silence controversy in the Netherlands, and the bringing about by royal pressure of
the Prussian religious union of 1817 may be cited. It
will be found, however, that in the great majority of
instances the tendency of Erastianism was not toward
unity, but away from it. It may be very plausibly,
if not convincingly, argued that the partiality of the
Synod of Dort was due to the employment of force
by the Stadtholder to imprison or otherwise prevent
the attendance of the Arminian representatives. The
religious history of England and Scotland affords
ample evidence of this tendency. Even a liberal
Erastianism like that of Elizabeth, which aimed by
legislating average opinion into the state religion to

effect the maximum of "comprehension" of the various types of belief, failed utterly to promote unity. Both the Brownism and the Presbyterianism of the period fed upon the widespread hostility to the state control of conscience, and this anti-Erastian spirit was to take new forms in the following century. Perhaps there was no wiser alternative for Elizabeth's statesmen; but it seems at least possible that a closer solidarity would have been obtained if there had been less insistence on uniformity and if a measure of autonomy had been accorded to the church itself. The age of Erastianism was the age of schism in the English Church; and with the suppression of her means of self-government, completed under Queen Anne, the vitality of the church passed largely into the Nonconformist groups. Had the Established Church been free to respond to the Evangelical Revival, Wesleyanism would probably not have been alienated and organically separated from it. Scottish church divisions have come about, with scarcely an exception, over some aspect of the question of submission or resistance to state interference. The Disruption of 1843 was due to the impatience of awakened religion toward unreasonable hardships imposed by the action (or inaction) of English Parliaments. While marking a fresh division in the church, it was an assertion of a principle of freedom indispensable to a healthy church life. Scottish church unions, on the other hand, have come about entirely without suggestion from the state, as the spontaneous product of the church mind. Few indeed are the instances in which the state has effected an ecclesiastical union in any country.

Cujus regio ejus religio meant a coercive uniformity

among the subjects of each prince; and Erastianism at most attempts no more than a compulsory unity internal to the state. This may conceivably serve toward a real unity, emotionally felt and socially lived; but such a result would be exceptional. In fact, Erastianism, both by its necessary territorialism and by its deprivation of corporate freedom, is a denial of Christianity itself. Like all the greater religions, Christianity is essentially other than national or territorial, and any state connection that so confines it to a certain degree denatures it. Christianity is no more true to itself when it is sectional than when it is sectarian. Neither can it prosper when the state deprives it of autonomous organization. There have been times when the aggressive spirit of organized Christianity has seemed to require a check from the state; but a church that is reduced to impotence by the state is more pitiable than a church that is persecuted. The church is naturally a free communion; it is still this if it suffers in exercising its freedom, but not if it ceases to exercise it. Communion dies under compulsion, and union itself becomes meaningless. The injuries inflicted by Erastianism on Protestantism, and the continual protest of great sections of Protestantism against the system, make it clear that Erastianism is ultimately as alien to Protestantism as it is to Romanism. There is, of course, a world of difference between the theocratic Erastianism[7] of

---

[7] This expression is justifiable on a strict interpretation of the word "theocratic." The religious claims of the Roman emperors, before and after their adoption of Christianity, were theocratic, and Byzantinism was a theocratic "Erastianism." The expression employed by some writers, to describe the Zwinglian state-church order, is "Inverted theocracy," by which is meant the opposite not of "theocracy," but of "hierocracy," or the rule of priests. Cf. W. T. Hobhouse, *The Church and the World in Idea and History*, p. 228.

Zwingli, Erastus, and Hooker, and the secular Erastianism of Hobbes and the Enlightened Despots, for whom not only the church organization but religion itself is subordinated to the omnicompetent state. The modern secularization of the state renders its Erastian claims, wherever they are asserted, intolerable to any vital Protestantism.

Confessionalism, under the limitations of national connection, exhibited a very defective expression of the spirit of unity. Unity was often intensively cultivated and genuinely experienced in the congregational life. This was true to a far greater degree than under Romanism. The sense of communion in the national or territorial church, and within the fraternity of the confession, was also vigorous in Protestantism, but this local intensiveness was gained at the sacrifice of much of the ecumenical outlook which Romanism was now attempting to revive. In the course of the seventeenth and eighteenth centuries, Protestantism, deeply involved in international and civil strifes, largely lost the ambitious vision of ecumenicity that had animated the sixteenth-century leaders. For certain reasons the vision did not entirely fade. The New Testament itself could not permit the complete loss of catholicity. The celebration of the Lord's Supper, with the scriptural words of institution, always led away from sectarianism and revived the sense of the universal. Theology too retained the substance of the catholic conception of the church set forth by the Reformers and embodied in the confessions. The unitive principle survived everywhere, though it was, in general, rather passively received than actively espoused.

There were, however, not a few active exponents of the principle, for whom once more union became a cause rather than a mere desideratum. The leaders of Protestant unionism in that period were faced by insuperable difficulties. Their achievements in the promotion of organic union were slight and disappointing. But they gave testimony to the survival of the unitive principle in Protestantism, and passed on to a later age the tradition of the quest for Christian reunion. Some of their ideas, projects, and activities must now be briefly reviewed.

2. Protestant Advocacy of Union on the Continent in the Seventeenth Century

The later sixteenth century was active with theological strife, especially in Germany. The Lutheran position had been strictly defined in the *Formula of Concord* (1580), which, by rendering impossible any accommodation with Calvinism, had really contributed to the separate growth of the latter. The Reformation had passed from the stage of hope and conquest to one of deflation. Theology was reactionary rather than constructive; fresh ideas were few, and where uttered they were met by the suspicion and anger of neurotic theologians, to whom, it would seem, irenic voices were particularly alarming. The Thirty Years' War saw Germany trampled by more purposeful nations, her culture ruined, her resources devastated, and her population thinned. Out of this strife, nevertheless, came no little good. The terrible experience of the conflict weaned theology in some degree from the unprofitable habit of controversy, and called forth in Pietism the expression of a practical Christianity. The Peace of Westphalia prepared the way for the Great Elector's policy of toleration, with momentous results for later times.

Before the opening of this most wanton of modern wars, admonitions to peace and union were offered in different quarters. Pacification merely, rather than unification, was the object of some of the conciliatory writers. Of these, John Arndt (1555–1621) is the most typical example. Arndt's *True Christianity* appeared in four books, of which the first was published in 1605 and the remainder in 1609.[8] Arndt was essentially an exponent of the *unio mystica* aspect of Luther's teaching, which for Arndt carried with it weighty ethical and social consequences. Without definitely transgressing Lutheran orthodoxy, he exhibits sympathies far beyond it, and particularly appeals for theological disarmament and the cultivation of mystical fraternalism. This does not, however, lead him to projects of ecclesiastical unification, which lay beyond his interest.

Another type of approach was that of John Valentine Andreae (1586–1654), grandson of a fighting Lutheran, Jacob Andreae. Having been deeply impressed by the community life of Geneva, which he visited in 1610, and having become acquainted, perhaps through Isaac Casaubon (1559–1619), the Genevan scholar who found a religious home in the Church of England, with the Utopian ideas of Francis Bacon, Andreae wrote his *Christianopolis*, which he dedicated

---

[8] *Vom Wahres Christentum.* Brunswick, 1605–09; Pertz, H. L., *De Johanne Arndtio ejusque libris qui inscribuntur: De Vero Christianismo* (1852); Ritschl, O., *Dogmengeschichte des Protestantismus*, IV, 202ff.

(January 1, 1619) to Arndt as its inspirer.[9] This joint influence of Bacon and the Genevan republic appears traceable in the references in this book to the "college" in Christianopolis, where "religion, justice, and learning have their abode," religion giving a unity to learning and to society. "So there would seem," he says, "to be a need of co-operation which only Christianity can give—Christianity which conciliates God with men and unites men together."[10] The Confession of Faith, which he reads from an inscribed tablet in Christianopolis, omits the issues in dispute at the time, while it accords with the Ecumenical Creeds. The longest of the twelve articles contained in it is that on "the Holy universal Church," which is "fed by the communion of the Eucharist . . . active in charity, generous in communion, powerful in excommunication, which, though distributed throughout the whole earth, the unity of faith joins," etc.[11] The definition is in accord with the ideas both of Calvin and of Melanchthon.

"Rupert Meldenius" is the name used by the author of a tract on union important because it furnished the cause with a useful slogan. The name is apparently obtained by an interchange of letters from Peter Meiderlin (Latinized: Petrus Meuderlinus), of whom little is known except that he was a learned Lutheran divine. His *Paraenesis votiva pro pace ecclesiae* (1626) closes with the inspired motto: "In things necessary,

[9] F. E. Held, *Christianopolis, an Ideal State of the Seventeenth Century*, quotes evidence for the Genevan and Baconian influence, pp. 15f., 27ff. In the dedication to Arndt the author says of his Utopian "colony" that it "has its source in that Jerusalem which thou didst build with mighty spirit against the wishes of the sophists." *Ibid.*, p. 131.

[10] *Ibid.*, p. 174.

[11] *Ibid.*, p. 176.

unity; in things not necessary, liberty; in both, charity." The tract was addressed to the theologians of the *Augsburg Confession.*[12]

On the side of the Reformed, the characteristic expressions of the unitive principle carried with them specific projects of negotiation and organization. This is true, for example, of David Pareus (1548–1622), a contemporary of Arndt, a leading Reformed theologian of Heidelberg. Pareus actively espoused the cause of union, and published an *Irenicum* in 1614–15.[13] His project is a resumption or expansion of that of Calvin, Beza and Salvard. The Protestants (Evangelicals) are already in agreement on all the fundamentals and on most theological points, and should proceed to complete agreement and make common cause against the papists. As the means of bringing about this unification, he would have a conference, and "a regular and free council." The project called forth much discussion, most of it on the Lutheran side, adverse.[14]

The great Arminian theologian, jurist and philosopher, Hugo Grotius (1583–1645), was also a great church unionist, and held that "since all Christians are baptized into the same name, therefore there ought

[12] K. Müller, *Kirchengeschichte,* II (2), 582, thinks the words a development from phraseology used by Casaubon c. 1612. O. Ritschl, *op. cit.,* IV, 445, associates it with pseudo-Augustinian writers. G. Krüger has briefly reviewed the question, and holds that Meiderlin felt the influence of the exponents of toleration, Sebastian Castellio and Jacob Acontius. "Über den Friedenspruch: *In necessariis unitas,*" etc., *Studien und Kritiken,* C. (1927), 154ff. The words were used by Richard Baxter in his *True and Only Way of Concord,* 1679, where they are referred to as "the Pacificator's old and despised words."

[13] *Irenicum sive de unione et synodo evangelicorum concilianda liber votivus,* Heidelberg, 1614–15.

[14] Leube, H., *Calvinismus und Luthertum in Zeitalter der Orthodoxie,* I, 59ff.; Ritschl, *op. cit.,* IV, 256ff.; *Realencyklopädie,* XIV, 689ff.

GROTIUS

to be no sects or divisions, among them."[15] In his
work on *The Way to Ecclesiastical Peace*, he brought
together a collection of documents on the subject of
Christian unity and drew up a "Brief Confession," in
which, like Andreae, he sought to include only the
doctrines essential to the faith.[16] Grotius looked beyond Protestantism to a complete unification.

The French Reformed Church in its National
Synod in 1614 adopted a proposal of Du Plessis Mor-
nay, the most prominent leader of the Huguenots of
that period, to promote the organization of a general
Protestant church. The name proposed was "Christian Reformed Church," thus excluding the use of the
party names, "Calvinist," "Zwinglian," and "Lutheran." In 1631, at the Synod of Charenton, the
French church agreed to admit Lutherans to communion and intermarriage.[17] The French theologians,
Moses Amyraldus and John Dalleus (Daillé), who
were influential in this synod, and later sought to
promote interconfessional unity, advocated the principle for which their German contemporary, Calixtus,
is famous, "the consensus of the first five centuries."[18]
In the early months of 1631 a few Lutheran and Reformed theologians met at Leipzig on invitation
of the Electors of Brandenburg and Saxony, and engaged in a protracted conference in which the Reformed
made liberal concessions and a large degree of agreement was reached[19]; but, according to the Lutheran,

[15] *De Veritate Religionis Christianae*, Book IV, sec. 11, quoted by
J. W. Buckham, "Heralds of a United Church," *Constructive Quarterly*, VIII (1920), 127ff.   [16] *Ibid.*
[17] Hering, K. W., *Geschichte der kirchlichen Unionsversuche*, I, 323ff.;
Ritschl, *op. cit.*, IV, 269f.
[18] Ritschl, *op. cit.*, IV, 285.
[19] Hering, *op. cit.*, I, 327ff.; Brandes, F., *Geschichte der evangelischen
Union in Prussia*, I, 93-111.

Mosheim, the unwarranted suspicion of the Wittenberg theologians nullified the result.[20]

The war, begun in Bohemia in 1618, soon spread into
Germany, which became its chief theater. The possibility of a general conference for union opened up in
Poland, a country undisturbed by the war, and whose
king, Ladislaus IV, was an enlightened and pacific
ruler. The proposal came from the king, and was
taken up by a Polish Roman Catholic provincial
synod at Warsaw, November, 1643. The primate
of Poland, Lubienski, issued an invitation to all the
"Dissidents," as the Protestant groups in Poland were
called, to send delegates to a conference.[21] But the
tone of this invitation destroyed any hope of a free
discussion; and four months later the king took the
project into his own hands. He issued March 20,
1644, an invitation couched in happier phraseology.[22]

The conference met in August, 1645, and continued
in animated discussion for three months. On the
Protestant side, the Lutherans, headed by A. Calovius
and J. Hülsemann, proved determined and unyielding.
The sessions were stormy and the conference ended
in futility.[23] It was marked by the presence of two

---

[20] Mosheim, J. L., *Ecclesiastical History*, Engl. ed. (1829), II, 217.

[21] The "Pax Dissidentium," agreed upon in 1573, had failed to prevent conflict.

[22] Both letters are given in German translation by Hering, *op. cit.*,
II, 3ff.; 6ff. He offers an opportunity to relieve the prevalent hatred,
which is due to dissension in religion. He appeals to all, as children of
the "Mother Church," to live as brothers and to come to agreement.
Another letter was issued December 1, reiterating the king's sincere
wish for union and peace and promising "a free and brotherly conference." "It rests in your hands," he says, "to end the century of separation."

[23] *Ibid.*, II, 40-63; Brandes, *op. cit.*, pp. 142-57. The attempt to find
a basis of union between Lutheran and Reformed was renewed in a
conference at Cassel in 1661. The negotiations followed suggestions of

of the greatest union advocates of the time, Calixtus and Comenius, of whom some notice must now be taken.

Of the German Lutherans of the period, the most outstanding champion of unity was George Calixtus (1586–1656), who was professor of theology at Helmstadt from 1614 to his death. Calixtus may be regarded as the greatest continuator of Melanchthon's irenical work. His father had been a pupil and admirer of Melanchthon, and at Helmstadt as a student he had felt the influence of the Melanchthonian humanist teachers, J. Casilius and C. Martini. He exhibits in greater degree than Pareus and most of the Reformed a friendliness toward the Roman Church, though he is not prepared to unite with an unreformed Romanism.

Calixtus attempted to give a new orientation in theology and on the basis of the Patristic tradition to cancel the issues of contemporary controversy. In this he was reviving the teachings of the Roman Catholic reformers of the previous century, George Cassander (1513–1566) and George Wicelius (Witzel) (1501–1573). Cassander had sought reunion on the basis of Vincent of Lerins' formula, *"Quod semper, quod ubique, quod ab omnibus creditum est."* These views at the same time appealed to certain Reformed theologians, and Grotius in 1642 edited Cassander's *Consultatio inter Catholicos et Protestantes* of 1564.[24] Calixtus in wide travels made himself acquainted with

John Dury. The participants failed to reach agreement. The conference helped, however, to arous. interest in its objects on the part of Frederick William the Great Elector, who gave some attention to projects of union about 1668. Leube, *op. cit.*, pp. 313ff.

[24] The *Methodus concordantiae* of Wicelius (1537) was republished by Conring of Helmstadt in 1659.

both the Roman Catholic and the Reformed Church, and possessed a sympathetic knowledge of their theologies. He felt strongly the influence of Calvinism, and adopted something of the Federalism of Cocceius.[25]

Calixtus' grand proposal for theology was regarded as dangerous and fantastic. It called for the cancellation of ten centuries of the historical evolution of thought, and seemed to repudiate not only medievalism, but the Reformation itself. His wide catholicity and intellectual sympathy condemned him in the eyes of the strict confessionalists, of whom Abraham Calovius (1612–1686 was the chief protagonist. As a result, Calixtus had a life-long battle to fight, and the fight was carried on after his death by his son, F. U. Calixtus (d. 1701), and others of his school. Lutheran theologians were clearly divided into "Syncretists" and "Orthodox," till the latter party had their position challenged by the new force of Pietism late in the century.

The entire work of Calixtus is marked by unionism, but his chief special treatises on the subject belong to the period from 1643.[26] His principal method, like that of Pareus, is the holding of synods. To these, he gives the same functions and the same relation to Scripture as we have remarked in the Reformers. He is a Conciliarist, opposing monarchy in the church, even where he admits it in the state. His conciliarism, however, is aristocratic. The council should con-

---

[25] Friedrich, H., *Georg Calixtus der Unionsmann des 17 Jahrhunderts: Inwiefern sind seine Bestrebungen berechtigt?* pp. 11ff.; Ritschl, *op. cit.*, IV, 247; 363-423; Leube, *op. cit.*, I, 256ff.; *Realencyklopädie*, III, 142; XXI, 399ff.

[26] Titles and dates are largely supplied by Ritschl, *op. cit.*, IV, 363ff. His *De tolerantia Reformatorum* was posthumous (1658).

sist not, indeed, of the ordinary clergy, bishops, and presbyters, but of the learned. "According to his view, it is to an aristocracy of learned theologians that the supreme direction of the church belongs."[27] Like Pareus, and, for that matter, Calvin, he clearly distinguishes between essential and nonessential doctrines.[28] On the former he asserted that a complete agreement already existed. The problem was, however, to obtain agreement on the question of what were nonessentials. Some doctrines which he classed as *adiaphora* were stoutly contended for by the Orthodox.

Another of the outstanding advocates of Christian union of the century was the great educator, John Amos Comenius (1592–1670).[29] He drew his inspiration largely from the *Unitas Fratrum*, of which he was the last bishop, and a church which "has a record of persistent striving after unity in essentials of Christianity and of brotherly co-operation with other Protestant bodies."[30] But he also strongly felt the influence of Pareus, who was his teacher at Heidelberg, 1510–14. He also formed a friendship with Andreae, whose correspondence partially inspired his

[27] Ritschl, *op. cit.*, pp. 395-97.

[28] In his *Desiderium et Studium concordiae ecclesiae* (1650), he sets forth nine points to be observed in the proposed unification, the first of which is that "matters necessary to salvation are to be distinguished from subordinate matters." Friedrich, *op. cit.*, p. 31. Cf. Ritschl, *op. cit.*, IV, 420. Gieseler, *Church History*, Engl. ed., IV, 589ff., quotes some paragraphs from this and some other works of Calixtus.

[29] Full information is given in an unpublished doctoral dissertation by Matthew Spinka, *The Irenic Program and Activity of John Amos Comenius*, University of Chicago, 1923. Spinka has used extensive Czech sources. The current interest in the subject should call forth the publication of this important study. The treatise sheds valuable light also on the educational ideals of Comenius, on which his modern fame chiefly rests.

[30] Spinka, *op. cit.*, p. 1.

educational ideas, and with the irenical Polish scholar, Samuel Hartlib, who while resident in England opened correspondence with Comenius, and gave publicity to some of his early work. Owing to the distress of the war, and the invitations which followed on the recognition of his ideas, Comenius traveled widely, and spent periods of residence in England and in Sweden. He was apparently approached regarding the presidency of Harvard College in 1642. He represented his church at the Conference of Thorn, where he must have met Calixtus. It was in 1648, the year of the Treaty of Westphalia, that he became senior bishop of the *Unitas Fratrum*.[31]

Spinka holds that the union ideas of Comenius were at first allied to those of Calixtus and Dury,[32] but that with the publication of his *Pansophiae Prodromus* (1637?) he reached independent ground on the question.[33] His early opposition to the papacy, however, suggests the effect of his association with Pareus. He never became entirely friendly to Rome. "Thou hast been our mother, but hast become our stepmother," he wrote, addressing the Church of Rome in 1648.[34] On the other hand, he engaged in animated controversy with the Socinians. In his early works he lamented the failure of the Protestants to unite. He cites with "indignation" what seems a modern instance of several groups in a small town each seeking to force the others to conform to it, while the simple folk "held to whatever came along" in the

---

[31] Spinka, *op. cit.*, pp. 15-55.
[32] See below, pp. 276ff.
[33] *Op. cit.*, p. 74.
[34] *Ibid.*, p. 82.

way of religion. In his last treatise, *The One Thing Needful*, Comenius says he has made irenic study and effort "his life-long occupation."

The change which Comenius' irenic program underwent consisted in an extension of the objective to that of an integration of all human culture under the leadership of religion. The goal of his *pansophy* was the knowledge of God. Philosophy and theology were to be allied, and knowledge was to proceed by the inductive method, with scientifically prepared textbooks and an international research college of learned men to be established in London, with the task of gathering and distributing fresh contributions to the sum of truth. The distribution involved a scheme for a world-wide mission of Christianity and culture.[35] Comenius was also an exponent of the conciliar idea, on a scale more ambitious than others dreamed of. His elaborate scheme for a council involved representation in it of every sect on earth bearing the name of Christian. Comenius applied his irenical and educational zeal to a wide range of contemporary problems. He proposed the invention of a universal language. He procured the translation of the Bible into Turkish. When England and the Netherlands were negotiating peace in 1667, he improved the occasion to write a tract on behalf of international Protestant union, entitled *The Messenger (Angelus) of Peace sent to the English and Dutch Legates of Peace at Breda.* In short, he entered every door of opportunity by which he saw any hope of contributing to world unification and Christianization.

---

[35] This is developed in his *Via Lucis* (1643, published 1668), reviewed by Spinka, *op. cit.*, pp. 115ff. (One cannot but feel the resemblance here to the projects of Raymond Lull.)

A third illustrious leader among Protestant unionists of the seventeenth century is John Dury (1596–
1680).[36] "John Dury occupied a unique position among
these irenic leaders. Certainly, the range of his irenic
efforts was broader than that of any other leader who
attempted to heal the divisions of Christendom in
the seventeenth century. . . . For fifty-two years
with unwearied zeal he devoted his life to what he
called the establishment of 'ecclesiastical pacification.' "[37] Nor was he merely a negotiator. He was a
forerunner of Spener in his emphasis upon practical
piety as against confessional orthodoxy. He was as
deeply concerned over the cause of missions as Comenius, and, without the latter's originality as an educator, he was equally with him devoted to educational
progress. But all his wide interests were subordinate
to the passion for Christian unity.

A conversation with C. Godeman, a minister of
Gustavus Adolphus in Prussia, led Dury in 1628 to
devote himself for life to this one cause. In this decision he was motivated, as he wrote in 1644, by "the
love of peace and quietness and the hope of doing good
to the Church of God." He made the acquaintance of

---

[36] I gratefully acknowledge the kindness of Professor J. M. Batten,
of Scarritt College, Nashville, Tennessee, in permitting me to use the
manuscript of his dissertation, *John Dury, Advocate of Christian Reunion*, in advance of its presentation for the doctorate in the University of Chicago. This amply documented work will render antiquated
all previous studies of Dury, and shed much light on the whole seventeenth-century history of continental and British Christianity. Mr.
Batten has also put at my disposal full manuscript copies of five of
Dury's most important pamphlets. In addition, I am indebted to
him for valuable suggestions on a number of the details of this chapter. Among other studies of Dury that of Leube, *op. cit.*, pp. 204-56,
is of special value for his continental work. A particular phase is examined by K. Brauer, *Die Unionstätigkeit John Duries unter dem Pro-
tectorät Cromwells*. A useful short article is by M. Spinka, "John Dury
the Peacemaker," *Christian Union Quarterly*, XIII (1924), 372ff.

[37] Batten, *op. cit.*, p. 10.

Comenius and of Andreae, as well as of the English ambassador Sir Thomas Roe, the Swedish statesman Oxenstierna, and others who were politically concerned for Protestant union. He began to form plans for the practical work of union. In England, 1630–31, he secured the approval of Archbishop Abbot, but not the official support of the Anglican Church, for his union project. Laud also gave him nominal support; of other English bishops, John Davenant, Joseph Hall, and William Bedell finally indorsed his efforts. His project was now outlined in a tract, *The Purpose and Platform of My Journey into Germany*. It was a clearly thought-out program to persuade influential persons to unite in prayer and in conference "to further the work of Christian peace and ecclesiastical unity between us [the Reformed] and the Lutherans." He hopes "to sett the divines of Germany, as many as are fitt, upon this work." With plans thus laid, he returned to Germany. The death of Gustavus (1632), who religiously and politically desired union, was a severe blow to Dury's hopes. Failing to obtain a general meeting of the divines, he labored with individuals and small groups in an attempt to convert the indifferent or hostile. He won the support of a considerable number, both of theologians and princes; though the unfortunate Frederick V of the Palatinate was unfriendly to the Lutherans and declined to co-operate. He engaged in extensive correspondence and circulated his own tracts. In these writings, he urged the emphasis on practical theology and Christian social ethics, and the purposeful cultivation of an irenical spirit by means of the schools and the pulpit. Ministers should be pledged at ordination to avoid a party spirit. With education should go negotiation. This was to proceed by a series of conferences representative of smaller and larger areas of the Lutheran and Reformed Churches, culminating in a joint representative conference to form a basis of general agreement. Finally, there was to be a General Assembly of representatives of Protestantism from all countries, which would determine creed, practical teachings, public worship, and polity for the united Protestant Church.

During later years Dury and his ceaseless propaganda became a factor in the churches of Germany, England, Scotland, Holland, and Sweden, to all of which he paid repeated visits. He accepted reordination from Archbishop Laud, but failed to secure thereby Laud's unequivocal support. He was for a short time a member of the Westminster Assembly, but the high Presbyterians came to distrust his liberalism. Without sacrificing his own plans, he became Cromwell's chief agent for union negotiation abroad. The death of Cromwell (1658), like that of Gustavus twenty-six years earlier, shattered hopeful projects. Undismayed, he resumed his labors and spent his later life in continuous union activity. He finally resided at Cassel, where he died at a ripe age in 1680. His last work, *The True Christian*, was written in French. In it he extends the project of union to include the Roman Catholics, and stresses the idea of the communion of saints, which a recent German writer concludes is the central motive of his endeavors.[38]   In

[38] "Das höchste Ziel, das Duräus und seinen Friedensbestrebungen erreichen wollte, war die Gemeinschaft der Heiligen (*communio sanctorum*). Er gab diesem Begriff eine inhaltsreiche Deutung. (A tract

his conciliar plan of union and in his religious emphasis upon communion, Dury stood firmly on the ground taken by the greater Reformers of the sixteenth century, while he reached beyond them in his teaching on toleration and mutual conciliation. The neglect with which he has long been treated by history has meant a profound loss to Protestantism; but, like Comenius and Calixtus, he is to-day being rediscovered.

The most notable union effort put forth in the late seventeenth century on the Continent was that of the philosopher Leibnitz. G. J. Jordan, in his admirable recent study,[39] has followed A. Pichler[40] in the view that "the religion of Leibnitz is more basic than his philosophy," and that his philosophy rests upon his Christianity. These writers have further shown that for fifty years Leibnitz earnestly sought the reunion of Christianity. Indeed, Jordan affirms that his qualities and learning "made him the greatest supporter of church unity that the world has yet known," and expresses amazement at the neglect which this aspect of his work has hitherto met with.[41]

G. W. Leibnitz (1646–1716), one of the world's greatest intellects, even in youth devoured the controversial literature of Lutheran, Syncretist, Calvinist, Arminian, Jesuit, and Jansenist parties. The friendship of the statesman Boineburg, adviser to many

---

of 1639 is here quoted in which Dury explains *communio sanctorum* in terms of *sympathia spiritualis* which means *conjunctio animarum . . . in operis mutuis*, etc.) In dem Ziel: sanctorum communio, findet das Lebenswerk des Schotten seine Krönung." Leube, *op. cit.*, pp. 240f.

[39] *The Reunion of the Churches, a Study of G. W. Leibnitz and his Great Attempt* (1927).

[40] *Die Theologie des Leibnitz* (1869).

[41] *Op. cit.*, p. 31; pp. 41f.

rulers, widened his practical outlook. His historical studies rendered him familiar with the teachings of the conciliar period, and his whole approach to the reunion question is that of a Conciliarist. He became familiar with such previous union projects as have been reviewed above.

The Treaty of Westphalia (1648) left three forms of Christianity recognized in Germany. Not long afterward reunion was proposed afresh from the Roman side. The career of C. R. de Spinola, a Spanish Franciscan, who in 1686 became bishop of Neustadt, in a measure parallels that of Dury in devotion to the cause of unity.[42] From 1661 he was engaged in union negotiation in Germany, and at least from 1667 with the consent of the Pope.[43] Spinola recalled the early Protestant demand for a council, and proposed admitting Protestants to membership in it "as visible members of the Catholic Church." Leibnitz was pleased and hopeful. G. W. Molanus (1633–1727), a pupil of G. Calixtus and a friend of Leibnitz, with F. U. Calixtus of Helmstadt and other Lutherans, engaged in conference with Spinola; and in 1683 Molanus presented to him a memorandum which contained what Jordan calls "the most liberal offer to the Church of Rome in the history of Irenics."[44] The document was modified later through the influence of Calixtus, and was published in 1691 under the title *Regulae circa Christianorum omnium ecclesiasticam*

---

[42] Hiltebrandt, P., *Die kirchlichen Reunionsverhandlungen in der zweiten Hälfte des 17. Jahrhunderts,* gives much information on Spinola, but this writer thinks him more politician than religious unionist (p. 36).

[43] Jordan, *op. cit.,* p. 47.

[44] *Ibid.,* p. 53.

unionem.[45] This notable proposal emphasizes the necessity of forbearance over small differences, advocates the usefulness while denying the infallibility of councils, and sets forth a scheme for the meeting of a general council, to whose decisions assent is to be pledged in advance. Leibnitz afterward described the reception of the document in Rome. It was viewed with satisfaction, but, owing to troubles in France, Rome postponed all concessions to Protestants. Leibnitz wrote treatises in favor of the project, and on the general question; and his *Systema Theologicum*, which has been shown to bear the influence of Grotius, was intended to support these negotiations, and was left unpublished because they broke down.[46]

Another phase of the union effort of Leibnitz, in which he was again associated with Molanus, appears in his correspondence with the Gallican leader Bossuet, who became Bishop of Meaux in 1681. The correspondence between these truly great men began over literary matters in 1679,[47] and turned to the religious issues in connection with Spinola's efforts in 1683. In 1691, Molanus prepared a fresh memorandum, *Private Thoughts on the Method of Reuniting the Protestant with the Roman Catholic Church*, and Leibnitz sent a copy of it to Bossuet on condition that it should not be made public.[48] Bossuet replied with *Reflections on the Memorandum of Molanus*, which left some hope

---

[45] The document is analyzed by Jordan, *op. cit.*, pp. 56-62.

[46] *Ibid.*, Chap. IV. Following Pichler, Jordan thinks Leibnitz entirely sincere in this book, which has in various ways been explained as something else than a revelation of his own views.

[47] Jordan, *op. cit.*, p. 145, following Foucher de Careil, *Œuvres de Leibnitz*, I, 59.

[48] The *Cogitationes Privatae* are analyzed at length by Jordan, *op. cit.*, App. II.

of reunion, but raised issues which could not be resolved. On both sides there is full adherence to the conciliar method of settling matters in the church. This was a Gallican principle, and was written into the famous Gallican Articles of 1682, of which Bossuet was the author. Bossuet too makes no claim of papal infallibility. He talks, however, of the infallibility of councils, a notion that was foreign to Leibnitz' mind. Leibnitz at first hoped to make something of the point that France had not accepted the Decrees of Trent. Bossuet was determined not to yield here. "Show me a French Catholic," he demands, "who does not accept the creed of Trent."[49] The correspondence closed with a letter of Leibnitz of February 5, 1702.

This correspondence, with its futile close, indicates the contrast between two great minds, indeed, between two types of mentality. On Bossuet's side the fundamental conception is that of a static body of belief fixed by infallible councils; and Trent was sanctioned by him on this basis of infallibility. For the progressive mind of Leibnitz, all conciliar decisions were reformable in the light of larger truth and changing conditions; for he was at once a Conciliarist of the Gerson type and the chief founder of the Aufklärung.

3. PROTESTANT ADVOCACY OF UNION IN THE BRITISH ISLES IN THE SEVENTEENTH CENTURY

Whereas on the Continent the matters disputed between the theologians had to do largely with the question of the Eucharist, in Britain the points in

---

[49] Dimier, L. "Bossuet's Correspondence with Leibnitz," *Constructive Quarterly*, VI (1918), 628.

debate rather concerned the constitution and worship of the church. Knox had desired union between the Reformed churches of the two kingdoms, but his *faux pas* in writing the *First Blast of the Trumpet against the Monstrous Regiment of Women* (1557) alienated the good will of Elizabeth both from himself and from Geneva. The Scottish church took on a presbyterial polity, while that of England remained episcopal and liturgical. A vigorous effort to unite the two churches followed the union of the crowns (1603). It was natural that King James should favor a religious uniformity in his two kingdoms, and that he should favor the religious system of the majority nation. Embittered against Presbyterianism, which he saw to be opposed to absolute monarchy, he was anxious to subject the Scottish church to episcopal government.

Scotland submitted to a combination of Episcopacy and Presbyterianism in 1610, and some modern Scottish churchmen have praised this mixed polity as agreeable to fundamental Presbyterian theory.[50] When he, and later Charles I, proceeded to press for liturgical changes, Scotland was roused to vigorous opposition, and the reaction completely restored Presbyterianism (1638). In the next stage the movement was reversed, and Scottish and English Presbyterianism attempted a conquest of the Church of England. The Westminster Assembly was called by Parliament in order that there should be set up a church government "most agreeable to God's word, most apt to procure and preserve the peace of the church at home, and in nearer agreement with the

---

[50] Cooper, J., *Reunion, a Voice from Scotland*, 1918.

Church of Scotland and other Reformed Churches abroad."[51]

Before this crisis was reached the attempts of King James to alter the usages in the Church of Scotland[52] led to controversy, in course of which a group of Aberdeen scholars, who felt the liberalizing influence of Arminius, supported the king's policy as in accord with ancient Catholic practice. Distinguished among the "Aberdeen Doctors" was John Forbes (1593–1635), of Corse, son of Patrick Forbes, Bishop of Aberdeen (1618). In 1629, in an earnest effort to allay the strife, he published his *Irenicum* in two books.[54] Amid much detail, the essential argument of the work is that the changes proposed are in nonessential matters, and that on such matters it is wrong to separate from the church.[55] It was to "the lovers of peace and truth in the Church of Scotland" that John Forbes addressed his book. At the same period William Forbes (1585–1634), an Aberdeen man who in the year of his death became Bishop of Edinburgh, reached out more widely in the direction of catholic unity. His *Modest and Pacific Considerations*[56] has been compared to Pusey's *Eirenicon*.[57] The high

---

[51] Beveridge, W., *A Short History of the Westminster Assembly*, App. I, pp. 147ff.

[52] *Articles of Perth*, 1618. [53] Macmillan, D., *The Aberdeen Doctors*.

[54] *Irenicum amatoribus veritatis et pacis in Ecclesia Scotticana*. The popularity and influence of the work appears in the fact that it was reprinted in 1636. A revised edition which he left in manuscript appeared in 1703. Selwyn, E. G., *The First Book of the Irenicum of John Forbes of Corse*, p. 33.

[55] *Ibid.*, p. 130.

[56] *Considerationes modestae et pacificae controversarium*, etc., published 1658.

[57] Selwyn, *op. cit.*, p. 5. The work has been published with an English translation in the *Anglo-Catholic Library*. William Forbes was not strictly one of the "Aberdeen Doctors," but was closely affiliated with them. Archbishop Laud is said to have purchased his unpublished manuscripts. Macmillan, *op. cit.*, pp.172f.; pp. 263f.

Episcopal or Anglo-Catholic leaders, Bishop Launce-
lot Andrews (1555–1626) and Archbishop William
Laud (1573–1645), craved union on divine-right episcopal principles, and looked away from the parties in
England to the Greek and the Roman Churches.
Roman emissaries discussed the terms of union with
the English Church in this period, and the words
of one of these, Christopher Davenport, who as
a Recollet took the name Franciscus de Sancta
Clara, that the Anglican *Articles* were "patient but
not ambitious of a Catholic interpretation" (1633)
are significant in the light of later Anglo-Catholicism.[58]

Shortly before the meeting of the Westminster
Assembly, an attractive union proposal came from
the distinguished Anglican scholar James Usher
(Ussher) (1581–1656), Primate of Ireland (1626).
Ulster, after the "Plantation," was the meeting-
ground of the Scottish and English Church systems.
The pacific mind of Usher, a strong Calvinist whom
James I feared and disliked for his Puritan leanings,[59]
sought the means of unifying the two churches in
Ireland. In accordance with much previous opinion,
including that of Cranmer, he believed that bishop
and presbyter differ only in rank, not in order.[60] He

[58] Davenport (1598–1680) was a brother of John Davenport, Puritan divine and founder of New Haven, Connecticut. His *Paraphras-
tica expositio articulorum confessionis anglicanae* was written in 1633.
Ollard, L., and Crosse, G., *Dictionary of English Church History*, article
by Ollard on "Reunion," p. 504; p. 507; *Catholic Encyclopedia*, article,
"Davenport, Christopher."

[59] Carr, J. A., *Life of Archbishop Usher*, pp. 115ff.

[60] "I have ever declared my opinion that *Episcopus et presbyter gradu
tantum different non ordine*. Consequently where bishops cannot be
had, the ordination of presbyters standeth valid." Carr, *op. cit.*, p.
272. He accordingly held valid the ministries of the churches of France
and the Netherlands.

285

was impressed by the recognition of this fact in the ancient Celtic church (to whose history he made a highly important contribution), and saw the advantages of the Scottish Presbyterian system with its distribution of authority. In 1641, having left Ireland, he published his *Reduction of Episcopacy Unto the Form of Synodical Government Received in the Ancient Church.*[61] This compressed document, in four sections of paragraph length, projects a combination of the two systems. Usher proposes the employment of the church-wardens and sidesmen to administer local discipline, carrying serious cases to a monthly synod. He advocates the appointment, on the basis of an old statute, of suffragan bishops to the number of the rural deaneries (like the ancient *chorepiscopi*), under whose presidency is to be held a monthly synod of all the rectors who shall decide matters by vote. From this body appeals would go to the diocesan synod. The latter, to meet once or twice a year, would consist of the suffragans and some or all of the rectors in the diocese, and would have power to revise the acts of the district synods. Above the diocesan synods would stand the provincial synod, of which the archbishop or his nominee would be moderator. A national council, consisting for England of the combined Provincial Synods of Canterbury and York, might also sit every third year, when Parliament was in session. Usher gives to his "suffragans," who are the ministers of small areas, though not merely of single congregations, the power of jurisdiction and of ordination. Without using the terminology of

---

[61] Usher, *Works*, XII, 527ff.

Presbyterianism, he makes, in some respects, an approach to that system.[62]

Usher was not a member of the Westminster Assembly, and no attention was given by it to his moderate counsels. The rise and military strength of Independency placed out of consideration for a time any concessions to episcopacy. The polity framed by the Assembly, while left elastic in details, was essentially that exemplified by Scottish, French, and Dutch Presbyterianism. The recognition of the lay elder ("other church-governors. . . . Which officers reformed churches commonly call Elders"), in the *Form of Church Government* issued by the Assembly (1645), corresponds in principle to a detail of Usher's plan; but the Assembly gave no recognition to the episcopal ideal.

The Westminster Standards were conceived on principles too narrowly Presbyterian to afford a basis for lasting unity in the English Church, and the failure of an unsympathetic Parliament to enforce them left the situation in England quite unsolved. Notable efforts to co-ordinate the divergent elements, in voluntary associations mainly of Presbyterians and Independents, mark the period of the Protectorate. With the death of Cromwell, 1658, these efforts were continued, while the reviving sentiment for episcopacy also called forth hopes of a general comprehension.[63] There is some probability in the detailed account given

---

[62] Archbishop Robert Leighton of Glasgow, c. 1670, advocated a settlement on principles similar to those of Usher in *A Modest Defense of Moderate Episcopacy.* Leighton, *Works*, II, 142ff. Modern Anglicanism, with its synodical organization, is probably nearer in principle to Usher's plan than was the Laudian church.

[63] Shaw, W. A., *A History of the English Church 1640–1660*, II, 152–74; Walker, W., *Creeds and Platforms of Congregationalism*, pp. 453ff.

by Stoupe, a Huguenot in England, to Gilbert Burnet, of a project of Cromwell (c. 1657), for a general Protestant Council to match the papal Congregation *de Propaganda fide* which since 1622 had been placed in control of the missions of the Roman Church. In this scheme the world was to be divided into four provinces, with paid secretaries, and Chelsea College was to be restored and used as a center. The whole scheme was to be amply endowed, and administered by seven councilors.[64]

The figure of Richard Baxter (1615–1691) is prominent in the union movements of this period. A moderate Presbyterian, Baxter was ardently devoted to Protestant union in England, and was prepared to make concessions in any direction that promised results.[65] At the Restoration he, with other Nonconformists, proposed to the king a settlement on the basis of Usher's proposal.[66]

From the Episcopal side an approach was made by Edward Stillingfleet (1635–1699), in his *Irenicum, a Weapon-salve for the Churches Wounds* (1661).[67]

---

[64] Burnet, G., *History of His Own Times*, 1833 ed., I, 141f. The project is evidently related to a favorite idea of Comenius, who was offered Chelsea College by Parliament for his Pansophic College (1641). Spinka, *op. cit.*, p. 132.

[65] His *Christian Concord, or the Agreement of the Associated Pastors and Churches of Worcestershire* (1653), *Catholic Unity* (1654), *Universal Concord* (1660), *The Cure of Church Divisions* (1670), *The True and Only Way of Concord* (1679), and the (autobiographical) *Reliquiae Baxterianae*, ed. by M. Sylvester (1696), may be consulted. See also Powicke, F. J., *The Life of Rev. Richard Baxter*, pp. 163ff.; *The Rev. Richard Baxter under the Cross*, pp. 185ff.; Slosser, G. J., *Christian Unity, its History and Challenge*, pp. 50ff.

[66] Sylvester, *op. cit.*, Part III, p. 274. On his friendship with Usher, see Powicke, *Life*, pp. 126f.

[67] A. A. Seaton shows reasons for revising the commonly accepted date of 1659. *Theory of Toleration under the Stuarts*, App. IV, pp. 341ff.

Stillingfleet gives a thoughtful analysis of the debate on divine right in church government.[68] He distinguishes what Scripture commands from what it merely records, and by a lengthy argument concludes that apostolic practice was not universally binding. On the basis of what is merely *justum*, or in accordance with the law of nature, as also on the basis of what Scripture commands (*jussum*), neither Presbyterianism nor episcopacy can make out a case for itself in divine right (*jus divinum*). But neither is necessarily unlawful; either may be useful and commendable, though not unalterable. The idea that presbyterial ordination is unlawful is, he says, "a stranger to the Church of England." He notes that Cranmer, Parker, Whitgift, and Hooker agree that no special polity is commanded, and that Calvin, Beza, and Melanchthon, while holding parity of presbyters to be primitive, yet approve of espicopacy as in certain cases lawful and expedient. The true and traditional principle of church government for Stillingfleet is not divine right, but "prudence," and "convenience." His proposals resemble those of Usher in the reduction of the extent of dioceses, and the restoration of the functions of the presbyters as a senate to the bishops.[69] This book was widely influential notwithstanding the fact that its author later became a supporter of the episcopal claims against Baxter.

---

[68] Divine right notions had prevailed among both Episcopalians and Presbyterians. For the most notable assertion of the doctrine on the Presbyterian side, see *Jus Divinum, The Divine Right of Church Government*, by sundry ministers of London, 1646. (Republished with an appendix, New York, 1844.) See also the study of the views of the divine right Presbyterians by J. N. Figgis, *Divine Right of Kings*, pp. 267ff. ("Jus Divinum in 1646").

[69] See especially Chap. VII, §§ 4-9, and Chap. VIII (pp. 368ff.) of 1662 ed.

In the Savoy Conference for unity in 1661, the bishops were unconciliatory. The Act of Uniformity of 1662 required episcopal ordination, and sent out of service nearly two thousand ministers whose consciences could not allow them to accept reordination. This was a fresh beginning for Nonconformity. A number of schemes of comprehension won considerable support in the following years,[70] but no formula acceptable to the bishops could be found. They were determined that there should be no "reduction of episcopacy."

The first highly placed churchman after Usher to propose a modification for comprehension was Archbishop John Tillotson (1650–1694), who felt the influence of Presbyterianism and of Latitudinarianism, and whose wife was a niece of Cromwell. Tillotson became primate in 1691.

William III had been a Presbyterian, and came to England pledged "to establish a firm union of his Protestant subjects," as he was reminded by Dr. William Bates at the head of a Nonconformist delegation soon after his reign began. William made encouraging utterances: he hoped, he said, to see the Church of England a lively type of heaven. It was recognized that some concessions were to be made to rising Nonconformity. Ideas of toleration were now widely favored,[71] and comprehension was regarded by some not as the accompaniment, but as the alternative of toleration. The Toleration Act of 1689 gave considerable relief to the major groups of dissenters.

---

[70] Notable were the efforts of Orlando Bridgeman, Keeper of the Privy Seal, in 1667 and 1674.

[71] Seaton, *op. cit.*, pp. 45ff.; Russel-Smith, H. F., *The Theory of Religious Liberty in the Reigns of Charles II and James II*, pp. 2f.

A bill for "uniting their Majesties' Protestant subjects" was also brought before Parliament, and essential clauses of it failed of adoption in the Lower House only because "the votes being equal it was carried in the negative." John Locke wrote to Limborsch (to whom he had addressed his *Letters on Toleration* three years before) that the bishops were opposed; and Birch says that "some who moved the bill set on their friends to oppose it."[72] Tillotson was the main promoter of the comprehension scheme. He now got William to summon Convocation, and prepared for his fellow bishops a list of "concessions which will in all probability be made by the Church of England."[73] But no "concessions" were made.

4. The Survival of Unionism on the Continent of Europe in the Eighteenth Century

The eighteenth century opened with little definite progress toward union as a legacy from the seventeenth; and it was itself marked not so much by union movements as by a gradual growth of the social attitudes that were to make possible union at a later date. The seventeenth century had witnessed the rise, in Prussia and England, of the spirit and practice of toleration, and the eighteenth was to see the triumph of that prin-

[72] Birch, T., *Life of Dr. John Tillotson*, pp. cxiv-cxvi.

[73] These included: "Those who have been ordained only by presbyters shall not be compelled to renounce their former ordination"; they are, however, to receive conditional or "hypothetical" (Birch) reordination in this or like form: "If thou art not already ordained I ordain thee." Those ordained in foreign reformed churches were not to be reordained. Birch gives the document, *op. cit.*, pp. cxxf. Conditional ordination had been advocated by John Overall (1560–1619), Bishop of Norwich, who, in the case of a Huguenot, de Laune, presbyterially ordained in Leyden, suggested the formula "If thou beest not already ordained." Birch, *op. cit.*, pp. 170ff.; Mason, A. J., *The Church of England and Episcopacy*, p. 79.

ciple elsewhere. The bitter denunciations sometimes exchanged between the religious groups in this period are protests against the new order of toleration acquiesced in by the majority. "It must be said to the credit of the century we are treating," Hagenbach remarks, "that such [controversial] talk as this seemed to great men's ears like the rude noise of an angry or drunken man heard in the distance; that the most fiery of the zealots began to complain very naïvely that they were losing the market for their controversial writings; and that people even preferred to read the ungodly writings which were favorable to ecclesiastical union."[74] The new force of Pietism strongly resisted the embattled Orthodoxy of Lutheranism, and gradually modified Lutheran attitudes toward the Reformed; while the triumph of the Aufklärung, and the religious indifferentism of the policy of Frederick the Great (1740–1786), conduced to the breakdown of interconfessional barriers. The foundations not of Lutheranism merely, but of religion itself, were tested under the stress of new ideas. Biblicism tottered under the impact of criticism; and it was evident that insofar as they were literalistic, the thought systems of the Reformation had had their day. Reconstructive forces appeared in the Christian humanism of Herder and in the new theology of Schleiermacher. It is significant that Schleiermacher's important work begins not with an attempt to compare Lutheranism and Calvinism, but with an apologia for religion itself, addressed to its educated despisers.[75]

[74] Hagenbach, C. R., *History of the Church in the Eighteenth and Nineteenth Centuries*, Engl. ed., 1869, I, 108.

[75] *Reden über die Religion, an die Gebildeten unter ihren Verächtern* (1799).

The Protestant unionist tradition survived in the period between Leibnitz and Schleiermacher, and was embraced by the more enlightened and progressive ecclesiastical thinkers. Prominent among the irenical Lutherans was Christoph Mathew Pfaff (1686–1760) of Tübingen.[76] In 1720 Pfaff published a *Pacific Address to the Protestants* in which he revived the view that the different Protestant communions were essentially at one. Unity in exact detail is not possible; hardly can we find two persons who believe exactly alike. Nor is such identity of belief in detail desirable, but merely a unity in the fundamentals of the faith. On other matters we must treat each other with charity. His associate Klemm supported his efforts, advocating the abandoning of controversial preaching.[77]

Probably no religious leader of the eighteenth century surpassed in concern for Christian union Count Ludwig von Zinzendorf (1700–1760), the patron and organizer of the Moravian Church. This fact is illustrated in his whole career, and especially in his correspondence with the Cardinal Louis Antoine de Noailles, the defender of the French "Appellants" after the suppressive bull *Unigenitus* (1713). This illuminating correspondence (1719–1728) has now been reviewed and partially published. It reveals a remarkable friendship between the aged prelate and the

[76] Pfaff was the author of *De originis juris ecclesiastici* (1719), a notable book on polity, proposing the "collegial system" of church government. See K. D. Macmillan, *Protestantism in Germany*, pp. 134ff. On Pfaff's work as a whole see Stolzenburg, A. F., *Die Theologie des J. F. Buddeus u. des C. M. Pfaff*.

[77] Stolzenburg, *op. cit.*, pp. 132ff.; Hering, *op. cit.*, II, 342, 344f.; Pariset, G., *L'État et les églises en Prusse sur Frédéric-Guillaume*, I, 223ff.

youthful count. In these letters Zinzendorf shows the influence of John Arndt, of whose *True Christianity* he sponsored a French translation which he dedicated, without asking consent, to the Cardinal (1724). He saw the Catholic Church in all communions, and was hopeful of the realization of a wider unity through missions. Apparently neither correspondent seriously influenced the other's views.[78]

Among the Reformed, the outstanding irenic spirits were S. Werenfels (1657–1740) of Basel, J. Osterwald (1663–1747) of Neuenberg, and J. A. Turretin (1671–1737) of Geneva. These men were called "the Swiss Triumvirate." Together they led the Swiss Reformed Church away from the narrowing tendencies that had produced the *Formula Consensus Helvetica* (1675). Through their efforts this reactionary document was abandoned (1723); and the correspondence of Turretin with Archbishop Wake and with King Frederick I of Prussia shows that the object in view was the removal of offense to other churches. In 1707 Turretin informed Frederick that "the Genevan church had always held that the Protestants of the two confessions were one in all that was essential to religion." Through the influence of the "Triumvirate" Swiss Protestantism was liberalized in dogma and the Reformed unionist tradition was revived. All three were consistent advocates, by speech and pen, of Protestant union.[79]

---

[78] Salomon, A., "La catholicité du monde chrétien d'après la correspondance inédite du comte Louis de Zinzendorf avec le cardinal de Noailles," *Revue d'histoire et de philosophie religieuses*, VI (1928), 430-66.

[79] Turretin's principal work in this connection, *The Cloud of Witnesses*, was suggested by his correspondence with Wake. The full title is *Nubes testium pro moderato et pacifico de rebus theologicis judicio et instituenda inter Protestantes concordia* (1719). It was translated into

Unionism was strongly encouraged by the first king of Prussia, Frederick I. In the latter part of the century, the advocacy of local or general union continued. Among the writers and promoters of the cause in Germany were Dr. J. G. Tollner,[80] Koster of Epping, and H. S. Van Alpen of Stollberg, whose *Patriotic Appeal for a General Religious Union* appeared in 1800.[81] But the period was marked, on the whole, by the growth of secularism and the decline of the church sense. The principle of toleration was often espoused in a way that could scarcely be distinguished from religious indifferentism, and the consciousness of the *communio sanctorum* was weakened in comparison with the earlier period. The secular Erastianism of Frederick the Great and the equally Erastian reactionism of Frederick William II offered little opportunity for a spontaneous union movement in Prussia, the leading state of Germany.

5. The Survival of Unionism in England in the Eighteenth Century

In England, as on the Continent, the eighteenth century witnessed little active espousal of unionism; but the habit of toleration became fixed, and modern religion has reaped benefits even from the indifferentism and individualism of that age. The unitive principle was by no means entirely obscured. Deism

---

English as *Discourses on the Fundamental Articles of Religion.* On the Swiss Triumvirate see Wernle, P., *Der Schweizerische Protestantismus im XVIII Jahrhundert,* I, 481ff.; Good, J. I., *The Swiss Reformed Church since the Reformation,* pp. 169ff.; Hagenbach, *op. cit.,* I, 112ff.; Articles in *Realencyklopädie,* XXI, 106ff.; XIV, 516ff.; XX, 166ff.

[80] Author of *Das Abendmahl des Herrn,* 1756, and *Die Leiden des Erlösers,* 1757, in which he advocated unity with the Reformed. *Allgemeine deutsche Biographie,* XVIII, 427ff.

[81] Hering, *op. cit.,* II, 429ff.

itself, insofar as it was positively religious, was an attempt at religious comprehension on a scale broader than Christianity. An intellectual catholicity was a marked feature of the period. The Evangelical movement was linked in Wesleyanism with the Arminian theology. Wesley combined with a high Anglican sense of communion the church ideas of Stillingfleet and Lord King, whose remarkable book on the Primitive Church convinced him that "bishop" and "presbyter" were identical in early Christianity.[82] The Church of England, in servile subjection to the state, was too enfeebled to respond officially to the new movement. Wesley was far more concerned for the church than were most of the bishops. But his pathetic patience in seeking to keep his followers attached to Anglicanism was exhausted at the end of his life, when, in meeting the situation that had arisen in America, he proceeded with other presbyters to ordain ministers to serve the Methodist congregations in that (now independent) country (1784). As at the Reformation so in Methodism, the apparent seceders were actuated not by a spirit of schism, but by a greater catholicity than the official representatives of the present church. In large degree the same judgment is true for the Scottish seceders of 1733 and of 1762. They stood for church principles against the supine policy of the "Moderates" in accepting a harsh Erastianism. Yet among both Moderates and Erastian Anglicans, there were some who acted on the

---

[82] King's book, *Enquiry into the Constitution, Discipline, Unity, and Worship of the Primitive Church*, appeared in 1691. He held, with Usher, that presbyters and bishops were different *in gradu* but equal *in ordine*, and declared for synodical government. See pp. 62ff., p. 66 of the 1841 ed. Wesley read the book in 1746.

motives of a catholic unionism which they saw imperiled by the tendencies of the new movements.

Of less importance than these general changes are the specific projects of reunion in the century. The correspondence of Archbishop William Wake (1657–1737) and Louis Ellies Dupin (1657–1719), doctor of the Sorbonne, and editor of the *Works* of Gerson, was instituted by Dupin, when the French Gallicans were in distress over the Bull *Unigenitius* (1713). A former Huguenot, William Beauvoir, then Chaplain to the English ambassador in Paris, acted as intermediary. Dupin's *Commonitorium*, presented to Wake in 1718, is an examination of the *Thirty-nine Articles*. The degree of his acceptance of the Articles is striking, but the differences are striking too. Like Bossuet, and contrary to the Articles (XXI), he declares that general councils are infallible; and he holds to the Seven Sacraments against Art. XXV. Other differences, though minimized, were substantial. Wake decided to end the matter; but resumed correspondence when fresh efforts of the Pope brought fresh opposition in France. But the Gallicans were defeated, and Dupin's papers were seized some months before his death (1719).[83] Wake was, however, not a Laudian, but a liberal churchman, and he was no less interested in the Swiss Protestants than in the Gallicans. He corresponded not only with J. A. Turretin of Geneva, but also with Waldensian and Dutch Reformed leaders. In the same period, the Nonjurors, whose divine right

[83] Lupton, J. H., *Archbishop Wake and the Project of Reunion;* Overton, J. H., and Relton, F., *The English Church 1714–1800,* pp. 23f.; Pusey, E. B., *An Eirenicon* (1865). Considerable detail on other eighteenth century Anglican-Roman approaches is given by J. W. Legg, *English Church Life from the Restoration to the Tractarian Movement,* pp. 393ff.

principles forced them to secede from the Church of England under William III, entered into negotiation with Eastern Orthodoxy; but differences of belief emerged, and when Wake informed the Patriarch of Constantinople of their schismatic position in England, the negotiations were dropped.[84]

The Nonconformist groups showed little concern for corporate union in the eighteenth century. By the *Heads of Agreement*, 1691, a temporary union was accomplished between Congregationalists and Presbyterians.[85] It was soon disintegrated, however, owing to theological controversy. Salter's Hall, London, subsequently became a center for meetings of the dissenting groups; until Arianism caused a disruption in 1719.[86] Co-operation in the "Dissenting Academies" was maintained, however, and political rights were sought by a joint committee which represented the "Dissenting Interest," and were called the "Dissenting Deputies."[87] We find among the dissenting groups little desire or expectation of reunion with the Establishment. Before the Evangelical revival these groups showed no great vitality. With the revival wider outlooks came. The new spirit entered deeply also into the important group of Evangelicals in the Church of England. The so-called "Clapham Sect" of social reforming leaders, of whom Wilberforce is the most distinguished, neglected theology for practical Christianity, and escaped sectarianism. To this

[84] Overton, J. H., *The Nonjurors, their Lives, Principles, and Writings*, pp. 451ff.

[85] Walker, W., *op. cit.*, pp. 440ff.; Bogue, D., and Bennett, J., *A History of the Dissenters* (1833), I, 381ff.

[86] Colligan, H., *Eighteenth Century Nonconformity*, pp. 23ff.; Bogue and Bennett, *op. cit.*, III, 214ff.

[87] Clark, H. W., *History of English Nonconformity*, II, 190.

group was attached Richard Cecil (1748–1810), who, long before Newman, conceived of the Anglican church as offering a *via media* for the reunion of Christianity.[88]

The last years of the eighteenth century witnessed the rise of a movement that gave some promise of union. In that century the Protestant nations took the lead in the expansion of European commerce, and Protestant missions followed trade and colonization. The Evangelical Revival in Britain, combined with the opportunity presented in her expanding empire, called forth in that country at the end of the century a series of notable missionary organizations. From the beginning of Protestant missions there had been a unitive tendency on the movement, and the Anglican Society for the Promotion of Christian Knowledge had co-operated with the Lutheran missions inspired from Halle Pietism. In some of the missionary societies whose organization in the last decade of the century marks a new beginning in missionary enterprise, the note of a universal Protestantism was strongly present. At the founding of the London Missionary Society (1795), Dr. David Bogue exclaimed amid the applause of a huge and enthusiastic audience which could hardly refrain from one general shout of joy: "Behold us here assembled with one accord to attend the funeral of bigotry. . . . I could almost add, Cursed be the man who shall attempt to raise her from her grave."[89]

---

[88] Overton and Relton, *op. cit.*, p. 192, quoting Cecil's *Remains*.

[89] Similar sentiments were expressed by Doctor Haweis, another of the founders of this society, and by other speakers. Lovett, R., *History of the London Missionary Society*, I, 35, 38; Bennett, J., *Memoir of David Bogue*, p. 184.

In their high expectations the missionary zealots of that time could not foresee the length of the process by which missions were to promote church unity. So long as the supporters of missions were few in each denomination, they naturally sought association across denominational lines. Later, when through their efforts the churches themselves were converted to missions, the work became more distinctly a denominational matter. But at a still later stage with the expansion of missions and the increasing recognition of the requirements of the indigenous churches, the basis has been laid for the development of a progressive interdenominationalism that seems in the nature of the case to have union as its goal.

6. CONCLUSION

Throughout the seventeenth and eighteenth centuries, even in the times of Protestantism's greatest depression and weakness, the vision of catholic unity was by no means lost by its leaders. The Thirty Years' War and the subsequent era of reconstruction saw a series of ardent advocates of the cause of unity of whom Calixtus, Comenius, Dury and Leibnitz were men of eminent capacities, who made a contribution of permanent value chiefly in the field of ideas. The influence of their work cannot be traced in organization, but it contributed to the perpetuation of the unitive principle, and led to its resumption by later writers and leaders. The conciliar idea was prominent in the unitive projects of the age, whether these were confined to Protestantism or conceived on a more general scale. Emphasis was laid too by the leaders on the notion of Christian communion in its practical expression in national and international religious fellowship and corporate unity. In the British aspects of the movement amid a variety of interests, there emerged in particular the significant question of ministerial orders. Efforts to Anglicize the Scottish Church and to Scotticize the Anglican Church, in turn failed. Divine right ministries, exclusively Episcopal and exclusively Presbyterian, were irreconcilably opposed. Usher attempted peace by mingling the two; Stillingfleet and many unionists of the Restoration era were prepared to solve the antithesis of divine right claims by making ministry and government merely economic matters to be adjusted according to expediency. For conscious adherents of episcopacy, it has always been possible to affirm either that episcopacy is essential to a church, or merely that it is preferable to other forms of government—in other words, that it is of the *esse* or of the *bene* (or *melius*) *esse* of the church. This question emerged strongly in English union and comprehension proposals of the seventeenth century. The Act of Uniformity, 1662, seemed to pronounce upon it in excluding from the Church of England ministers not episcopally ordained. Yet no doctrinal pronouncement binds the church to the narrowly episcopal view, and the tendency has been to assert it mainly for practical and traditional reasons. The question is a live one in modern unionism as a whole. In the language of Archbishop Söderblom of Upsala: "The real frontier (in the union problem) is within the episcopal part of the church, between those who consider a certain external order, here the historic episcopal office, necessary to the true congregation of Christ . . .

301

and those who do not. The former favor statutory religion; the latter have the evangelic view."[90]

The eighteenth century, when the established churches of Europe were greatly debilitated, exhibits relatively little evidence of Protestant unionism. Its survival, through that period both on the Continent and in Britain, is, however, clearly demonstrable. The growth of religious toleration and the rise of critical and philosophic thought undermined confessionalism and favored interchurch reciprocity; but in the secularism, Erastianism and religious indifferentism that prevailed, the sense of communion in the church was weakened.

The growth of toleration was a marked feature of the whole period. While it sprang in part from secular policies, and its advocates were not always concerned for the church as such, it was consciously espoused, at least in degree, by the advocates of union. Its adoption, as a habit of government and society, constituted an essential prelude to the later advance of unionism. The spirit of interdenominational good will and co-operation was strongly felt and expressed in the missionary movement, which, stimulated by the Evangelical Revival in Britain, organized strongly at the close of the century. This movement offered the churches a common objective in foreign work, which was to prove a permanent incentive of unionism.

---

[90] Söderblom, N., *Christian Fellowship* (1923), p. 34. Reprinted by permission of Fleming H. Revell Company, publishers, New York.

CHAPTER VIII

THE REVIVAL OF THE UNITIVE PRINCIPLE AND CONTEMPORARY ASPECTS OF PROTESTANT UNIONISM

1. THE REVIVAL OF UNIONISM: THE PRUSSIAN UNION OF 1817

THE revival of unionism of which we are deeply conscious to-day definitely though almost imperceptibly began about a century ago. What is meant by this general statement is that for approximately a hundred years the movement has been cumulative. It would be idle to expend effort in giving date and circumstance for this change. It might plausibly be connected with missionary interdenominationalism, or with the Prussian Evangelical Union, or with the beginning of the reunion of Scottish Presbyterianism, or with the Oxford Movement, or with the Evangelical Alliance. It will be more historical to say that in the Revolutionary and Napoleonic period Protestantism, already stirred in Britain by Evangelicalism, gained everywhere new breadth and sympathy, and at the restoration of peace felt the urge to a religious integration from which unionist literature and effort were revived.

Let us give our attention first to Germany, and especially to Prussia, the state which now took the lead in the movement toward German nationalism. In Prussia the Hohenzollerns had early politically favored a consolidation of the Lutheran and Reformed

Churches; and to Frederick William III (1797–1840), after the War of Liberation, the time seemed ripe for a definite move. Partly in response to growing sentiment and partly from his own inclination Frederick William adopted a policy of union and reform; but the hand of the ruler was too heavy upon the church to permit of the best results. Even if we adopt the very favorable view of Geffcken that "the union he desired was quite as little a work of calculating political wisdom as of confessional indifference; it was the pure outflow of personal piety and church sentiment,"[1] it remains true that his methods were arbitrary and his success incomplete. In a sense his policy was a return to that of Frederick I, who a hundred years earlier had more cautiously striven for interconfessional unity. But a new Prussia and a new Germany were arising. The national spirit had revived, and a new moral and religious energy was exhibited in the abundant literature of the age. The king's resistance to political constitutionalism rendered him an unpopular ruler, and he undertook his confessional union in defiance of a fresh outburst of Lutheran confessionalism represented by Claus Harms of Kiel. The true friends of union were in the following of Schleiermacher, whose ideal was a union not of confession but of worship, obtained by consent, not by rough-shod force, and who, therefore, could not fully support the royal policy.

The king's summons, September 27, 1817, to both branches of Protestantism to unite in communion on the occasion of the approaching tercentenary of the Reformation with a view to forming "one united Evangelical Church," "was hailed with delight in

---

[1] Geffcken, F., *Church and State*, Engl. ed., 1877, II, 170.

Berlin and elsewhere," and the churches were thronged for the union meetings.[2] Harms, however, theatrically issued a set of "95 theses" on the three hundredth anniversary of Luther's (October 31), in which he appealed to Lutherans "not to consummate the act over the bones of Luther. They might revive, and then woe betide you."[3] Opposition found expression elsewhere, especially in Saxony. A synod of Berlin ministers, under Schleiermacher's influence, voted in favor of a union of worship without fresh dogmatic statements, a proposal out of accord with the wish of the king, who wanted a new consensus. Thus the prospect of success for the king's plan was dimmed from the first.

While the question of a consensus waited, difficulties arose with regard to both polity and worship. In 1815 Frederick William had restored the consistories, which had been discontinued in 1808. A commission which he appointed, responding to public opinion, urged the establishment of presbyteries in each community, with synods for the "circle" (*Kreis*) and the "province," subject to the general consistory of the state. The king generously favored this synodical system, which would have given the church some measure of autonomy. But his minister, Altenstein, opposed the plan, and by a policy of delay prevented its application.[4] The king's attempt to introduce a

---

[2] Fuerster, E., *Die Entstehung der preussischen Landeskirche*, I, 283; Macmillan, *Protestantism in Germany*, pp. 175f.; Kissling, J. B., *Der deutsche Protestantismus 1817–1917*, I, 4f.; Geffcken, *op. cit.*, II, 171.

[3] "Als eine arme Magd möchte man die lutherische Kirche jetzt durch eine Kopulation reich machen. Vollziehet den act ja nicht über Luthers Gebein! es wird lebendig davon und da—wehe euch!" Rocholl, R., *Geschichte der evangelischen Kirche in Deutschland*, p. 463.

[4] Geffcken, *op. cit.*, 174; Fuerster, *op. cit.*, I, 285.

common ritual was scarcely more successful. The *Agenda*, or new liturgy, drew its name from the language of army orders. It had been introduced in the garrison at Potsdam in 1816, on the king's initiative. In 1822 he began a policy of extending its use throughout the kingdom. But everybody found fault with it. The Reformed complained that it was too Lutheran, the Lutherans that it was Catholicizing, though on some points conceding too much to the Reformed. Schleiermacher severely criticized the king's arbitrariness, and the great majority of the clergy resisted the imposition of the *Agenda*.[5]

The long struggle that ensued cannot here be detailed. The whole story shows the futility of any church union that is not a spontaneous church affair. If in advance of all his actions the king had consulted with the strong body of liberal-minded unionists among the ministers, and formed a policy for which they took responsibility jointly with the government, the outcome would probably have been different. As it was, the "Prussian Evangelical Union," which produced a church without a general polity, a common worship, or a common statement of belief, and without any adequate sense of religious unity, can obviously be called a union only with reservations. It was only in the Rhine provinces and in Westphalia, where synodical government had already arisen in Lutheranism, that the two churches, by synodical action, became really consolidated into one church (c. 1835). There, however, Reformed and Lutheran confessions were formally retained. In other parts of the Prus-

---

[5] Kissling, *op. cit.*, I, 10-12; Geffcken, *op. cit.*, II, 175-6.

sian state, and of Germany,[6] the result was to secure the joint co-operation of the two confessional groups with the state, a system of which the advantages were mainly political and the disadvantages were suffered by the church. Nonconformity arose, but as compared with that of England, remained insignificant, and the principle of church autonomy received little expression.

2. THE REVIVAL OF UNIONISM IN THE BRITISH ISLES

In the British Isles the movement was entirely spontaneous, and manifested itself chiefly in the advocacy of union from a variety of angles. The most notable practical aspect was the union of the vigorous Secession groups, the Burghers and Anti-Burghers, in Scotland (1820). This union followed similar action on the part of the same groups in Canada (1817) and in Ireland (1818). It was the beginning of the series of steps by which Scottish Presbyterianism has now reached almost complete unification. Scotland too had her notable advocates of the principle of Christian unity. In 1821 Dr. Thomas McCrie, a Secession minister and a capable historian, published his *Unity in the Church, her Divisions and their Removal.* McCrie writes in part to vindicate the Secessionists from the charge of schism; but his book shows a vigorous conception of the unity of the church universal, and a vivid hope of the visible realization of union. For Scotland he anticipates that "the Westminster Standards may form a rallying point around which the

---

[6] For the unifications effected in other German states in the same period, see Kissling, *op. cit.,* I, 25-47.

scattered friends of religion in this land shall meet and again happily combine" (p. 174). The Disruption which detached from state control a great part of the Church of Scotland in 1843 was led not by schismatic spirits, but by men whose church principles were strong. In 1845 we find Thomas Chalmers and Robert Candlish contributing, along with Secessionist, Reformed Presbyterian, and Congregationalist ministers, to a series of *Essays on Christian Union*. The writers of these essays are all thorough, if somewhat cautious church unionists, most of them a little alarmed against Tractarianism, but hopeful of the ultimate unification of Protestantism in both England and Scotland. Chalmers himself sets no limits to Christian union. "We confess ourselves," he writes, "sanguine for a union still more comprehensive than that which we are immediately aiming at, and by which not only the smaller but the larger differences of the Christian world will be harmonized."[7]

The close of the Napoleonic era brought Britain into co-operation with Continental powers for the political integration of Europe,[8] and both Anglicanism and Nonconformity began to form fresh contacts with Continental churches. The activities of the Scottish evangelical Robert Haldane (1764–1851) in Geneva and elsewhere (1816–), of the Methodist Charles Cook (1787–1858) in Southern France (1818–), of the Anglican John Charles Beckwith (1789–1862) among the Waldenses (1827–), are indicative of the revival of British religious internationalism.

The subject of communion again attracted the in-

---

[7] *Essays on Christian Union*, p. 17.

[8] See A. Phillips, *The Confederation of Europe*.

terest of theology in this period. It was not alone
among High Churchmen that this note was being
struck. Thomas Arnold (1795–1842) was the earliest
of a line of English liberal theologians who profited
by the early results of critical thought and sought a
broadened reconstruction of theology and of the church.
Arnold asked for "comprehension without compromise," and believed it possible to integrate the religious
forces of England on the basis of the fundamental
realities on which all agreed.[9] In 1842 appeared
Archdeacon H. E. Manning's *The Unity of the Church*,
a book of some scholarship in which a measure of
theological liberalism struggles with literalistic notions of authority and a rigid episcopalian conception
of the church. In 1851 Bishop H. B. Wilson in his
Bampton Lectures on *The Communion of Saints* again
exhibited the Broad Church interest in the corporate
life of the church.

The Oxford Movement had its principal forerunner in a friend and admirer of Wesley, Alexander
Knox (1757–1831),[10] who desired to see the Anglican
Church liberated from the pressure of secular Erastianism and had a deep sense of the values of corporate
religion. These are the outstanding features of the
movement in its early stages. The Tractarians craved
a great function for their church as the *via media* or
meeting ground of Catholicism and Protestantism.
For the authority-craving mind of Newman the ultimate solution of the ecclesiastical problem was to
enter the Roman obedience. E. B. Pusey (1800–

---

[9] *Principles of Church Reform*, 1833, and other works. "His soul
was possessed of the vision of Christian unity," says V. F. Storr, *Development of English Theology in the Nineteenth Century*, p. 106.

[10] Storr, *op. cit.* pp. 85-91; Brilioth, Y., *The Anglican Revival*, pp. 45-53.

1882) remained loyal to Anglicanism and to the *via media* principle. From 1845 he and Keble joined in circulating prayers for Christian unity. In 1857 he fostered a society for prayer on behalf of union. Cardinal Manning secured the condemnation of this society at Rome in 1864, and issued an attack upon the Anglican Church. Pusey's reply to this was his famous *Eirenicon* of 1865.[11] Pusey here reasserts the *via media* argument, and contends as Newman had done in Tract No. 90 (1841), though with more candor, for the compatibility of the *Thirty-nine Articles* with the Tridentine Decrees.[12]

The interest of Nonconformists in unity is attested by the work of the popular Congregationalist writer John Harris (1802–56), whose *Union, or the Divided Church Made One* appeared in both England and America (1838). He rejects any project of union by subjugation or absorption, and declares for mutual forbearance and fellowship. Though his theology is not that of to-day, much of his argument strikes a very modern note.

In 1845 the initial steps were taken toward the formation of the Evangelical Alliance, and the organizing meeting took place in London, August 19, 1846.[13] The bicentenary celebration of the Westminster Assembly, the writings of S. S. Schmucker of Gettys-

---

[11] *The Church of England a Portion of Christ's One Holy Catholic Church and a Means of Restoring Visible Unity. An Eirenicon*, 1865; a second and a third *Eirenicon* appeared 1869 and 1870. Cf. Ollard, S. L., *Short History of the Oxford Movement*, pp. 259ff.

[12] An interesting feature of the treatise is the extensive analysis of Dupin's *Commonitorium*.

[13] *Evangelical Alliance, Report of the Proceedings of the Conference Held at Freemason's Hall, London, 1846.* Davis, J., "The Evangelical Alliance, its Origin, Objects and Operations," in *Evangelical Alliance, Proceedings, Essays and Addresses, 1873*, pp. 189ff.

burg, Pennsylvania,[14] and a letter of William Patton, a New York Presbyterian, were factors in the origin of the Alliance. It took for its motto the formula of Rupert Meldenius, which Baxter had repeated: "In things necessary, unity; in things indifferent, liberty; in all, charity." But the Alliance suffered from the adoption of an antiquated theological platform; and its leaders generally shrank from any outspoken advocacy of corporate unity. Its service to the advancement of unity was nevertheless considerable. The warmth of its internationalism, the exchange of information afforded by the often able papers and discussions to be found in its reports, and the vigorous assertions of the moral force of Protestantism on questions of the rights of religious minorities, made it a factor of no little importance in developing an all-Protestant consciousness throughout the half century in which it flourished.

3. THE OLD CATHOLICS

Within Germany a new unionism was developing. A writer whom Döllinger calls "an influential clergyman" in 1863 anonymously published *Pax Vobiscum*,[15] a book advocating union between Protestants and Roman Catholics, and Pastor Schulze, of Berlin, at a time of intense political feeling over the Vatican council, offered "A Word of Peace,"[16] which made large concessions to Roman principles. The declaration of papal infallibility (1870) was strongly opposed within the Roman obedience, and a group mainly of

---

[14] Slosser, *op. cit.*, pp. 178ff.

[15] *Pax Vobiscum, die kirchliche Wiedereinigung der Katholiken und Protestanten historisch-pragmatisch beleuchtet von einem Protestanten.*

[16] *Ueber romanisierende Tendenzen, ein Wort zum Frieden*, 1870.

German opponents severed connection with Rome. Seeking episcopal orders, this group turned to the Jansenist separatists of the Netherlands and adopted their name of "Old Catholic." The Old Catholic movement proved its catholicity by earnestly seeking intercommunion with other non-Roman, episcopally ordered churches, and by a not unsympathetic attitude to Protestantism. The Bonn conferences of 1874 and 1875, initiated by the Old Catholics and participated in by Anglicans and Easterns, were of significance not so much for the theological terms agreed upon as for the novel exhibition of an ambitious effort toward Catholic reunion on the part of these communions.[17]

The outstanding leader of this movement was J. J. I. von Döllinger (1799–1890), who had early felt the influence of the liberal Roman Catholic J. A. Möller (1796–1838), author of a book on church unity and of a more famous work on symbolics.[18] Döllinger gave in 1871 a course of lectures on reunion, which were rendered into English by a hearer, and published in 1872.[19] The work called attention to the historic aspects of the reunion problem. Its merits, and the wide sympathy with Döllinger's struggle, gave it an extensive circulation among Protestants. Its author had evinced an interest in reunion long before the Vatican Council, and he felt that by

[17] *Report of the Union Conferences . . . at Bonn,* 1870, Ed. Reusch, F. H., tr. Buel. For the "theses" adopted in 1874 see pp. 196ff.; for the *Articles* of 1875, pp. 199ff.

[18] *Die Einheit in der Kirche oder das Prinzip des Katholicismus* (1825); *Symbolik oder Darstellung der dogmatischen Gegensätze der Katholiken und Protestanten.*

[19] *Lectures on the Reunion of the Churches,* tr. Oxenham, 1872. (German edition, 1883.)

the Infallibility decree Rome had "made union with her impossible."[20]

He and his associates gained their chief importance by their advocacy of a Catholic union. Theologically the Old Catholics, like the Evangelical Alliance, were unprogressive. A degree of understanding was arrived at between these two movements. Some Protestants were invited as observers of the Bonn conferences; and the Old Catholics sent cordial official greetings to the 1873 meeting of the Alliance.[21]

4. THE UNION MOVEMENT IN AMERICA

The notorious multiplicity of sects in the United States of America may obscure the fact that a large number of minor but substantial reunions have taken place in that country. The history of these efforts would fill a volume, and has not been adequately written.[22] We must confine our treatment to some indications of the advocacy of the unitive principle as indicated in a series of writings. The call to united prayer issued by Jonathan Edwards in 1747, at the suggestion (1746) of twelve Scottish ministers, instituted the practice of the "concert of prayer" in which a spirit of local Christian unity was promoted in thousands of communities for a long period.[23]

---

[20] *Ibid.*, p. 136.

[21] Schaff, D. S., *Life of Philip Schaff*, pp. 252ff.; pp. 317ff. *Evangelical Alliance Proceedings, Essays and Addresses*, 1873, pp. 485ff.

[22] See, however, F. Lynch, *The Christian Unity Movement in America;* W. A. Brown, *The Church in America;* and Slosser, *op. cit.*

[23] An interesting post-Revolution echo of this is *Circular Letters, containing an invitation to the ministers and churches of every denomination in the United States, to unite in their endeavors to carry into execution the "Humble Attempt" of President Edwards, to promote explicit Agreement and visible Union of God's People in Extraordinary Prayer, for the revival of Religion and the advancement of Christ's Kingdom on Earth.* Concord, 1798.

Thomas Coke, the early Methodist leader, corresponded (1791) with Bishop William White, of the Protestant Episcopal Church, with a view to a union of the Methodists with the latter; and later (1798) was in correspondence with the Bishop of London and the Archbishop of Canterbury on the same question.[24] In this period (1792), Bishop Madison of the Protestant Episcopal Church proposed a conference for union with other communions.[25]

A prominent phase of unionism in America was that led by Thomas and Alexander Campbell which resulted in the formation of the new denomination known as the Disciples. Thomas Campbell attempted to interpret his Scottish seceder Presbyterianism in the catholic terms of the Westminster Confession, which would extend communion to all Christians "as God offereth opportunity." He was censured by his presbytery for extending the invitation to communion to all Christians in his Pennsylvania congregation, and in 1809 published his *Declaration and Address*, designed "to restore unity, peace and parity to the Church of God." Believing that it is the function of religion "to unite men to God and to each other," he invites "brethren of all denominations" to join a "society" (not a church, he insists) that shall seek the reformation and unification of the whole church.[26] The "society" soon began to take on the character of a separate denomination; but throughout its history

---

[24] The letters are given with comments in White, W., *Memoirs of the Protestant Episcopal Church*, pp. 208ff.; pp. 424ff.; and in Drew, S., *Life of the Reverend Thomas Coke*, pp. 228ff. Coke made generous proposals which suggest the strength of his surviving Anglican sentiments.

[25] Tiffany, C. C., *History of the Protestant Episcopal Church*, pp. 388f.

[26] The document is given by P. Ainslie, *The Message of the Disciples for the Union of the Church*, pp. 145ff.

its leaders have continued to show concern for church unity.

In the thirties there began to appear a series of books in advocacy of union, emanating from different Protestant groups. Abraham van Dyke, of the Dutch Reformed Church, published his *Christian Union, or an Argument for the Abolition of Sects*, in 1835. Van Dyke was anxious to eliminate the names of the different groups, as occasions of sectarianism. He appealed to ministers and laymen, including newspaper writers, in all denominations, and pointed out the possibility of Christian union in a country like America, where the churches were unfettered by religious establishments. The book was welcomed in some quarters, and not soon forgotten;[27] but the ease with which the author hoped to heal the church's wounds led to criticism.[28] A more fundamental proposal was that of the distinguished Lutheran scholar of Gettysburg, Pennsylvania, S. S. Schmucker (1799–1873), entitled *A Fraternal Appeal to the American Churches*, 1838. Schmucker laments the sectarian training of youth, and the prevailing "idolatry" of the founders of sects. Luther, Calvin, and Knox are now like Paul, Apollos, and Cephas for the Corinthians. His proposal is for a close federation under the name of *The Apostolic Protestant Church*, with branches called Lutheran, Episcopal, Presbyterian, etc. He lays emphasis upon the practice of communion, ministerial, ecclesiastical, and sacramental. He advocates a

[27] We find it quoted largely by J. P. Campbell, *A Plea for Christian Union*, 1860.

[28] Hurst, J. F., "The Irenic Movements since the Reformation," in Shields, C. W., and others, *Church Unity: Five Lectures delivered in the Union Theological Seminary*, New York (1896), pp. 131ff.

common statement of faith to include the Apostles' Creed and a short Protestant confession. In the form of the latter which he suggests the doctrine of the church is taken from the *Westminster Confession*.[29] Schmucker formed a society for the promotion of Christian union, and published other influential writings.[30] He was well qualified by historical knowledge to appreciate the viewpoints of different Protestant groups, and his work made a deep and lasting impression in many quarters.

Probably the Protestant Episcopal Church can boast in this period more books in advocacy of union than any other church in America. These books in general are based on the *via media* argument, and a number of the writers propose the mere adoption of the standards of their own denomination as the solution of the problem.[31]

5. THE CHICAGO QUADRILATERAL

The influence of America in the modern revival of unionism is seen in the origin of the Chicago-Lambeth Quadrilateral. This historic document was first in substance formulated by a member of the growing unionist party in the Protestant Episcopal Church led by Bishop W. A. Muhlenberg. This group exhibited a liberal attitude to other churches, and Muh-

---

[29] 2d ed., 1839, pp. 128ff.

[30] Slosser, *op. cit.*, pp. 178ff., stresses the influence of his *Overture on Christian Union*, 1845, in connection with the origins of the Evangelical Alliance.

[31] For example, *Hints on Church Union*, by a Presbyter of the Protestant Episcopal Church, 1836; and a rather facetious book by F. S. Mines, a convert from Presbyterianism, entitled: *A Presbyterian Clergyman Looking for the Church* (1857). A well-written early typical book of this class is Bishop T. H. Vail's, *The Comprehensive Church*, 1841, (2d ed. 1879).

lenberg proposed modifications of Anglican standards. In 1853 he got the Convention of Bishops to accept a resolution liberalizing the rules for the admission of ministers. After the Civil War the temporarily severed Northern and Confederate churches were reunited, and the spirit of union was nourished in this act (1865). In 1870 appeared the notable book by W. R. Huntington, *The Church Idea.* Huntington's final chapter (Chap. VII) treats of the Anglican Church as "the Church of the Reconciliation," and defines the "true Anglican position" in four principles "which make the Quadrilateral of pure Anglicanism," and which the English state church has "muffled in a cloud of nonessentials." On the basis of this Quadrilateral he proposes to seek Christian reunion.[32] The book added to the strength of Muhlenberg's following and in the subsequent years unionism continued to gain support in the church. In 1886 a memorial signed by more than eleven hundred clergy and more than three thousand laymen was presented to the General Convention meeting in St. John's Church, Chicago. The committee then appointed to draft a resolution on union presented a remarkable statement which incorporated Huntington's four requirements.[33]

It has caused regret in some minds that the terms of the Quadrilateral have been taken by themselves as a *sine qua non* of unity, while the Preamble has been

[32] Fifth edition (1928), pp. 115ff. Cf. Huntingdon's Bedell Lectures, *A National Church,* 1898, with a useful bibliography of English titles on the history of Christian union effort.

[33] *Journal of Proceedings of the Bishops, Clergy and Laity of the Protestant Episcopal Church in a General Convention, October 6–28, 1886,* pp. 78ff.; Tiffany, C. C., *A History of the Protestant Episcopal Church in the United States of America,* pp. 557ff.

forgotten.[34] The latter declares (section 4): "This church does not seek to absorb other communions, . . . but, rather, co-operating with them . . . to discountenance schism," etc.[35]

The Chicago declaration laid down the principles of (1) Scripture as the revealed will of God, (2) the Nicene Creed, (3) the Two Sacraments, and (4) the Historic Episcopate.

6. THE LAMBETH CONFERENCES AND RECENT PROGRESS OF THE MOVEMENT

The Lambeth Conference of 1888 gave world significance to the Quadrilateral. The series of Conferences at Lambeth had been inaugurated in 1867, following a suggestion which came from the Provincial Synod of the Canadas, 1865. By resolutions of the Australian and of the Canadian branches of Anglicanism, the Conference of 1888 was urged to take action for union.[36] The Chicago proposal was the ready instrument for the corporate affirmation of the conference. With slight modifications of clauses 1 and 2 it now became the Lambeth Quadrilateral.[37]

The adoption of the Quadrilateral marked an important stage in the revival of unionism. It appeared to simplify and clarify the whole issue. At once discussion swung from the detailed balancing of confessions to the consideration of four concise proposi-

[34] Hall, Francis, "The Anglican Movement for Reunion," *Anglican Theological Review*, VIII (1925), 100.

[35] Tiffany, *op. cit.*, p. 558.

[36] In Canada union sentiment had been expressed in the Presbyterian and Methodist unions of 1875 and 1884, and the Anglican Synod had appointed committees for conference with these churches for wider union.

[37] Davidson, Archbishop R. T., *The Five Lambeth Conferences*, pp. 122f.; pp. 158f,

tions. In the Church of England it was looked upon primarily as a possible basis for "Home Reunion," but it was soon the subject of discussion everywhere. It was obviously more attractive than Tractarian unionism to evangelical Protestantism. On only one of the four points was there any serious difficulty for the non-episcopal churches. In the response of these churches it soon appeared that the principle of the "historic episcopate" would require a great deal of explanation to make it acceptable to them.[38] The interpretations of the expression offered by Anglicans were in general not satisfactory to Free Churchmen; and there appeared little promise of fulfilling the function of *via media* on the side of the non-episcopal communions. Union between these groups themselves was, however, stimulated. Finding the approach to Anglicanism difficult, they turned, notably in Canada, to projects of union with each other. On the other hand, Anglicanism was repulsed by Rome. In 1896 the Pope emphatically refused to recognize Anglican ordinations.

Not until the Great War had humbled the churches and revived the desire for the widening and deepening of Christian communion, was further progress possible. The Lambeth Conference of 1920, with its moving "Appeal to all Christian People," set forward the cause of union in the psychology of Christendom. This utterance marks, indeed, a new stage in the modern revival of unionism. It offers distinct sug-

---

[38] See, for instance, the *Report of a Conference on Christian unity held in Toronto, April 24th and 25th,* 1889, and the significant book by C. W. Shields, *The United Church of the United States* (1895), Chap. IV, "Denominational views of the Quadrilateral," pp. 111ff.; also the same author's essay: *The Historic Episcopate* (1894).

gestions of an interpretation of the ministry sufficiently conciliatory to attract churches which practice presbyterial ordination.[39] It sets forth frankly the principle that "the truly equitable approach to union is by way of mutual deference to one another's consciences." In subsequent conferences Anglicans and Free Churchmen jointly agreed that in the projected united church of the future episcopacy should be retained, but it should be "representative and constitutional," and its acceptance should not involve the adoption of "any particular theory as to its origin and character."[40]

The negotiations between the Anglican and the Free Churches showed evidence of great concern for union on both sides. The discussions ended (1925) without other tangible result than the rise of a union literature that is rapidly educating the churches into a realization of the problem and possibility of union. Anglicanism has not officially and unambiguously accepted non-episcopal ministries, and the non-episcopal churches refuse reordination. The next stage of progress in England seems to wait on the solution of this question; but the gain in good will and understanding since 1886 is incalculable; and the common pressure of the social tasks of the churches will hardly permit them long to desist from reunion effort.

It lies beyond the purpose of this book to describe the voluminous literature in advocacy of church unity which has appeared in the past half century. Much of it has been of superficial and ephemeral character, though not necessarily without value for its purpose

---

[39] Bell, G. K. A., *Documents on Christian Unity*, pp. 1ff.

[40] Bell, *op. cit.*, p. 150 (1922).

of arousing interest where hitherto this has been lacking. It is doubtful whether any even of the more searching studies of recent years has exercised a distinctive influence upon the course of the movement.[41] Apparently, a stage has now been reached in which, while any fresh light on practical and historical aspects of the movement will be welcomed, nobody's personally conceived project or opinion will receive much attention. The whole problem is now felt to rest broadly upon the shoulders of the responsible leaders of Christianity and upon the Christian people in all groups. The churches have already so far learned the substance of the teachings of the prophets of unity that they have begun to consider or undertake, as churches, activity in the cause. At the same time, the practical community problems faced by the churches increasingly suggest union as a means of their solution.

The widening range of union effort is exhibited in the almost countless number of contemporary projects for reunion in which Protestant churches are concerned. The church press is constantly reporting fresh negotiations, and in this respect developments have been particularly rapid in America during the past year or two. Many Protestant communions have

---

[41] Among the thoughtful books on the subject as a whole one may with some hesitation select Lacey, T. A., *Unity and Schism;* Wallau, R. H., *Die Einigung der Kirche vom Evangelischen Glauben aus;* Smyth, N., and Walker, W., *Approaches Toward Christian Unity.* A useful article is Tollinton, R. B., "Reunion, the Present Situation," *Hibbert Journal,* XXVII (April, 1929), 438ff. Informing on many points of the history is Slosser, G. J., *Christian Unity, its History and Challenge.* Sir James Marchant has edited a collection of essays, by representative leaders of the great communions of the world, entitled *The Reunion of Christendom.* On special fields, Athearn, C. R., *Interchurch Government,* and Woods, F. T., *Lambeth and Reunion,* may also be noted.

participated in the "Faith and Order" movement, initiated in 1910 at the suggestion of the Protestant Episcopal Church.[42]   The faith and order conferences, like the Quadrilateral, have called forth more discussion on "order" than on "faith," and so far have yielded nothing more than increased good will and understanding, especially on the question of the ministry. Of very different purpose were the "Life and Work" conferences at Upsala 1917 and Stockholm 1925.[43]   The "Life and Work" movement rests on a pragmatic approach to the unity problem, which for some minds offers the best promise both of the achievement of unity and of its value when achieved. It may be participated in, indeed, merely from a realization of the value of co-operation, with indifference to organic union, but the logical tendency of a union in Christian work to a union of worship and organism cannot be ignored. The principle of co-operation has been succinctly stated by Dean Shailer Mathews in the words, "The way for Christians to get together is to work together."[44]

The Federal Council of Churches of Christ in America[45] has successfully carried on co-operative effort on a large scale, and has steadily grown in im-

---

[42] Bell, *Documents on Christian Unity,* pp. 15f.; *Faith and Order: Proceedings of the World Conference, Lausanne, August 3–21, 1927,* ed. H. W. Bates; Woods, E. S., *Lausanne, 1927;* Soper, S. D., *Lausanne, the Will to Understand;* Laun, J. F., *Die Konferenz von Lausanne.*

[43] Deissmann, A., *Die Stockholmer Weltkonferenz;* Brent, C. H., *Understanding, being an Interpretation of the Universal Christian Conference on Life and Work held at Stockholm, August 15–20, 1925.*

[44] Mathews, Shailer, "Protestantism, Democracy and Unity," Journal of Religion, IX (1929), 183ff.

[45] Macfarland, C. S., *The Progress of Church Federation in America to 1922; The Churches of the Federal Council;* Cavert, S. M., *Twenty Years of Church Federation.*

portance and effectiveness since its inception over twenty years ago. It does not lie within the province of this study to survey the manifold activities of the Council or to examine the structure of the local and general organization by which it enables twenty-seven denominations to combine important religious and social tasks. The Federal Council is already doing some of the things which a united church would do. Its Department of Research is a bureau for the scientific study of the whole social environment in relation to church tasks. It contributes, too, to the experience of church fellowship by conferences and retreats, and through the associations involved in the joint labor of committees. It achieves a measure of unity between groups so widely divergent that their corporate unification is at present out of the question. While by its constitution it explicitly conserves "the full autonomy of the Christian bodies adhering to it," the first of the five objectives which it avows is: "To express the fellowship and catholic unity of the Christian Church." In co-operation with the Home Missions Council it now lends aid in the local expression of catholic unity through the unification of charges in divided and overchurched communities.

In response to the needs of such communities there has also grown up during the last two decades a series of Community Churches which have become to a certain degree associated into a unified movement. This movement represents the craving for a unitive instead of a divisive presentation of Christianity in small towns and villages, and its comparatively rapid growth is evidence of the strength of that desire. There has been some apprehension lest the result would be

merely the addition of a new denomination. A plan
is now projected, however, by which Federal Council,
Home Missions Council, and Community Churches
will be allied in the prosecution of the "Five Year
Program," already launched by the Home Missions
Council, to unify the Protestant churches in communities of less than one thousand population.[46]

As such experiments increase in number and prove
successful in the smaller communities, there will inevitably be an increasing tendency to apply the method
in larger centers. Indeed, the experience of the Federal
Council has led some participants to the judgment
that it is preparing the way for more advanced measures of unification than have yet been adopted. In
this connection it may be appropriate to quote the
recent words of one of the Council's three General
Secretaries:

The spirit of co-operation abounds; the day of denominational asperities and intolerance has passed. The new
spirit awaits the clothing of itself in a suitable body. The
pressure of the growing sense of brotherliness is breaking
the sectarian bonds. The ideals of fellowship demand a
technique of co-operative action.

More than this is appearing. The experience of co-
operation has awakened desire and expectation that mere
co-operation is not able to satisfy. Some larger union calls,
and its call will be heard. What it may be or how it will
come about may yet be obscure, but that it is coming and
coming fast, men and women of prophetic vision are
assured.[47]

Similar councils of the denominational churches
have been established and have accomplished impor-

---

[46] Home Missions Council, *Annual Report, 1929*, pp. 26, 56; *Federal
Council Bulletin*, XII, 5 (1929), pp. 15ff.

[47] Moore, J. M., in Cavert, *op. cit.*, pp. 39f.

tant tasks in Great Britain and on the continent of Europe. In the Church Peace Union and the World Alliance for Promoting International Friendship through the Churches many churches have undertaken to co-operate for the maintenance of international peace. Both these organizations took their rise in 1914; the latter held its first conference at Constance in the opening days of the Great War.

7. THREE EXAMPLES OF UNION ACHIEVEMENT

The practical results of the modern revival of unionism can already be counted in an impressive series of acts of union. These unions have been formed partly under the inspiration of the growing literature and also to a large degree in response to the needs of churches in facing their social tasks. In some instances much progress has been made with relatively little theoretic discussion of principles. Two effective motives may probably be discerned in all cases: the desire for communion and the demand for efficiency.

The unions actually consummated differ in respect to the degree of diversity among the uniting groups. On this point illustration may be furnished by reference to three of the more notable instances. In the Scottish union[48] which was consummated October 2, 1929, no fundamental question of polity or of doc-

---

[48] Logan, R., *The United Free Church, an Historical Review, 1681–1906;* Fleming, J. R., *The Church in Scotland, 1843–1874;* Cooper, J., "The Church of Scotland and the whole Church Catholic," *Contemporary Review,* CXVII (1920), 45ff.; Curtis, W. A., "Reunion in the Scottish Church and the Proposed Articles," *Hibbert Journal,* XVIII (1920), 240ff.; Lord Sands, "Church Union in Scotland," *Quarterly Review,* CCXXXIII (1920), 205ff.; Balfour, Lady Frances, *Memoirs of Lord Balfour of Burley;* Cairns, D. S., *Life and Times of A. R. MacEwen;* Martin, A., "Church Union in Scotland," in Marchant, *op. cit.,* pp. 185ff.

trinal standards has had to be solved. The greatest difficulty lay in the Secessionist assertion of voluntaryism as a principle, against the principle of ·establishment. Voluntaryism was not adopted by the Free Church (1843), whose leaders still desired that state connection which because of abuses they were forced in conscience to forego. When, after long negotiation, The United Presbyterian Church and the Free Church united in 1900 to form the United Free Church, the issue of voluntaryism was already largely outgrown. Its survival has been a minor factor in the subsequent negotiations; but in general the practical view was taken that the state connection was valuable so long as the church was safeguarded against the abuses from which it had formerly suffered. The enlightened parliamentary legislation of 1921[49] largely removed fears on this score, and all outstanding points were finally settled. The reunion of the Church of Scotland eighty-six years after the Great Disruption is a highly impressive fact which cannot but affect deeply not only the Presbyterians, but other furcated denominations throughout the world. Scottish Episcopacy still stands outside the united church, as do the reactionary fragments of Presbyterianism, the Free Presbyterians and the remnant of the Free Church (the "Wee Frees"), groups which failed to keep the pace of the advancing movement a generation ago.[50]

Somewhat more divergent were the units which went to make up the United Church of Canada.[51]

---

[49] Bell, *op. cit.*, pp. 170ff.

[50] A notable parallel to the Scottish union is seen in the approaching union of British Methodism which is now virtually assured.

[51] United Church of Canada, *Record of Proceedings of the First General Council*, pp. 57ff. (Historical Sketch); *A Statement Concerning Ordination to the Ministry in the United Church of Canada;* Morrow, E.

This followed a century of progress in unification by which Presbyterianism (1875), Methodism (1884), and Congregationalism (1906) had each internally united to form a nation-wide communion. Between these denominations theological differences had largely vanished; all three had about equally responded to the influence of modern thought. In meeting their tasks of church extension and foreign missions they had to some extent approached each other also in polity. The effect of the discussions inaugurated in the late eighties on the initiative of the Anglicans was to discourage the hope of a union in which the Anglican Church would participate with any of these presbyterially ordered churches, but to suggest the possibility of a union of these churches themselves. Negotiation and practical co-operation led to a definite union project which was clearly formulated in 1902. Anglicans and Baptists, for widely different reasons, declined (1906) to participate in the formation of a Basis of Union. The Basis was virtually completed in 1908. A Presbyterian minority resisted the movement, and when union was effected this group seceded and obtained large concessions in property. The United Church of Canada stands in guaranteed freedom, so far as the state is concerned, to revise its standards and unite with other communions without loss of identity. Further, by the Basis of Union and the utterances of its leaders it stands committed to

L., *Church Union in Canada;* McNeill, J. T., *Church Union in Canada, an Estimate of Doctor Morrow's Book;* McNeill, J. T., *The Presbyterian Church in Canada, 1875–1925,* Ch. XVI; Johnston, A. J., *The Larger Fellowship;* Kilpatrick, T. B., *Our Common Faith,* with Introduction: "A Brief History of the Church Union Movement in Canada" by K. H. Cousland; Wilson, R. J., *Church Union in Canada After Three Years.*

the principle of wider union, both within and beyond the Dominion.

The Canadian union strikingly proves the possibility of the harmonious and advantageous blending of the three denominational groups of which it is formed. It does not, however, span the gulf between episcopal and non-episcopal churches, since all three of the uniting churches practiced presbyterial ordination,[52] and the United Church has a typically presbyterial or conciliar polity.

A promising attempt to link such churches is being made in India. The Presbyterian Church in India was formed in 1904. In 1908 its synod of South India was released from the union to unite with the churches in connection with the London Missionary Society and the American Board (Congregational), thus forming the South India United Church. Since 1919 this church has been in negotiation with the Anglican Mission Church, and in 1925 the Wesleyan Church in South India joined the discussions. A basis of union has been prepared which solves the question of ministry by the adoption of a constitutional episcopate under careful guarantees of responsibility, and the recognition of existing ministries. Final reference to the constituted authorities of the negotiating churches is still necessary, and the union will hardly be consummated before 1934.[53] A movement has

[52] The *Statement Concerning Ordination* put forth by the General Council (1926) presents an extended and documented historical argument for the recognition of the orders of the ministers of the United Church of Canada by other Christian Churches.

[53] Manshardt, C., "Movements Toward Christian Union in South India," *Journal of Religion*, VI (1926), 614ff.; Banniga, J. J., "Progress in Christian Union in South India," *Christian Union Quarterly*, XVIII (October, 1928), 128ff.; Philip, P. O., "Special Correspondence From

now been set on foot for a wider unification to embrace the proposed Church of South India and a group of churches of North India.[54]

The South India project adds, to the types that have been fused in the United Church of Canada, the Anglican and episcopal elements. The Church of England is vitally concerned, and the completion of the movement may prove to depend on the attitude taken by the forthcoming Lambeth Conference of 1930. Its success, if achieved, will be a prophecy of future union movements of a sweeping character. It will not mean, however, that Anglicanism surrenders its alleged function as *via media*. It is true, as we have seen, that Anglican orders were rejected by the Pope in 1896. The friendly post-war Malines conversations ended, too, in futility.[55] But, on the other hand, notable progress has been made in establishing accord and intercommunion with the Eastern Orthodox churches and with the episcopally governed Lutheran Church of Sweden.[56] The position of Anglicanism in the whole field of unitive effort thus remains a central one.

The Indian project, if effective, will be the first instance of a union across the dividing line of episcopal and presbyterial polity. It is rendered possible by a

India" (Poona, April 26, 1929), in *Christian Century*, May 29, 1929, p. 772; Azariah, V., "The Anglican Church in India," in Marchant, *op. cit.*, pp. 281ff.; Waller, H. M. (Bishop of Madras), *Church Union in South India, the Story of the Negotiations*, 1929.

[54] See the *Indian Witness*, LIX, 242ff.; 265ff. (April 17 and 24, 1929).

[55] *The Conversations at Malines, 1921–1925* (Oxford Press, 1927). It is not surprising that the most serious difficulties were found "with regard to the special position of the Pope in the Church," p. 87.

[56] Bell, *op. cit.*, pp. 44ff.; Douglas, J. A., *The Relations of the Anglican Churches with the Eastern Orthodox Church;* Riley, A., "Anglican and Orthodox," *Church Quarterly Review*, CI (1925), 124ff.

lively sense of the needs of the country and by the fact that since 1888, and especially since 1920, the "historic episcopate" of the Quadrilateral has been semiofficially interpreted in such constitutional terms as not to repel the presbyterially governed churches.

8. CONCLUSION

Social and international movements of the Revolutionary and Napoleonic era seem to have conditioned the modern revival of the unitive principle. For a century the quest of union has enlisted increasing interest and effort. The Prussian Union left much to be desired; but a spontaneous movement for unity later became manifest in Germany. In Scotland a new interest was revealed; in England both Tractarians and Broad Churchmen in different ways cherished a vision of future reunion. The Evangelical Alliance cultivated a warm internationalism. The Chicago-Lambeth Quadrilateral drew attention to the issue of the "Historic Episcopate," and the Lambeth Appeal of 1920 marked a stage of advance. Attention has been directed to the unions achieved in Scotland and Canada, and to the South India project, of which the last-mentioned holds promise of overcoming the barrier between historic ministries. This and related topics are amicably discussed in conferences of the "Faith and Order" movement while the "Life and Work" conferences sought general unity of action on human conditions. The century has been fertile with projects, experiments and expectations: and it has witnessed concrete achievements that have reversed the former divisive trend.

CHAPTER IX

THE ECUMENICAL REVIVAL

THE above title is a phase employed in my classroom lectures for many years before I read the statement by W. A. Visser 't Hooft: "Mrs. Söderblom remembers that the Archbishop preferred to describe the movement as the ecumenical revival."[1] The Introduction to this book called attention to a new spirit in the Protestant communions, "a common desire to seek their own liberation into a wider fellowship." The intervening decades have seen the movement then emerging advance with mounting force. It is a revival not only in that it renews the ancient emphasis upon Christian unity, reaffirmed in the best thought of the Reformation, but as a re-invigoration of Christianity itself. To those who have foretold the dissolution of Protestantism or the abandonment of Christianity, it can only be disconcerting. But many, both within the church and without, have not yet taken the measure of its importance.

1. HOW IT CAME ABOUT

The ecumenism of today is by no means a Protestant movement only. It receives invaluable contributions from Easten Orthodoxy and from Anglo-Catholicism. But insofar as it draws its strength from Protestantism it represents the re-emergence of elements inherent in

---

[1] W. A. Visser 't Hooft, *The Meaning of Ecumenical* (London: S.C.M. Press, 1953), p. 24.

THE ECUMENICAL REVIVAL

the Reformation. Its energizing concepts are to be
found in sixteenth-century writers. It is not born of
the theologies of our era, though nourished by them.
It is itself giving new vitality to theology in every
branch of the church. It has been affected by a com-
plicated set of historical circumstances, so that its
sources and causes are multiple and somewhat elusive.

Future historians will ask why it was in the present
century that the ecumenical movement first found
opportunity. Some of their answers already suggest
themselves. The unprecedented ease of travel and
communication and the innumerable cultural, political,
and commercial contacts thereby formed and maintained have fixed in most minds a "one world" concept
affording a psychological background for a worldwide
Christian movement. We cannot evaluate the part
played by Christianity and its widespread missions
in creating this new world consciousness which is now
an asset to it. Even the peril of a war of ultimate
destruction calls forth strong efforts to foster world
community and renders more urgent the ecumenical
task. Standing on the brink of world ruin, we discover
the absurdity of alienation from other Christians who
share our prayer for God's peace.

An indispensable service has been rendered by a
choice company of dedicated leaders,[2] men who deserve
an honored place with the devout and sagacious churchmen of past ages. Through their work together,
their addresses and writings, coupled with the industrious efforts of competent organizers and local group
leaders, and an abundance of informative literature,

---

[2] For lively sketches of the major and some of the minor figures, see
Stephen Neill, *Men of Unity* (London: S.C.M. Press, 1960).

332

the gospel of Christian world fellowship has been carried to a widening audience. Biblical and historical scholars, too, have helped to change the atmosphere in church circles as they have consciously viewed their tasks in an ecumenical light.

Yet all these and like considerations are insufficient to explain the vast and strange revival we are witnessing. There are indefinable spiritual and emotional forces at work in it. Men who came together with denominational particularities to defend found themselves thinking their way forward with those of other backgrounds. "We may gratefully claim," says the Edinburgh Affirmation (1937), "that the Spirit of God has made us willing to learn from one another."[3] A Roman Catholic observer at the Evanston Assembly (1954) said with conviction: "For a time Evanston was a place where the Holy Ghost breathed."[4]

2. "ECUMENICAL"

Shortly after the initial publication of this book the words "ecumenical" and "ecumenicity" began to gain currency in our language in their now familiar sense. These words were sparingly used in the above chapters. But "the ecumenical outlook" claimed for the Reformers (ch. II) had reference to the catholicity or wholeness and worldwideness of the church, both of the church invisible, the body of saints known only to God, and of the defective visible church, which they found in a ruinous state. Their task of reform was "to build again the ruins" of the true

---

[3] Lately reprinted in Norman Goodall, *The Ecumenical Movement* (London: Oxford University Press, 1961), Appendix II, p. 205.

[4] Eva-Maria Jung, "Roman Catholic Impressions of the Evanston Assembly," *Ecumenical Review*, VII, 1955, p. 125.

church, part by part as was necessary, but with a live concern for the whole. The word "unitive," which runs through the presentation of the theme, was used to suggest the craving for unity over any area and at any level. To the Greeks *oikoumene* was the entire area of the earth where men dwelt, a term in human geography. Our historians of culture have been making convenient use of "ecumene" in tracing early man's geographic expansion. With the modern movement, "ecumenical" has increasingly taken on a unitive connotation along with its basic reference to extension over the earth.

As stated above (p. 115), the *Form of Presbyterial Church-Government* holds in view the functioning of "synodical assemblies" which may be "ecumenical." The conception of "synodical assemblies" in the minds of the Westminster Fathers was of conciliar bodies having jurisdiction. The developing organization of the ecumenical movement is otherwise conceived. When in 1919 Nathan Söderblom wrote: "What I advocate is an ecumenical council of the Churches," he added: "This should not be given external authority."[5] All the leaders have been anxious to repudiate the suggestion that they were planning a "superchurch."

3. THE WORLD COUNCIL OF CHURCHES

No narrative of the long sequence of local, national, and worldwide meetings by which the ecumenical revival has been advanced can be crushed into these pages.[6] Following the epochal conferences of "Life

---

[5] Quoted by Goodall, *op. cit.*, p. 64.

[6] An ample account to about 1948, with some data for the early fifties, is found in *A History of the Ecumenical Movement*, edited by Ruth Rouse and Stephen Neill (Philadelphia: Westminster Press, 1954).

and Work" at Oxford and "Faith and Order" at Edinburgh in 1937 it was decided to continue these movements in one council, and the name adopted was "World Council of Churches." As over against "ecumenical council" this was a happy choice, since that term had been pre-empted by Roman Catholics and was in general use by historians for the twenty councils recognized as of universal authority by the papacy, to and including Vatican I.[7] After a decade "in process of formation," a decade which included a world war, the World Council was organized at the Amsterdam Assembly of 1948. It describes itself as "a fellowship of Churches which accept our Lord Jesus Christ as God and Saviour." Its function is "to offer counsel and provide opportunity of united action," and explicitly not "to legislate for the Churches." Lack of jurisdictional and legislative powers does not prevent the World Council from exercising weighty influence upon its member churches.

At New Delhi in 1961 the great step was taken of amalgamating the International Missionary Council with the World Council of Churches. The I. M. C. had a forty-year record of vigorous activity, rendering valuable service through its many departments, facilitating arrangements for comity among missions, and co-operating with various agencies of the ecumenical movement. Through it the missionary tradition of the nineteenth century is perpetuated in the World

---

[7] It was Samuel McCrea Cavert who, when the question of a name came before a small committee presided over by Archbishop William Temple, proposed "World Council of Churches." Dr. Cavert was then General Secretary of the Federal Council of Churches in America (Goodall, *op. cit.*, p. 64). Dr. Cavert does not recall that the traditional meaning of "ecumenical council" was discussed.

Council's activities. Many of those best acquainted with missions discern in their modern development the most potent factor in the rise of the ecumenical movement itself. Certainly the impact of Christian missions on the modern world has been incalculable, and not the least phase of their influence has been upon the sending churches.

The World Council operates through a large Central Committee and a small Executive Committee, and through world assemblies of delegates from the participating churches meeting at intervals of about six years. The member churches now exceed two hundred in number, and include Eastern Orthodox Churches of Greece and Russia, the Orthodox Patriarchates of Alexandria and Antioch, the Reformed Church of Hungary, and numerous recently formed or united churches of Asia and Africa. From its headquarters in Geneva it keeps watch for the interests of Christ's Kingdom in every land, co-operating with the national councils and with units inherited from the International Missionary Society. Its Ecumenical Institute at the Château de Bossey is a busy training school for service in the movement. Through its Division of Interchurch Aid and Service to Refugees it brings merciful relief to countless victims of distress. Its constant concern for the peace of the world was signalized by a nobly worded "Appeal to All Governments and Peoples" adopted by the New Delhi Assembly.[8]

4. Anxieties

All this structural expansion is to some as disquieting

---

[8] Visser 't Hooft, ed., *New Delhi Speaks* (New York: Association Press, 1962), pp. 22ff.

as it is impressive. Will the lively spirit of the revival be one day smothered under a spiritless bureaucracy? The alarm has been sounded by various writers, some of whom imply that the mischief has already begun.[9] Without adopting the heresy that all bigness is badness, we do well to be wary of the demons that tend to infest flourishing movements. An experienced and discerning participant in its committees points to certain unwieldy features of the organization, uncomfortable anomalies in the relationships of World Council and national councils, and the embarrassing growth of world agencies of merely denominational activity.[10] A prominent leader and spokesman of the movement has expressed apprehension lest the very existence of the World Council may serve weak consciences as an excuse from any painstaking effort toward further union.[11] There is questioning about the objectives sought, and to be sought. A scholarly long-time advocate of Christian unity has offered a caveat against the ill-considered pursuit of an unattainable goal, proposing a more modest aim, the union of disrupted denominational families.[12]

All such anxieties should be fully weighed. The revival will cease to revive anything unless diligent and prayerful watch is kept against the creeping paralysis of institutionalism. Constitutional changes may be requisite that every part may function effec-

[9] Keith R. Bridston and Walter D. Wagoner, eds., *Unity in Mid-Career, An Ecumenical Critique* (New York: Macmillan, 1963); same authors, "Haloes in the Ring," *Christian Century*, Jan. 2, 1963.

[10] Henry P. Van Dusen, *One Great Ground of Hope* (Philadelphia: Westminster Press, 1961), pp. 118ff.

[11] Neill, *Men of Unity*, p. 167.

[12] Matthew Spinka, *The Quest for Church Unity* (New York: Macmillan, 1960), ch. iv.

tively. And it is vanity to applaud utopian objectives while neglecting the tasks necessary for attainable ones. In this matter, however, there is involved the primary Christian doctrine of the "One Church, Catholic and Holy," unbounded by place or race or time. Each minor union is a step in bringing this principle to realization, and belief in the principle is the best incentive to any unitive effort. It will not let us rest with small gains. The achievement of one union creates the impulse to seek another. We should be concerned in due proportion with both near and distant goals. Nobody in Geneva or elsewhere can chart the future progress of church unification. Welcome, though inexplicit, is the New Delhi statement of aim: "The Lord . . . constrains us to seek the unity which he wills for his Church here and now."[13] Spontaneity is essential, and local or area conditions may suggest unitive actions. It is being realized that the challenge of deterioration in the great cities cannot be met by denominationally directed measures, and that this calls for the cultivation of the ecumenical spirit on the local scene. Every selfish denominational or racial interest is placed under judgment by the crying needs of men.

5. Some Church Unions Completed and Projected

The formation of the United Church of Canada (above, pp. 326ff.), despite the losses attending it, has produced a harmonious and statistically prosperous communion active in missions and social services. Declaring its aim "to foster the spirit of unity," it invites union with other Canadian churches. Con-

---

[13] Visser 't Hooft, *New Delhi Speaks*, p. 92.

versations with the Anglican Church in Canada through a joint committee have made some progress. The Church of South India (above, pp. 328f.) was finally launched in 1947, after protracted discussions. The issue of the ministry was examined from every angle in weighty writings. Episcopal and presbyterial ministries were mutually recognized, to be finally unified after thirty years, new ordinations being by bishops. That such a union of polities should prove viable at all has lent encouragement for the formation of churches of even wider comprehensiveness. In negotiations now proceeding in North India, Pakistan, and Ceylon, churches practicing believers' baptism only are participating with pedobaptists, and complete unification of ministries at the outset is proposed. Under compulsion by an unsympathetic national government a still more inclusive union produced the United Church of Japan, which has survived the war and freedom and shows impressive vitality, notwithstanding the withdrawal of Anglicans, Lutherans, and some Presbyterians. In the Philippines a union of Presbyterians, Congregationalists, and United Brethren was enlarged in 1948 by the addition of Evangelicals and a unit of Methodists to form the United Church of the Philippines. In general the growing indigenous churches of Asia and the outlying island nations tend strongly to leave behind them the denominational phase and to form united churches that address themselves in a natural way to the whole people among whom they work.

Areas of "rapid social change" include most of three continents, Asia, Africa, and South America. An All Africa Church Conference in 1958 set up a provisional

committee which is strenuously promoting the solidarity of African Christianity against the background
of a society everywhere shifting. To similar purpose
was the All Latin-American Conference of 1961.
Amid political excitements and economic transformation a prompt move forward of the Christian forces
is of the highest importance.

Following the Scottish-Presbyterian union of 1929
ecumenical advance in the British Isles has been
largely a matter of conversations between churches
and of valuable published studies. The British Council
of Churches is associated with the Scottish Churches
Ecumenical Committee in exploring ways toward
union and in guiding common action in various social
ministries. While Presbyterian-Episcopal antagonisms
have passed into history some of the convictions
behind them are still held so strongly as to make any
general unification of British churches a somewhat
remote goal.

It is not possible here to recite the record of newly
united churches in the United States, but some examples may be recalled. The Methodist Church
(U.S.A.) formed of three units in 1939, and the United
Presbyterian Church in the U.S.A., 1957, combining two
branches of the denomination, drew together long-
severed church families. Similar was the formation
of the Lutheran Church in America, 1960, uniting
four Lutheran churches which represented somewhat
divergent national origins. Unions of Congregationalists with some Disciples in 1931 and of Reformed
and Evangelical churches in 1934 led to the formation
in 1957 of the United Church of Christ. The coming
together within a few years of groups so dispersed

shows the unpredictability of such action.

Projects for wider unions than these have been put forward from time to time. Chiefly before the public at present is that launched by Eugene Carson Blake, Presbyterian leader, with the approval of James A. Pike, Episcopal Bishop of California, in December, 1960, looking toward the formation of a church "reformed and catholic" with a polity combining episcopal and presbyterial elements. The Protestant Episcopal Church, the Methodist Church, the United Church of Christ, and Blake's own denomination were named as first negotiators, with a welcome out to others favorable to the principles set forth. These include credal orthodoxy along with theological freedom, the scriptural sacraments, and a realization of "local communion and common witness in all the places where men live." The churches have responded. A meeting of delegates took place in Washington in April, 1962, and formed a continuing body called "the Consultation on Church Union" with President James I. McCord of Princeton Seminary as chairman. There is strong expectation that in time something will come of this and that it will assume a dimension far exceeding any of the church unions hitherto achieved.[14]

6. RESPONSE TO POPE JOHN'S INITIATIVE[15]

A change has come across the ecumenical landscape by the new direction of Roman Catholicism. Despite

---

[14] In *The Challenge to Reunion*, compiled and edited by Robert McAfee Brown and David H. Scott (New York: McGraw-Hill, 1963), more than a score of writers treat the proposal from many angles.

[15] Books and articles on Pope John and Vatican II are abundant. Protestants wishing to understand the approach of Roman Catholic scholars in Europe will do well to read *The Council, Reform and Reunion* by Hans Küng (New York: Sheed and Ward, 1962), and *The Ecumenical Council, The Church and Christendom* by Lorenz Jäger (New York: Kennedy, 1962).

early negative answers to approaches made on behalf of the ecumenical movement, the papacy has of late years begun to permit and encourage friendly contacts with Christians of other communions. Since 1943 the unrestricted study of the Bible by Roman Catholic scholars has been actively pursued. A reciprocal willingness to engage in conversations on doctrinal and social concerns has been developing, and Protestants find themselves described not as heretics but as "separated brethren," often with emphasis on the noun. But nobody who rejoiced in the changed atmosphere was quite prepared for the cordial initiative of Pope John XXIII. Having announced to astonished cardinals on St. Paul's Day, 1959, his intention to call a new Vatican Council, the late Pontiff, in numerous utterances and personal contacts, convinced even cautious observers of his informed zeal for Christian unity. He likewise, by manifesting Christian goodness, won the homage of millions whom he did not expect to share all his opinions. Future ages will remember how we all, as it were, looked on wide-eyed while the octogenarian Pontiff, stricken by a mortal disease, with a frail octogenarian cardinal, Augustin Bea, S.J., at his side, charted a revolution in the greatest and most conservative of Christian communions.

We shall be deeply concerned in what the Council, now scheduled to resume meetings in September, 1963, may under the guidance of Pope Paul VI determine on the unity issue, and on the related matters of Scripture and tradition, worship reform, and the doctrine of the church. But forecasts seem to point to the implementation of Pope John's policy. Already

POPE JOHN XXIII AND VATICAN II

much has been changed that can never be changed back. What seems of most importance is the patent fact that we are now, for the first time since 1541, in mutually respectful dialog with Roman Catholic spokesmen, with every promise that it will continue. It is hardly an exaggeration to say that the ecumenical revival has laid hold on Christendom, shedding a wave of religious friendliness throughout the world. A thoughtful kind of Pentecostal revival was much in the late Pope's expectations for the Council, involving far-reaching "modernization" and reform. The beginners of the non-Roman Catholic ecumenical movement would, if they were with us now, rejoice and be glad. The chorus of Protestant approval does not mean a tremulous and headlong rush to embrace all that is papal—the behavior of minnows when bait is let down into their pool.   Nothing like this is anywhere desired. With the Orthodox and other participants in the World Council, we shall be in discussion with Roman Catholic scholars and thinkers for a long time. It is an exchange for which they are well equipped, and for which our ablest young men ought to prepare themselves. They will need a great deal more Latin and Greek, and more familiarity with Patristic, Medieval, and Reformation writings, than present theological students usually acquire. But if the spirit now engendered prevails, the participants will not find themselves matching wits with competitors, but together appropriating the riches of the Christian heritage. The organization of union is always of far less importance than its spirit. A new stage opens for the advance of Christianity in freedom, communion, and charity. Thus may be built the only effective counterforce against the crude and cruel materialism, the moral deterioration, and the psychic confusion that threaten mankind.

CONCLUSION

This book was conceived as a reinterpretation of Protestantism resting on an examination of Reformation facts and writings and of some phases of later history. I was convinced that, despite certain superficial indications, a unitive principle inhabits the Protestant mind. The additional chapter maintains continuity with the original argument, while dealing briefly with later developments. The ecumenical movement of our time has advanced with increasing momentum and has already profoundly affected nearly all segments of organized Christianity. It has attracted the attention of a great number of scholarly inquirers whose approach is from a variety of ecclesiastical angles. It will be for future writers to assess the entire range of causes and motives for this transforming movement. Certainly nearly all active Protestantism is either clearly within it or favorable to its aims. Most of the recent church unions noticed above have been virtually confined to Protestant groups. But "Protestant" was originally a designation applied from without to the signers of a very special protestation, and extremely few denominations have chosen to adopt it. In the ecumenical movement we hear little of this historically convenient but sometimes embarrassing name. Unitive Protestantism must always have interests beyond Protestantism as popularly understood, since it affirms the belief of the Reformers in the holy catholic church. Much has been written about the possibility or desirability of an ecumenical theology. It is well to realize the degree in which every theology of any weight is ecumenical. Nevertheless the age requires new formulations of theology framed in minds completely aware both of the tradition and of today's need for valid interpertations of Christianity in its present setting amid human society. The theology of the remainder of this century cannot be Roman Catholic or Orthodox or Protestant in any restrictive sense of these words. Theology is at last completely out in the open. If it becomes quarrelsome, the disputes are as likely to be within the communions as between them. And with a wider spread of discussion perhaps fewer new sects will be born in the assured certainty of ignorance. When the Reformers indentified *ecclesia catholica* with *communio sanctorum* they were stressing the New Testament concept of *koinōnia*, the inviolable bond of fellowship among Christians, in which all exercised a mutual priesthood, giving and receiving benefits, and enriching one another's lives thereby. In historic Christianity from an early date we have inadvertently or culpably violated this fellowship, impoverishing our experience and nullifying our testimony. The hour is great with hope. Once again the world takes note that "these Christians love one another."